Twee

ALSO BY MARC SPITZ

Fiction

How Soon Is Never?

Too Much, Too Late

Nonfiction

We Got the Neutron Bomb:
The Untold Story of L.A. Punk
(with Brendan Mullen)

Nobody Likes You: Inside the
Turbulent Life, Times, and
Music of Green Day

Bowie: A Biography

Jagger: Rebel, Rock Star,
Rambler, Rogue

Poseur: A Memoir of Downtown
New York City in the '90s

Twee

THE GENTLE REVOLUTION IN MUSIC, BOOKS, TELEVISION, FASHION, AND FILM

Marc Spitz

!t itbooks

AN IMPRINT OF HARPERCOLLINS PUBLISHERS

TWEE. Copyright © 2014 by Marc Spitz. All rights reserved. Printed in the United States of America. No part of this book may be used or reproduced in any manner whatsoever without written permission except in the case of brief quotations embodied in critical articles and reviews. For information address HarperCollins Publishers, 195 Broadway, New York, NY 10007.

HarperCollins books may be purchased for educational, business, or sales promotional use. For information please e-mail the Special Markets Department at SPsales@harpercollins.com.

FIRST EDITION

Designed by Shannon Plunkett

Library of Congress Cataloging-in-Publication Data has been applied for.

ISBN 978-0-06-221304-4

14 15 16 17 18   OV/RRD   10 9 8 7 6 5 4 3 2 1

For Tracey Pepper. Please try to avoid skimming over the parts
that do not involve Glasgow in the early '80s.

If it weren't for the nervous people in the world, we'd all still be eating each other.

—Guido (Eli Wallach),
in Arthur Miller's screenplay for
John Huston's *The Misfits*, 1961

Contents

Introduction: Hello "Brooklyn!"   1

1 The Mean Reds   23

2 Younger Than That Now   58

3 The Wild Things   82

4 Sixteen Again   102

5 I'm a Loner, Dottie, a Rebel   114

6 Blue Boys   126

7 Meet the Tweetles   137

8 Slings at the Corporate Ogre   150

9 "You're in High School Again"   168

10 Do Something Pretty While You Can   188

11 *Sic Transit Gloria*   203

12 Extremely Loud and Conveniently Local   233

13 Welcome to the Mumble   245

14 It'll Change Your Life   269

15 Dorks Incorporated   286

16 Culture Teasing   305

Epilogue: The Last Donut   313

Bibliography:
     Books; Magazines, Websites, and Podcasts; Interviews   317

Appendices:
     A Thoughtful but Danceable Playlist   331
     A Reader, Books Both Joyful and Sad   334
     A Queue for Many Warm and Quiet Evenings In   336

Acknowledgments   339

Introduction

Hello "Brooklyn!"

Summer 2013

In which I, a fourth-generation Brooklynite, marvel at the trans-
formation of my former home from working-class immigrant
stronghold and rent haven for a few dozen pioneering artists
to open-air supermarket for the privileged and precious. I then
quickly dispense with shock, subjectivity, and (most) personal
anecdotes in order to scientifically explore how the inhabitants of
the new Brooklyn, epicenter of Twee, as well as a sort of global
"Brooklyn" are possibly helping the world become a kinder, closer,
and cooler place. "Brooklyn" is accomplishing this, in part by em-
bracing artists and objects once-arcane and niche, all of which can
be grouped under the vintage, transparent plastic umbrella of the
often pejorative term Twee. *Twee, in short, may not be all bad.*
For one, it's now the most powerful youth movement since Punk
and Hip-Hop. It may not be all new, either. For decades Twee
has been a school of the larger catchall Indie and a home to the
Indie kids who held a close bond with Hello Kitty and the Lovin'
Spoonful as well as if not in place of being versed in J. G. Ballard,
the harsher end of Neil Young, and Slint. Slowly, however, Twee

is growing and absorbing its Indie host. All things Twee are very Indie. All things Indie are not necessarily Twee . . . yet.

NOTE: When "Indie" is referred to in this book, it's on the gentler rim of the spectrum of tone and mood ranging from sunny to pitch-black: from the upbeat Free to Be You and Me *soundtrack to the dour "Needle in the Hay" sequence in* The Royal Tenenbaums.

At times, the story of the rise of Twee will be anecdotal; the making of a Twee-seminal album (the Smiths' self-titled debut, Belle and Sebastian's Tigermilk*) or a film (Whit Stillman's* Metropolitan, *Noah Baumbach's* Kicking and Screaming*) or key literary works (*The Catcher in the Rye, The Diary of a Young Girl, The Bell Jar, *the* McSweeney's *titles) that changed minds and, eventually, common behavior on a grander and grander scale. Other times, the chronicles of Twee-nia will simply consist of the charting of struggle and progress; the slow transporting of the Twee ethos (bullying is bad, perennials are good, so are Christmas and owls) out of the bedroom and into the streets. Technological advances and new ideas (YouTube as the modern diary) or even the rise of an Epicurean notion (there's more to pickles than green food coloring and a pinch of dill) will be considered as well.*

I will chart a half century of pop cultural revolution from the postwar '50s to the present; gentle at first, but now seemingly unstoppable. I will also, hopefully, provide you with a satisfying, funny, and educational read that may even inspire some questions along the lines of, "Wait a minute? Am I Twee? And if so, do I need help?" (If you do, there are some useful lists at the end of the text.)

They line up by the cash machines outside the asphalt yard of the Bishop Loughlin Memorial High School on Clermont Avenue. A Gothic structure, it stands across from the 108-year-old Masonic Temple, which now occasionally hosts Indie-rock shows organized by the "Masonic Boom" collective. The young men here mostly have mustaches, some waxed and twisted into spiny points. Others have thick lumberjack beards that are also carefully groomed. They're all skinny but seem somehow out of shape and slow, like koala bears. The women wear little makeup. Many have cut their hair in the pixie style that suggests Jean Seberg or have grown out bangs to evoke Anna Karina, Julie Christie, and other '60s film stars. They wear vintage granny dresses with Doc Martens and a discreet amount of black eyeliner, or loose, carefully worn-in tees, some silk-screened with the faces of other vintage legends: "Hanoi Jane"–era Fonda or the young, snappish Bob Dylan circa *Don't Look Back*.

Outside the fences, draped with tattered flags, faded school banners, or burgundy-and-gold faux Moroccan tapestries, there are opportunists on these grounds too. They're simply selling ice-cold water. These Brooklynites make no fashion statements and thus seem decades older than their customers even when they are contemporaries.

A scattering of eco-Punks distributes flyers from their worn canvas satchels. This literature contains tips and scoldings and general instructions for saving Brooklyn, which increasingly means saving the world. The tourists bear this out. They've journeyed, thousands of them every season, from Japan, Germany, France, Brazil, and Iceland, all drawn to this lot and others like it. Since 2001, the number of visits to New York City has increased from around 35 million annually to nearly 53 million, with a large percentage who might not have even considered a trip to Brooklyn a decade ago now making *Manhattan* their second destination; hence luxury hotels like the chic but bohemian Wythe, a converted waterfront factory, opening in Williamsburg. Brooklyn has become not just a borough of New York City but rather an idea, an aesthetic, a selling device, an industry, and a dream of some kind of global Narnia where everyone has the right books, clothes, shoes, records, cookies, and pickles. Everyone is young and most of the young are Twee.

There are similar marketplaces like the Greenpoint, Brooklyn, Flea all over the world. In 2013, one no longer has to be in Brooklyn—the borough, the county, the former "hood"—to be in Brooklyn. Austin is "Brooklyn." In fact, some argue that Austin was Brooklyn before Brooklyn was "Brooklyn," but lackadaisical or just plain mellow, the weird Texas hamlet never really had the right fuck-you attitude and Eastern drive to lead a culture-penetrating charge (most of us have seen *Slacker*). Parts of Chicago and L.A. (Silver Lake, Echo Park, Highland Park) are now "Brooklyn." Paris is "Brooklyn." "Among young Parisians, there is currently no greater praise for cuisine than "très Brooklyn," "a term that signifies a particularly cool combination of informality, creativity, and quality," wrote the *New York Times*'s Julia Moskin in 2012 in a feature about the kind of food trucks that line the back of this yard like a smoky, meaty, or vegan convoy, smelling of curry and mint and brisket and steaming rice. In Egypt and Syria and elsewhere in the Middle East, the young want their "Brooklyn" too. And both Brooklyn and "Brooklyn" keep Twee and its designs, chief among them the freedom (and often the daring) to be soft in an increasingly hard world, alive and thriving.

When the late Apple visionary Steve Jobs envisioned a sort of global, utopian, design-driven planet where all are connected no matter what religion, creed, gender, province, or class one belongs to, he was tapping into a sort of scale model of the current "Brooklyn" in which Mose Allison, Animal Collective, and Drake live in harmony in the cloud, and gluten-free vanilla whiskey biscotti or a cavalry hat made from repurposed felt are status symbols because of their purity, are in because of their outré status, desirable and marketable because they deserve to be; because they are good. We aren't quite there yet, not completely. There are imposters, knockoffs, and faux Brooklyn crafts. The old divides remain as well. All one needs to do is jog up out of the subway exit and onto the street, under the giant mural of slain rapper and "old Brooklyn" saint Biggie Smalls, to instantly detect these schisms in the new, hyper-gentrified Brooklyn.

Jobs died of cancer in October of 2011 before really learning whether this color- and class-blind vision could possibly hold. (It still remains to be seen.) Biggie never lived to see what happened to the corners where he used to sell crack and battle-rhyme. The realities of life inside the Twee model for the world are complicated. Today, most "street" Brooklynites are college educated, white, and affluent, or at least middle class, with semidisposable incomes, or at least enough cash on hand to search for a Galaxie 500 album on vinyl rather than simply downloading (or stealing) it. "I personally think of the modern Indie aesthetic as a lifestyle," says Tamara Winfrey Harris, a writer and blogger who has explored this divide with humor and frankness on her blog *What Tami Said*. "It relates to people with a lot of time on their hands to ride around on bikes with giant wheels and stick birds on things. There would be a cost to a black man or a black woman walking around in holey clothes they got in vintage stores. That's not to say black men in suits aren't rousted in stop and frisk," she adds of the city's controversial policy of randomly targeting its citizens regardless of whether or not they have committed or are about to commit a crime. "But you are probably increasing your chances [if you are wearing vintage clothes]."

Few speak as openly of the divide between class and race, but on a bright, hot Saturday in Greenpoint, Brooklyn, it's certainly detectable. A middle-aged African-American man in a sweat-soaked navy T-shirt (sans 1960s icon or personal statement about loving bacon) has set up a pile of old issues of *Jet, Ebony,* and *Vibe* magazines to sell on the sidewalk.

"Nineties, man! Nineties! You got it!" he says, hoping to impress a group of bemused white kids in thick glasses as they pass. "Retro!" They don't stop. They're on their way to the aforementioned cash machine and then to the Flea, to browse coffee mugs etched with ducks, owls, squirrels, and foxes; old green glass Coke bottles; hatboxes printed with violets and daisies; fake-fur cropped jackets; and wind-up, spark-spitting King Kong, Godzilla, and Creature from the Black Lagoon toys. I wonder, in my darker nights of the soul, "Am I writing a book for well-off white people?" But I press on and remind myself that to even question that is part of the problem. Twee, like Punk and Hip-Hop, no matter who pioneered it, is at its best pure and open, a meritocracy and a good party. This is why it's lasted. "Profile the aesthetic, tell the history, and you will be okay." Still, it's hard to ignore that many of these old brownstones and apartment complexes used to belong to working-class, nonwhite families. Greenpoint used to be a real, livable neighborhood with low rents that attracted first immigrants and then pioneering artists. Now it attracts the arty, and the next few waves of artists savvy enough to feed their need for all things Twee. The divide can cause fleeting moments of discomfort during an otherwise idyllic weekend outing. Some of these new residents stand fascinated by a local wood-carver's booth. He's set out a plastic sign indicating that he will happily accept Visa, AmEx, MasterCard, and Discover for his decorative whittled logs. Brooklyn has simply boomed, and few booms are graceful or without collateral damage. The number of business establishments in Kings County grew from around 37,000 in 1998 to nearly 50,000 in 2011. Since 1990, the population has increased by nearly 300,000 with a whopping 222,842 falling between twenty-five and twenty-nine years of age. Of Kings County's 2.5 million residents, according to Census Bureau data, nearly 50 percent are white. Nearly a quarter of the population is under eighteen. One is almost assaulted by the youth energy upon hitting the street, and the pockets of Old Brooklyn need and fatigue become things the mind can sometimes yearn to bypass.

"Williamsburg and Greenpoint replaced the East Village," says the droll and bold Brooklyn-based writer Jonathan Ames, one of those pilgrims who in the early 1990s moved to the still quiet, affordable family neighborhood just one subway stop from East Fourteenth Street in Lower Manhattan. The streets of Williamsburg were desolate after ten P.M. back then. Some of them smelled like gasoline, or burning chemicals. There was no view of Manhattan across the East River because massive, often abandoned Gothic factories obscured it. No developers had yet built the skyscraper condos that now edge the shore. "When the real estate developers gave artists these cheap lofts they were chumming the waters. 'We'll let artists live here and at some point a really cool café will open up and then the *New York Times* will write about that really cool café,'" Ames says. "After a while, if you said, 'I'm moving to DUMBO,' they wouldn't think you were moving there because you wanted to be in an art scene. You just wanted to be where all the restaurants and bars and young people are living."

The tall, gleaming condos lay empty and spooky for much of George W. Bush's second presidential term and well into Obama's first. I recall a sold-out Belle and Sebastian concert on the waterfront in late September of 2010 that basically took place in their shadow and seemed stranger for it. Here was a Twee superband that personified the new Brooklyn, playing their ballads and jaunty rock for an adoring crowd, but backdropped by ghost towers. With the election of President Obama in 2008 and the return of optimism, these haunted houses began to fill up, as did Bedford Avenue, Williamsburg's main thoroughfare, as crowded on a weekend afternoon as Times Square or Piccadilly. The pilgrims came back with a vengeance. Just as it was after the Second World War, we got a big scare with 9/11, and in the wake, all we wanted—us Westerners anyway—was youth, beauty, and food that made us feel special for selecting it.

TV got a lot better. So did hot sauce. "It's going to make your mouth happy," a woman hawking probiotic hot sauce promises to passersby inside the yard. Did probiotic hot sauce exist five years ago, when there was talk of another Great Depression? The Bush era aged us all, and some of us before our time. It enervated the actual young, and made the aging older before their time. Once it finally concluded, young and youngish Americans seemed to be determined to get their lost innocence back with a vengeance; even the thirty-somethings and young boomers wanted to reclaim some youth taken by fear and war and "truthiness" and . . . more fear. "I'm into this woodworking stuff," the mysterious Adam (Adam Driver) says during a rare and revealing moment from HBO's award-winning comedy *Girls*. Most days, as imagined by creator Lena Dunham, he's a cool customer, but clearly there's a part of his soul that is crying out for beauty and truth. Adam, who drinks milk like an infant, constantly and compulsively, is searching for the right way to grow up.

Some Narnias are not full of industrious souls. Rather, they are otherworlds, which simply enchant without stoking the urge to collect and consume. They're fantastical, mostly fictional. In Brooklyn and "Brooklyn" (the real world, if you will) you have to purchase the snow and the creatures and the experience itself. While it might seem folly to some, this retail-happy land is not without its share of genuinely inspired inventors. Among these aesthetes is the clever soul who has penetrated the lid of an old-fashioned glass mason jar and welded a metal straw to the top for sipping. It's not the lightbulb, the combustion engine, or the silicon chip, but America doesn't make these things anymore. What we produce is . . . "Brooklyn." It's our greatest export to the world right now, the way "Hollywood" was a half century ago and Silicon Valley was three decades later.

Another vendor has set out a basket of quills. They're glossy and long and, upon first glance, one can imagine someone writing a poem with them, dipping the tips into ink. "I haven't decided what to do with them yet," she says. "I'm just selling them. Sometimes I stick them through my hair."

Pursuing youth and beauty can be dangerous too. There are children, again mostly white, in shorts and sneakers, snapping off those old firecrackers against the asphalt, one after the next—"Pop! Pop! Pop!"—and cackling gleefully. Some are plucking rubber noses and wax lips from rough wood bins on the ground, and it occurs to me that they are acting the same as the adults around them who are look-ing for their initials among the rusted metal letters or inquiring about how the cucumber-mint lemonade comes together, percentage wise.

"There's much less interest from certain members of the young African-American community in joining," says Winfrey Harris, whose blog often deconstructs issues of popular culture and race, "in posing as Twee, and not growing up."

The actual children are the whimsy-obsessed offspring of a largely unchallenged generation. This generation used to be called X. Then came Y, or the Millennials. Today they've all combined, even along with some late-cusp baby boomers, and fused into some kind of multiheaded Generation Twee, or Twee Tribe, all the while breeding ever-gentler boys and girls with epicurean taste and a love for the formerly obscure and the baroque. To many this hydra is a serious threat to culture.

"Chiefly derogatory," warns the *Oxford English Dictionary* before de-fining the word *twee* as "excessively affected, quaint, pretty, or senti-mental." It's derived from the sound of a small child attempting to say the word *sweet*. Imagine a three-year-old pointing at a rosebush and observing, "Flower smells twee!" Now imagine a twenty-five-year-old man saying the same, or a sixty-year-old grandfather. Now imagine him dressed like a vested, precocious Truman Capote in 1948. Who wouldn't want to punch that guy in the ear?

But there may be virtue here as well, fighting to be noticed as the class and racial divides are slowly parsed and hopefully one day elim-inated. Twee, captial *T*, like Punk, captial *P*, is not merely a fashion statement or what Winfrey Harris correctly labeled a "lifestyle." It is all of those things, but only in the same reductive way that Punk was about three chords, torn tees, safety pins, and giving an old person the reverse victory salute. But Punk was also about "freedom," as Kurt Cobain famously stated, and Twee can be similarly liberating from the pressure to be cool, swaggering, aggressively macho, and old at heart.

"There's an intrinsic value and appeal," the writer Simon Reynolds says today of the movement's prevalent style and ethic. "Beyond saying it's class bound or race bound, there are intrinsic values and appeals to it. A handcrafting aesthetic is probably nicer than buying things at Target. The idea of being sensitive. The idea of guys not being dicks. The good outweighs the bad as an option or a way of being in the world and seeing yourself. I see the appeal of it. But it gets cutesy-fied. I went to an Etsy-type fair some months ago and there seems to be a big move from owls to narwhals, those whales with horns. Narwhals seem to be appearing on a lot of T-shirts, whereas the previous year it was owls. It does get a bit Twee. You can't get around that."

Like the most enduring youth movements, it's also strongly political; whether it pertains to preservation of a threatened methodology or the championing of green business acumen or simply pushing back against the pricks—virtually all Twee heroes, fictional and real, from Dumbo the flying elephant to Calvin Johnson (the monkish Indie label head) to Morrissey (arguably the King of Twee) to, most recently, Casey Heynes (the Australian teenager who body-slammed a menacing classmate and became a YouTube superstar after a lifetime of suffering for being shy and overweight) and Zooey Deschanel (the self-styled Queen of Twee), make their bones confronting cruelty, sometimes even as they inspire backlashes and voilence by nature of their very preciusness and often proud punchability.

"When I was twelve years old I put on my velour jacket and I wrote with my fountain pen—in my Moleskine notebook, which I had before it was cool—'Haters gonna hate,'" says actor and author John Hodgman, only half joking, "and I knew I was onto something." We are now in the era when the free-range, organically fed chickens have come home to roost.

Where there's an ethos and an ideal, there's going to be resistance. Twee yearns to welcome a spectrum: all professions, ages, types, and there is a growing awareness that if its reforms are to continue and the movement is to thrive and last, like Punk or Hip-Hop, it will have to address these issues of race and class. Its ethics, however, have remained concrete:

* Beauty over ugliness.
* A sharp, almost incapacitating awareness of darkness, death, and cruelty, which clashes with a steadfast focus on our essential goodness.
* A tether to childhood and its attendant innocence and lack of greed.
* The utter dispensing with of "cool" as it's conventionally known, often in favor of a kind of fetishization of the nerd, the geek, the dork, the virgin.
* A healthy suspicion of adulthood.
* An interest in sex but a wariness and shyness when it comes to the deed.
* A lust for knowledge, whether it's the sequence of an album, the supporting players in an old Hal Ashby or Robert Altman film, the lesser-known Judy Blume books, or how to grow the perfect purple, Italian, or Chinese eggplant or orange cauliflower.

* The cultivation of a passion project, whether it's a band, a zine, an Indie film, a website, or a food or clothing company. Whatever it is, in the eye of the Twee it is a force of good and something to live for.

These are the values that redeem the true Twee and separate them from the poseurs and hypocrites and weekenders and bad apples and, most egregiously, the cynics, who buy and sell bootleg versions of the aesthetic. A testament to the strength of Twee as a modern movement is the sheer volume of carpetbaggers eager to unload a version of it and the well-meaning, perhaps naïve souls who, knowingly or not, abet them.

"The buyer of $9 jam, after all, isn't another maker of $9 jam," the writer Benjamin Wallace pointed out in a *New York* magazine feature on the rise of this culture, "The Twee Party," published in the spring of 2012. "It's the guy whose multinational robotic assembly line spits out jars of $1 jam. Or it's his trustafarian son, the Global Jam Logistics heir. Or it's the private-equity guy who just off-shored GJL to a sweatshop in Bangalore," Wallace writes. Seventies Punk and eighties Hip-Hop were street-hardened and suspicious youth movements. Indeed, Twee is often a too-trusting movement, where the well meaning sometimes do not equal the well informed, those business starter-uppers who have not read Small Is Beautiful, the British economist E. F. Schumacher's 1973 bible for conscientious and eco-minded business decorum. For every genuinely conscientious Warby Parker, there are plenty of wolves out there in their Warby Parker–style nerd spectacles, emboldened by the voracious desire for curator culture. Thrift suddenly becomes *vintage* and anything edible can fall under the hard-to confirm-but irresistible term *artisanal*.

The microsuspicions of purity feed the macrosuspicion some hold for Twee; it's simply too lousy with frauds and impossible to truly purify or regulate. This, again, is no new battle.

"For the rich countries, they say, the most important task now is 'education for leisure,'" Schumacher writes (again, forty years ago!), "and, for the poor countries, the 'transfer of technology.'" As the world is Brooklynized will it truly be so, or will we make what Schumacher calls the "suicidal error" of assuming that so long as a product appears artisanal, it's all good? "The illusion of unlimited powers, nourished by astonishing scientific and technological achievements, has produced the concurrent illusion of having solved the problem of production." Shilling and collecting faster does nature no favors and remains part of the suicidal error.

Take the classic "Brooklyn Without Limits" episode of the sitcom *30 Rock*. Here, Tina Fey's character Liz Lemon is briefly enchanted by "Brooklyn Zack," a mystery utopian who "throws pool parties in Dumpsters" and, more important, cuts affordable jeans that make her ass look fantastic. "Big business is what's screwing up this country," Lemon tells her mentor, the realist Jack Donaghy (Alec Baldwin). "I live like a cowboy by buying quality locally made jeans [and] also eating beans out of a can due to impatience." This exchange perfectly captures the sense of cheap outlaw fix one gets from weekending in what was once a genuine bohemia. Lemon is quickly disabused of the notion that "stores like this are saving the world" when Donaghy reveals that Brooklyn Without Limits (a sort of stand-in for American Apparel) crafts its canvas messenger bags from unused "waterboarding hoods" and is secretly owned by evil empire Halliburton. Lemon must choose between her true personal/political values and the intoxicating smells and temptations of Brooklandia. She chooses the truth.

"We are told that gigantic organizations are inescapably necessary," Schumacher writes, "but when we look closely we notice that as soon as great size has been created there is often a strenuous attempt to attain smallness within bigness." Such will be the Zen-like challenge for the jam maker as we head toward what may literally become an endless summer. The gaint banking corporations that sponsor public bike exchanges are part of both the problem and the solution as we strive for some/equilibrium, or kind of Tweequilibrium.

But let's briefly, and happily, return to the books and records, since that, not fruit preserves or locally fished sea critters, is the real food for the modern tribal Twee—and again, it is a tribe, the Twee Tribe, not a singular generation. It has its elders and its newbies, and this strength in numbers has placed it above other subsets of the macro Indie or a kind of Perma-Punk; dubious offshoots like Sea Punk, Steampunk, or with regard to Hip-Hop, Gangsta Rap, or Booty Bass Rap. All Twee is one.

Naturally trusting (or yearning to be trusting) as it is, the Twee Tribe has already proven to be a very tricky one, perhaps the trickiest of them all, to join. Unlike Punk or Hip-Hop, an aspiring tribal Twee cannot get there simply via haircut or by turning one's baseball cap around. You have to read . . . a lot . . . and, generally, alone. You have to make friends with your Crosley suitcase turntable and record collection, your Criterion Collection, your 33 $\frac{1}{3}$ books, and your cut-out-and-pasted photos of dead film stars and authors. Simply taking yourself outside of society isn't enough. Once outside, you have to actually study. Twees cannot kick with the fray unless they carry a lot of cultural history in their heads, or at least on their devices: they are *Jeopardy!* contestants, boning up on Felt, the Swell Maps, Judee Sill, Anne Sexton, Michel Gondry, *Peanuts,* Roald Dahl, and *The Phantom Tollbooth.* And you don't only have to know those bands and books and filmmakers; you have to formulate an aesthetic around them. Take Belle and Sebastian's leader Stuart Murdoch. Handsome, pale, and vastly talented, Murdoch is a Gen Twee icon and one of those courageous, sensitive, perhaps too-smart figures we will chronicle farther along in these pages. In the mid-1990s, the Glaswegian dreamer was recovering from chronic fatigue syndrome and had to drop out of school and literally move back into his childhood bedroom. "When you're down and out, what you want is escapism," Murdoch told *Fresh Air* host Terry Gross in 2005. "At the period of time there was a core of groups in music that I listened to that took me somewhere else. And then I got very much into certain filmmakers as well. But then there reached a point where I wanted more escapism and more fantasy, and that's when I started to invent it for myself."

To listen to the audio commentary on a Blu-ray of a Wes Anderson film (he is another soul we will meet along the way here) is to enter a sort of confessional booth in which the director cops to shots he's stolen from dead heroes. This book will create a canon of sorts, and nearly every person mentioned will have a sharp awareness of other, sometimes greater canons. They aren't randomly chosen or reliant on coincidence or expediency or even the cosmic (perhaps I shouldn't point out that Holden Caulfield's middle name happens to be Morrisey, one *S* shy of the former Smiths' lead singer's handle). Many are connected either directly (*Peanuts* animator Bill Melendez, one of Wes

Anderson's heroes, got his start at the early Disney studios, working on marvels like *Fantasia*) or via a shared approach, with an adeptness at making original art from the sum of their influences—their imaginary friends and unmet heroes, as it were. Murdoch, Anderson, Dave Eggers, Andrew Bujalski, Miranda July, and, before them, Salinger, Schulz, Sendak, Gorey, Godard, Plath, the Velvet Underground, Jonathan Richman and the Modern Lovers, the Buzzcocks, Andy Kaufman, the Raincoats, the Smiths, They Might Be Giants, Whit Stillman, and Kurt Cobain are all unique and all precocious, impressionable, and, in this writer's reading, utterly, irrepressibly Twee. They are a kind of heroes' gallery of pajama people whose work will speak truth to the actually young and spiritually young for all time. They are sad Punks, scared Punks, angry nerds, violent femmes, bedroom sitters, undaunted idealists, and raggedy aesthetes, and they all share another aspect: lots of people hate them.

Even with regard to its artists, films, albums, and literature, and not merely its adherents in their cardigans, nobody is ambivalent about Twee. One either loves *Bugsy Malone*, Alan Parker's wry take on the 1930s gangster film with its all-child-actor cast talking like hoodlums and dames (the Tommy guns shoot whipped cream) and its jaunty, speakeasy score by diminutive Twee pop icon Paul Williams, or you think it's an enervating and endless cutesy-poo. Similarly, a young Michael Jackson's nasal, clueless rendition of the melancholy, world-weary Sinatra classic "It Was a Very Good Year" (from the Diana Ross television special when Jackson was barely a teen) is either adorable or insufferable. Again, children dressing and acting adult is only slightly less hate-making than adults who won't let go of childhood. Think about Morrissey, former lead singer of the Smiths, who is obsessed with the past and the passing of time and functions almost outside of society and certainly outside of the music industry as it stands, a sort of pure and righteous deity. Do you know anyone who lacks an opinion about him? The Smiths are either the brilliant band who "sang out to the slums" and "worked wonders for the strangled spirit," as Morrissey claims in his 2013 memoir, making a half dozen albums, all of them classics, and self-destructing just "as the songs were growing in stature"—or they are unlistenable.

Similarly, there are those who will see every Whit Stillman, Wes Anderson, Noah Baumbach, Sofia Coppola, Miranda July, or Andrew Bujalski film, know exactly what the pained bit of silence or pregnant pause *means* in every script, and feel the connection. And then there are the film critics like iconoclast Armond White, who will often dismiss them as pretentious and callow.

There are bibliophiles who purchase every new Dave Eggers, Jonathan Safran Foer, or Sarah Vowell book and fall asleep with them on their chests. Others roll their eyes and make quickly for the new James Elroy and a bracing whiskey and soda, snarling, "Good Lord, grow a pair!"

Recently some mourned HBO's cancellation of Jonathan Ames's *Bored to Death* after three highly Twee seasons, while others argued that three was three too many. Marc Jacobs unsuccessfully attempted to bring grunge fashion to the masses in the early 1990s, but then perfected his attack with his extremely Twee line of clothes and accessories that connected more organically with the precocious Indie spirit and featured actress Elle Fanning (star of Ms. Coppola's creeping, ponderous, but sunlit and beautiful *Somewhere*). Fanning is also frequently seen in Rodarte, another fashion house that is more like a dollhouse. Bookmarc, Jacob's bookstore, essentially re-creates a discerning Twee reader's shelves, its book buyers almost freakishly well-versed in the aesthetic. The outlets are now either havens for the smart, shy shopper or scapegoats for everything that's gone wrong with the 'hood.

If this book is about anything, it's about those who seem outwardly callow and frail but are secretly fearless. It's about geeks with guts.In a *New York Times* feature on the late David Rakoff (another hero of Twee lit), his editor Bill Thomas said this about Rakoff's posthumous novel in verse: "What is so special to me about the book is that it is the purest distillation of David's belief that we live in a world that is essentially cruel and indifferent, but there are remedies for that. And the remedies are kindness and beauty."

"It's so easy to laugh, it's so easy to hate," Morrissey sang during the bridge to the beloved Smiths ballad "I Know It's Over." "It takes guts to be gentle and kind." He throws a hard *g* into *guts,* as if to signal to his many followers that this is the key: *Guts!*

If Hip-Hop and Punk are about the now—"No future" or "Get rich or die trying"—Twee is decidedly about the then, even as it alters the present, possibly forever and (depending on whom you ask) for the better. And there is no more perfect "then" than an (often-idealized) boy- or girlhood. Of course, almost no Twee would truly want to return to high school, much less grade school, as it *really* was, but they keep the memory of themselves and their worldview at that time, the same way people carry Saint Christopher pendants. Lena Dunham even has children's book characters tattooed on her skin. Sofia Coppola nurtured an obsession with and even related to Kay

Thompson and Hilary Knight's fantastic if braggadocious Eloise. Much of the more abstract and smart-alecky Indie-rock lyrics owe a debt to Dr. Seuss and Edward Gorey. Dave Eggers and Spike Jonze nurtured a Maurice Sendak fixation all the way to a megabudget studio-film adaptation of *Where the Wild Things Are*. Bernard Waber's *The House on East 88th Street* provides a template for Wes Anderson's vision of urban romance and precociousness. Margaret Wise Brown and Clement Hurd's *Goodnight Moon* is read or referenced on both *The Wire* and *Mad Men* to signify a lost sense of innocence that these younger artists and burgeoning icons are so heroically struggling to grip forever.

Most classic children's books are told with few words, large type, and perfectly simple imagery rendered in pen-and-ink or watercolor illustrations that make the crazy, churning world seem calm and navigable. A good number of these books were literally created to be read before bed to fend off nightmares, and today, it seems they still do, only the nightmare is constant: dirty bombs, cyber bugs, global warming, exotic bird flu. The terror is as real as a Real Housewife.

The only thing scarier than death is the disappearance of youth. The Twee is both fascinated by and aghast at the passing of time as the body breaks down and the earth prepares to take us. Every child star's adult mug shot is an affront. They know that Wilbur the runt, saved by the obstinate Fern as he's about to be euthanized, then bottle-fed indoors, is going to be carted off to market as soon as he grows big enough. Five weeks, that's all he's got before he's bacon. But author E. B. White sensed that an out was needed, a bit of magical thinking: a benevolent spider who speaks with her web and keeps the hapless pig somehow eternally special.

In this way, White, Sendak, and Seuss become new romantic poets who all chose to look backward and celebrate childhood, nature, and individualism over herd think and scheming vulgarity and religious hypocrisy while remaining fully aware of how bloody and cruel things could get out there. And those who worshipped nature also knew well that nature itself, our growing and aging and sickening and dying, was the enemy.

There is a scene in the 1961 teen drama *Splendor in the Grass* where Natalie Wood's disturbed, horny, and terribly Twee Deanie Loomis rises before her high school class to deconstruct Wordsworth's ode "Intimations of Immortality," from which the film takes its title. Deanie stammers, "When we're young we look at things very idealistically, I guess. And I think Wordsworth means that when we grow up, we have to forget the ideals of youth . . ." She promptly bursts into tears and rushes out of the room, bound for a good, long rest at a sanitarium, but you see her point, and Wordsworth's. We all have to face the inevitable, and this is what makes Twee so sweet and so controversial. It's the French resistance, armed with one fight song after another, marching into battle singing, "We don't have to change at all."

With "the easy access to every aspect of pop music now there's no strain or risk involved for the listener," Morrissey observed in the middle of the last decade, when he was in his late forties. "There's nowhere to hide or to find the hidden and the forbidden for yourself—it's all on vulgar display. Certainly when I was younger than I am now it was very unusual to come across any other living human who actually heard the records that you heard and it was very unusual to discuss lyrics with somebody. But these days of course with the Internet and so forth and the obsession with knowing as much as possible—it's all become meaningless where everyone knows everything instantly."

Similarly, as Simon Reynolds once observed, "The Indie scene is struggling to protect 'innocence' in the face of a sophisticated culture." And that was in 1986! If anything can dilute the movement's power, it's the movement itself; hence the appearances of an organized campaign against Twee mainstreamers like Zooey Deschanel and Lena Dunham.

Once confined to the bedroom, Twee is now beyond viral, but will this mean the eradication of bullying, blight, ignorance, misogyny, three *Human Centipede* films, the Kardashians, and the Real Housewives? Will it save humankind or, as many haters fear, soften it to the point of inertia or implosion? It depends on whom you ask: William Blake's Lamb or his Tyger. This book provides no conclusions (that's your job), only a sense of history and trajectory. I will lay out how a segment of society got here and pushed the Twee aesthetic along, and where are we going as a new, hybrid generation. The Twee Tribe, with its teens and sixty-year-olds, its carpetbaggers and narcs and exploiters and its saints, pushes the movement daily, hourly, by the second and millisecond, toward its destiny. Is that a good place for humankind, or an even worse state than the one we are already in? I offer few opinions, beyond an aside or two. As you read on, I hope your own opinion about this—the slowest, strangest, and most polarizing of all the great postwar youth movements—coalesces as you encounter Anne Frank, Holly Golightly, Edward Gorey, Plath, Seuss, Morrissey, Murdoch, Zooey Deschanel, and a fuck-lot of kittens.

Chapter 1

The Mean Reds

1945–1963

In which an idealistic but haunted collection of artists, industrialists, actors, poets, songwriters, and one teenage girl (posthumously) endeavor to piece back together a broken world and make it new, safer, and more beautiful using hope, vision, and even memories of the horror and pain they'd seen and suffered.

While members of "the Greatest Generation" are passing on with each new year, their sacrifice, their stories, and the violence and destruction that they survived still affect our modern popular culture well over a half century on. Children are taught by schoolteachers about the great battles of the two world wars and the impossible cruelty and inhumanity of the Holocaust. But the postwar years also gave rise to a dozen or more unconventional and unofficial teachers who took on this task either directly or, often, by sharing their own mental scars. Here we are considering the artists, those among the survivors who wrote or sang or imagined and virtually invented a new world that somehow reclaimed whimsy, hope, idealism, and kindness in the face of battle and soon, the Cold War's long nightmare. Whimsy was not merely frivolous to these beleaguered but resilient men and women, but rather absolutely necessary for the survival of the species. Openheartedness, a loud, primal yowl of honesty, or a whispered plea for sweetness was not embarrassing or unseemly or, most crucially, unmasculine here but instead a powerful expression of grief and fear that instantly made any other kind of outpouring seem trite and guarded.

Walt Disney, born in Chicago in 1901 to itinerant and hardscrabble working-class parents, was witness to both world wars of the early and mid-twentieth century. The young Disney was handsome, with a wide forehead, an elegant nose, a strong chin, and a mischievous glint in his eye. Driven by patriotism and a desire to escape his rough upbringing, he was all too eager to serve in World War I. Alas, he was too young. Perhaps portending of his future ingenuity, he forged his passport and traveled overseas anyway, into the action. During the war, he drove a Red Cross ambulance in France, tending to the mangled and the dead.

Although he was the youngest male in the Disney clan, the war girded him and he grew up quickly. By the time he returned to America, he had the kind of preternatural focus that makes presidents and empires. Animation was still a new art form then, with technology seeming to develop by the hour. Walt Disney drew and sketched characters and intended to study these new techniques to bring them to life, both as a vocation and a means to entertain what he had directly perceived as an increasingly dangerous and dark world. In his early twenties, while his peers were gallivanting to the hedonism-stoking new jazz sounds, Disney sat alone in the library studying textbooks. Here is a trope we will see over and over again as we go on, the solitary party-misser lost in a world of books but destined to emerge, ironically, as the centerpiece of an even greater revelry one day. The largely European visionaries that enthralled Disney, inventors like Émile Cohl and Ladislas Starevich made two-dimensional figures dance and move as if conjuring spirits and company off the page. By the 1920s, Walt and his brother Roy had formed a company and were making their own films. Each new expensive and rare camera, lens, or filter provided a sense of fun—and a lack of shame, as there seemed no right or wrong way to operate them. The Disney Company entitled their product Laugh-O-Grams in cheerful tribute to both the folly that the machines inspired and their determination to return laughter to a post–World War I America.

The young Walt Disney was a gambler, frequently risking his entire fortune on ambitious projects. But he had his pragmatic side as well. Sensing the power of a strong brand, he endeavored to create a prototypical mascot that would, he hoped, be his key to wealth and power. This ill-fated creature was ironically named: Oswald the Lucky Rabbit. Oswald the Lucky Rabbit is all but forgotten today, but the poor guy bears more than a faint resemblance to Disney's greatest icon and spiritual avatar, Mickey Mouse: a broad smile, long black ears, and shorts to cover his modesty. Mickey (for a very brief time Mortimer, until Walt's wife suggested otherwise) was created in 1928. In early shorts like "Plane Crazy," he was bright, filled with ingenuity and patience—all the best qualities of the American worker. When we first heard him (it was Walt's own voice) in "Steamboat Willie," we had a high, happy, plucky voice to go with the ears and the shorts. Most of all, Mickey had hope in the face of adversity, making him—if not Walt Disney himself—the first American Twee icon, and certainly the most enduring.

When Walt Disney first journeyed to Hollywood in the late 1920s, he had little money and no entry to the studio lots. There were few prospects, but the young man had determination, a battle-tested sense of whimsy, and an almost holy frivolity. And he had Mickey. For a while, he attempted to be a live-action, conventional film director of live actors, but when that didn't pan out he and his partners fell back into what they had to admit was a more natural path: breathtakingly inventive, enchanting, and sometimes quite darkly themed animation.

The lack of fear of darker, often morbid subject matter—clearly drawn from the war—and the fact that the Disney studio shop was one of the first independents, setting up in a big house far from the gilded lots of Paramount and Warner Bros., further establishes Disney's Twee bona fides. He was Indie when Indie wasn't cool. Perhaps a little Goth too. Goth culture is about nothing if not about making something joyful and positive about horror and, well, death.

"The Skeleton Dance" is as macabre as popular child-aimed art gets. The visions of World War I never really left him, but a decade on, the young Walt Disney was combating them with humor. One of the first and most famous of the seventy-five short films he made early in his independent studio career, "Dance" virtually set the template for Tim Burton's oeuvre. (Burton pays homage to it in the animated 2005 film *Corpse Bride*.)

"The Skeleton Dance" concerns a graveyard late at night. A dance troupe of skeletons sneaks from their crypts and boogies to Edvard Grieg's "March of the Trolls" (orchestrated by future Bugs Bunny composer and arranger Carl Stalling). Other Silly Symphonies take on classic children's fables like "The Three Little Pigs" (also not exactly light fare). The shorts were inventive technologically, with both "The

Skeleton Dance" and Mickey Mouse's 1928 debut "Steamboat Willie" receiving sound in postproduction. Soon audiences were flocking to see whatever the Disney studios would come up with next, and Mickey would appear along with a list of superlative-worthy subjects in Cole Porter's 1934 standard "You're the Top." The deeply colorful "Flowers and Trees" from 1932, hand painted in an age when even movie stars lived in black and white, won a special Academy Award.

Feature films came next, many of them with vast crews and budgets that even in the mid-1930s exceeded millions of dollars. *Snow White*, based, again without fear of darkness, on a Gothic Grimm's fairy tale, was a blockbuster in 1937, and *Pinocchio*, arriving in 1940, would eventually prove a hit as well, albeit upon re-release. The films started a tradition that continues to this day: they are aimed at children, are embedded with a variety of morality messaging, but they manage not to offend their adult moviegoing companions, rather reconnecting them to some of the heartwarming goodness that they may have lost to time. The message goes down easy when rendered in Technicolor with animation that was the modern equivalent of fine art. Then came the Second World War.

Pinocchio opens, as war overseas is escalating, with what some consider one of the most serene and joyful moments in cinema history: a hobo-ragged Jiminy Cricket (given a smooth, Bing Crosby–esque voice by Cliff Edwards) singing "When You Wish Upon a Star." The song itself, rivaled only by Henry Mancini's "Moon River," may be the ultimate Twee anthem. Moonlit, alone, and at peace, Jiminy Cricket delivers what would become Disney's de facto message: "When you wish upon a star, makes no difference who you are, anything your heart desires will come to you." If you take the leap—and in a time when the larger world population is about to make its discovery of Auschwitz and the bombings of Dresden, Hiroshima, and Nagasaki loom, that very leap is foolish—you will be rewarded.

The Beach Boys' fragile Brian Wilson, born in 1942, two years after *Pinocchio* and one after America entered the war, never got over the message or melody of "When You Wish Upon a Star." Years later it would inform the first masterpiece to distinguish the Beach Boys from a dozen other Southern California surf-rock purveyors, the ballad "Surfer Girl." Later still the Beach Boys would pay direct homage to the ethos with "Disney Girls (1957)," a nostalgic ode to childhood: "Oh, reality, it's not for me, and it makes me laugh. Oh, fantasy world and Disney girls, I'm coming back."

No matter one's age and no matter how disturbed by cataclysmic events outside one's room, the song implies, all one has to do is spot Jiminy Cricket's star and make a wish.

Pinocchio himself is the by-product of a wish of faith. He is the creation of the lonely wood-carver Gepetto, who lives alone with a goldfish and, yes, a cat (Figaro). Gepetto's workshop is visited one night by the Blue Fairy, who rewards the old man for all his lovingly crafted toys, clocks, and music boxes by granting his wish that his beloved Pinocchio come to life. Of course, there's a catch. He is, after all, still just a walking, talking piece of pine.

"You have to prove yourself to be truthful and unselfish," the fairy warns Pinocchio, "then you will be a real boy."

"The Bully," the bête noire of the humanist Twee hero, is taken to task far back in Disney's oeuvre too. Another early Silly Symphony is the fairy tale "The Ugly Duckling" (1939), with the namesake duck mocked by his fellow ducks until one day he is revealed to be a graceful swan. Then there's the case of *Dumbo* (1941), quite literally a circus freak, delivered by the stork to his mother, an elephant in a traveling circus, who loves the calf unconditionally despite his enormous ears. Dumbo, of course, becomes the star attraction of the circus, those ears acting as a pair of gliders that enable him to fly around the big top. "Beware of who and what you pick on," Disney seems to be saying.

It's ironic that many of these films were popular all across the European movie market at the same time that the most thuggish, institutionalized, and deadliest wave of bullying and intolerance was sweeping the continent. 1n 1938, the year that *Time* magazine proclaimed Adolf Hitler Man of the Year, Disney produced a short film version of the pacifist children's book *Ferdinand the Bull*.

In the age of modern warfare, questions about the nature of humankind began to be taken on by pop culture; it was no longer simply the province of escapism and lighter fare aimed at children. Even the young could not avoid philosophical issues. Are we born or made evil? Hitler was once a baby, just like every other baby in the nursery, or was he different? In the eighteenth and nineteenth centuries, such things were still fairly cut-and-dried: the devil was real and so were angels. But in the postindustrial secular age, debates about what exactly contributed to our nature and when it began could no longer be dismissed. A new, difficult, and relatively sophisticated kind of secular morality, so prevalent in the Disney films, became commonplace among nearly all popular children's entertainment. Munro Leaf and Robert Lawson's Ferdinand begins life in their slight but powerful 1936 book—and the Disney film two years later—as a misfit (as most Disney heroes do). His mother frets that he is "not like other bulls." He is a loner. While his peers count off the days until they are big and strong enough to go to the city and fight in the arena against the heroic matadors, Ferdinand has no such interest. "Why don't you run and play with the other bulls?" his mother pleads. But Ferdinand is content to sit under his tree and smell the flowers. Two years pass and Ferdinand has not changed his ways, but of course nature has unavoidably altered him. The bull calf is now stock strong and massive.

By chance, as a car from Madrid is passing through town, Ferdinand has the misfortune of sitting on a bumble bee. Ferdinand rises, snorts, and bucks, impressing the men who then take him into the city and redub him Ferdinand the *Fierce*. Hype fills the bullring to capacity as the greatest matadors vie to be the first to take on Ferdinand, but when they draw their blades, he refuses to fight. It's the anticlimax of the season. Frustrated, the Spaniards are forced to cart him back to the cork tree, where he lives out his days in peace.

Ferdinand, often interpreted as a commentary on the Spanish Civil War, was a merchandizing sensation in 1938 as the German army was secretly plotting to invade Poland and begin a thousand-year Reich of world domination. The bull who refused to fight would appear on playing cards and board games and as children's toys; he was a triumphant outsider and resister who would not buckle to thugs, a Twee archetype for the ages even three quarters of a century later. Elliott Smith, Twee cinema-soundtrack stalwart and lost boy of Indie rock, had the bull tattooed on his flesh.

The clever Emo-soul Punks Fall Out Boy would pay homage with the title of their breakthrough 2005 album *From Under the Cork Tree* (the tree where the gentle bull loved to lie and dream).

The war itself hit the Disney studios hard in the bank book as well as in the soul of its increasingly dark but still crucially child-friendly subject matter. Case in point: when the hunters come after Bambi and his mother in the most notorious scene from that eponymous 1942 film, some of the animators reportedly suggested that the audience be shown the adult deer's bloodied corpse in the snow. Disney absolutely refused.

Combat during the First World War had helped steel the young Walt Disney's spine, but as a middle-aged businessman with a family to support and a studio to run, losing a large percentage of the European market was a blow. The Disney lots were no longer making enchanting features; they were housing Lockheed aircraft. Disney began stark propaganda films such as *Victory Through Air Power*, a still technologically stunning but dour manual for "neutralizing the opposing state." Walt Disney being a natural storyteller, these harsh realities are couched in history lessons designed to gin up patriotism with the tale of the Wright brothers' triumph at Kitty Hawk. Yet at heart, this is a Disney film about killing—particularly the most efficient ways to kill and destroy the enemy. The man who brought us the dancing mushrooms of 1940's astounding *Fantasia* was now animating bombardiers and explosions.

Disney's enterprise would of course survive the war, and thrive, rebounding with more feature-length smashes like 1951's *Alice in Wonderland*. By then, the man himself was through with violence and pain. The weariness was a long time in coming. *Lady and the Tramp* (1955), yet another classic, was "dedicated to all dogs," the implication being that loyalty and simplicity were not only admirable but worthy of great reward. The titular Tramp is a cynic, commenting at one point, "The human heart has only so much room for love and affection," but Disney proves him wrong in film. Lady melts the street-smart mutt's heart, later inspiring a classic monologue in Whit Stillman's *The Last Days of Disco*: "Essentially it's a primer on love and marriage directed at very young people, imprinting on their little psyches the idea that smooth-talking delinquents recently escaped from the local pound are a good match for nice girls from sheltered homes." Disney himself had a place in mind where all were welcome and even the most reprobate and recidivist scoundrels and "chicken thieves," as the Tramp was, would be welcome and somehow redeemed. That same year, Disneyland, a real-life Narnia, albeit one with a carefully maintained image and a perhaps disingenuous facade, opened to the public.

Disneyland was made to last forever, immune to the vicissitudes of fashion. Built on acres of orange groves near Anaheim, a conservative bastion of Southern California, it was conceived from the start, at the beginning of World War II, as a wholesome sanctum where our values and core freedoms, protected by the loss of young life overseas, would be kept safe, and where children would be encouraged to dream. Walt Disney and his crew envisioned, or "Imagineered," a haven where employees were mandated to be cheerful and that would suggest simple, rugged, plucky, small-town America: Main Street, U.S.A.

The carnivals that Disney recalled from his childhood were prurient and dirty. Disneyland, and later Disney World in Florida, would be different. Happiness was part of the attraction, as were Mickey and his pals Donald and Goofy and his girlfriend Minnie. Disneyland was subdivided into a series of "lands": Frontierland. Tomorrowland. A "place" is somewhere that you simply are, but a "land" is a place to explore, in this case without the danger and intrepid spirit that actual exploration requires. None of the corners of the villages were sharp; they were all rounded. The threat of earthquakes was played down, as each structure resembled a kind of large dollhouse. There were no pests, despite the discarding of tons of uneaten food and garbage. The place was artificial and larger than life, rather than reinforced, ready for nature's hard realities.

Disney, now in his midfifties, became a father figure full of hard-won calm for our newly prosperous but still recovering country. He appeared at movie premieres and on the new medium of television as a smiling, comforting presence. To share in his vision of goodness and innocence over evil, one could, in the TV age, now swear allegiance to Mr. Disney and Mickey Mouse. Unlike the Communist Party, the Mickey Mouse Club was a perfectly acceptable organization and would provide children, and young adults, a sense of both belonging and well-being, for a small price and perhaps a gesture of allegiance (donning a yarmulke-like skullcap affixed with plastic mouse ears).

For adults, to enter Disneyland was to re-enter childhood. Grown-ups were encouraged to take their children, once they had them, and experience that childhood together. Turn on *The Mickey Mouse Club,* which ran on the ABC network starting in 1955, and you could get a smaller dosage of the highly comforting and perfectly Twee spirit Disney invented and tended. By the 1960s, with the world once again in tumult, Disney's security force had grown adept at neutralizing those who saw the Magic Kingdom as a metaphor and therefore a perfect place to protest. Today, Disneyland remains a second and often preferable reality, and also an immovable one. Even in the age of terrorism and bag checks, warring and spying, it's as safe and solid as it was back when it opened in '55; anachronisms like the iPod are discouraged among the staff, and hot dogs, probably the least safe thing in the park, will always be on the menu.

Two other key keepers of the postwar spirit of hope and invention as a balm for horror and destruction were Disney's contemporaries: the primly dressed but aggressively wry couple Charles and Ray Eames. The Eameses were dashing, immaculately attired designers, architects, and filmmakers who are most famous for their body-hugging plywood and later plastic chairs, conceived of a series of new kinds of houses, modular and perfect for the returning soldier and the family he would inevitably start. The Eameses themselves—Charles in his tweed suit with pipe and bow tie, and Ray with her smart dresses and pulled-back hair—were Twee Tribe elders. And unlike Disney, who cut a rather conservative figure, the Eameses seemed Twee creatures in themselves, posing together in staged, publicity-type shots atop a motorcycle or pinned by a series of metal racks.

The Eameses were personalities, hosting great, whimsical dinner parties at their dream house in the middle of a wood in the Pacific Palisades up the California coast from Disneyland. They often served flowers as dessert to invited guests. Today *Eames* is a diluted word, used by eBay vendors to describe vaguely modern furniture, mostly of the Ikea variety, or knockoffs, but in the late 1940s and '50s and through the '70s and '80s, the couple was joined in both a kind of life-as-a-movie sense of theatricality and a commitment to make the new world a more practical and beautiful place. As Wes Anderson's would be decades on, their clean-cut appearance and sense of palatable but progressive whimsy was catnip to corporate sponsors. As with Anderson's now-iconic American Express card ad, the Eameses' most famous film would be short: an innovative piece for IBM entitled *Powers of Ten*, "a film dealing with the relative size of things in the universe and the effect of adding another zero."

The 1977 short begins with a couple enjoying a picnic in a park in

Chicago, then zooms out, adding a zero to the distance measurement of the bird's-eye view over them until the viewer is taken out of the atmosphere and years away at the speed of light—and is then returned to the park.

In the years after World War II and through the horrifying and tense Cold War, the Eameses were among those artists who crucially reclaimed science and technology from those who would use it to destroy cities and people—the "Masters of War" that Bob Dylan would soon excoriate. The Eameses were Masters of Twee by contrast. Their sense of the highly personal craft that was meant for sale and consumption predated the Etsy revolution by a half century.

Of all the champions of sensitivity and gentleness as a weapon, perhaps it was the writers who gave the strongest voice and the most direct succor to the war-wounded. A book, like a Bible, can be held the way a child holds a doll, traveled with and referred to when the room begins to spin with vertigo and dread.

New Englander Theodor Geisel, provides yet another way out of despair and existential malaise, a swirling, colorful, almost violently whimsical proto-Twee pathway. He was already in his forties when World War II hit. Even before the American forces' engagement, Geisel became noteworthy for his scathing cartoons of Adolf Hitler—such as "Mein Early Kampf," which portrayed the dictator as a petulant infant in diapers (but with that famous mustache). Geisel even worked with *Ferdinand* cocreator Leaf on a recurring strip aimed at soldiers that featured a character named Snafu. As the German surrender drew to a close, he was deputized by the War Department to create an instructive film designed to give the Allies a plan for occupying and eventually reconstructing the defeated Reich. Given a major's rank, Geisel flew to Europe, ending up in Paris to screen the film directed by Frank

Capra and entitled, simply, *Your Job in Germany*. Comparing it to the books of Dr. Seuss is like comparing Disney's *Victory Through Aviation* to *Peter Pan*. It's as bleak and as practical as film gets. "The problem now is future peace," Geisel writes. "That is your job in Germany. Lay the groundwork for a peace that could last forever, or just the opposite. You could lay the groundwork for a new war to come!" A typical instruction is: "You'll see ruins. You'll see flowers. You'll see mighty pretty scenery, but don't let it fool you! You are in enemy country! Be alert."

Geisel himself remained alert after Paris, where he saw the devastation, the wounded, and the pointless and cruel anarchy of combat. This bred a kind of madcap, existential freedom, tinged with not a little anger, that would inform his later work, beginning in 1957 with the surprise hit *The Cat in the Hat* (under the pen name, of course, of Dr. Seuss). The titular Cat does what he wants despite the almost incessant protestations of a panic-stricken fish belonging to a pair of children he visits one "cold and rainy day."

The Cat wears a tall red-and-white chapeau that would, four decades on, be adopted by Ecstasy- and speed-fueled ravers as a sort of tribute to the anarchic feline's madcap stance. He is also probably a sociopath, and certainly an exhibitionist. "I know some new tricks!" he promises the children, and refuses to vacate when asked. The cat is, in a sense, chaos itself, made palatable for children. It's as if Seuss is saying, "Get to know this cat, because you will see him again . . . and again. Be cool when this cat comes around." As with Disney, darkness, angst, and a kind of implicit but not overstated realism that children instinctively appreciated were never too far from Seuss's enchantment through subsequent books like *The Lorax* and his holiday tale *How the Grinch Stole Christmas*.

The Seuss stories, as a series of wildly successful animated films and television specials attest, translated seamlessly to the then-new media. They were at once throwbacks to the fables and incredibly modern and fearless, almost Punk. The first of which, the live action *The 5,000 Fingers of Dr. T,* is downright anarchic. It's a surrealist waking dream about a piano lesson gone prepsychedelic. Cowritten by Seuss, the 1953 film is little more than a colorful set piece that warns against being too strict with the hard-practicing piano student. The evil Dr. Terwilliker exists in a dream world where he tends a mad vision of louder, faster concertos. Seuss's fatherless hero Bart Collins seems to ask, "Why bother?" A key to the author's appeal is that he has insight into this bit of childhood philosophy. The things adults prize often pale in comparison with pure fun. To have fun is to be alive.

This is not to say Seuss is a hedonist. From Seuss's early children's books, like *Horton Hears a Who!* (1954) to his *The Butter Battle Book,* four decades later, we find surface-simple stories that are deeply pregnant with morality (in the first case, a plea for tolerance and faith; in the latter, a Cold War parable about the dangers of hawkish fervor and the absurdity of mutually assured destruction).

Horton the elephant, like Ferdinand, is a gentle giant in the "Jungle of Nool" who communicates with a microscopic citizen of Whoville. None of the other wild animals (monkeys, kangaroos) can hear the Whos shout at Horton, and they dismiss him as crazy. "A person's a person, no matter how small," goes the moral. It's a plea for faith and tolerance by someone who has seen, firsthand, the testing of one and the absence of another. And it's aimed at children because Seuss posits that they are instinctively moral. The world corrupts. Nobody is born hateful.

In *The Butter Battle Book*, the absurdity of prejudice is highlighted just in case. Seuss's Yooks nearly destroy their rival Zooks for eating their toast butter-side down instead of up. Separated by a Berlin-like Wall, each side concocts more and more elaborate weaponry to prepare for a growing conflict; moving dubiously from slingshots to the "Eight-Nozzled, Elephant-Toted Boom-Blitz," *Butter Battle* ends on a vague note, a stalemate, with bomb shelters dug and both sides pointing intricate (but Seussian-ridiculous) weapons at each other. "We'll see," says an elder, when asked about what happens next, "We will see." One could be heavy, Seuss proved, even dour, without frightening off children or losing that crucial sense of whimsy. It was a rare and useful trick; and a must for any protest artist worth a damn.

In 1950 there were about 6 million TV sets in American homes. A decade later, there were upward of 60 million. Network programmers, with a huge demand to meet, turned to children's stories to fill the airwaves and provide a proto-version of what is now called "content." The 1939 filmed version of L. Frank Baum's fantastic *The Wizard of Oz*, for example, made its television debut in 1956 and has remained an annual event ever since. Like Walt Disney, Baum saw the world as it was—black-and-white, dour, dusty Kansas, with its horrible Ms. Gulch—and then as it should be: a Technicolor fantasy world run by the Lollipop Guild and the Butterfly League . . . and, of course, a few witches, two of them really bad people. "There's no place like home" is the takeaway from Oz, but the real wallop was and continues to be Judy Garland's rendition of Howard Arlen's dazzling ballad "Over the Rainbow" while still in Kansas, pre-twister. The film became a perennial because people continued to dream of that place as they recovered from the war—and, later, from the conflicts in Korea and Vietnam and even Iraq and Afghanistan. Wherever there is bloodshed, there will be the counterideal of "happy little bluebirds."

Oz, of course, was a phony, and Jerome David Salinger, strong jawed, dark, and handsome, was already becoming world famous for creating a character who reveled in pointing those kind of people out. Salinger, unlike Disney, came from a well-to-do family, but he stands alongside Mickey's inventor as perhaps the second great body of water that feeds all Twee streams, rivers, estuaries, and ponds. His influence on the aesthetic is equally vast, his body of work virtual Twee scripture. Salinger attended the highly regarded Valley Forge military school and before the war cavorted among society types at the Stork Club and other upscale watering holes. During the war, Salinger left that lifestyle behind and served in the 12th Infantry. He was among the soldiers storming Normandy Beach on D-day, June 6, 1944. His division fought its way through the snipers in Hürtgen Forest, where thousands of American soldiers lost their lives. As the war wound down, Salinger's regiment was among those who liberated an offshoot of the Dachau concentration camp. He saw firsthand the dead, naked bodies stacked like cordwood or buried in mass graves after the guards had fled. Later, as part of the ISI, he hunted and interrogated Nazis. Then he almost obligatorily lost his mind, briefly married, quickly divorced, and by the late 1940s became the celebrated author he had aspired to be since his prep-school years.

J. D. Salinger was broken by the world as it truly was, but he saved himself from destruction by inventing a seventeen-year-old boy. Unbeknown to most, Salinger took this boy overseas with him, in his head. The boy wore a crew cut, like a soldier, and adopted the same chain-smoking, foul-mouthed persona at times (masking, of course, a pained sweetness). He had drink and girls on his mind, this companion-creation. Holden Caulfield was conceived in New York City, during the aforementioned reverie, which was marred only by frequent rejection letters from the *New Yorker*. Holden came of age and entered into the Twee canon not only as a product of the war and its chilly aftermath but as a balm for it all. Holden knew the game was rigged. He was familiar with loneliness. Every date would end in tears. In "I'm Crazy," published in the Christmas 1945 issue of *Collier's* magazine, Salinger, using the first-person narrative device that would soon be the universally familiar, lets us in on his heroes' inner voices: "I kept saying goodby to myself. 'Goodby, Caulfield. Goodby, you slob.'" And suddenly, self-deprecation is sexy and tough and sad, a decade before Woody Allen became a popular stand-up comic and four before the Smiths' debut.

Holden is a mess. He flunks classes. He talks back. He loses his fencing equipment on the subway. (How does one lose fencing equipment?) But he's wiser than everyone else around him at once and sees through them with ease.

It's reductive—and, given Salinger's eventual disappearance into New England and his refusal to publicly analyze his stories and novels during much of his later years, nearly impossible—to say that Caulfield would not exist without the war. But Holden's undeniable, irresistible, unrejectable voice was burnished during combat, and he surely came to life by roadsides and in foxholes and tents in Europe. Holden the idea—and the *ideal*—required battle, horror, and recovery. His voice is resilient, wise, and wiseass. He will go on because he's young but also because he sees beauty among the terror.

"Life is a game, boy," Holden is told in *The Catcher in the Rye,* the novel Salinger had been planning and piecing together as he served. "Life is a game that one plays according to the rules."

"Yes, sir. I know it is. I know it," he replies to his elder. But in his head, which we've already been allowed into, he says, "Game, my ass. Some game. If you get on the side where all the hot-shots are, then it's a game, all right—I'll admit that. But if you get on the other side, where there aren't any hot-shots, then what's a game about it? Nothing. No game."

Seymour Glass, hero of "A Perfect Day for Bananafish," the short story that made Salinger famous before *The Catcher in the Rye* made him immortal, puts a bullet through his temple in a Florida motel room as his troubled girlfriend sleeps next to him. Shell-shocked, he's lost all hope. Holden Caulfield has some left, even if he finds the very concept sappy. His persistence makes him not only endearing but also a sort of beacon.

It should be said that there's also a practical appeal to Salinger's literary universe and its population, one not lost on modern storytellers like Woody Allen, Whit Stillman, or Wes Anderson. Salinger offers the real-life miserable misfit wretch something glamorous. His heroes are all beauties, first of all. They sip martinis. They smoke. They quip. They fence, or attempt to. They live in a Manhattan where it always seems to be cold and Christmas-aired. When we see them, through his words, we really see our ideal selves as physically attractive and troubled; our pain given a kind of train-station shoe shine. They are pop savvy as well, all versed in magazines, jazz, and movies even as they remain haunted. The Glass family alone is marked by suicide and combat death, but who would not want to join it?

Salinger himself, wandering Central Park dreaming of a life akin to that of his literary hero F. Scott Fitzgerald and rereading his rejection slips, knew this particularly perverse strain of urban envy well. Writers were lousy with it. Fitzgerald and his wife, Zelda, were drunk and doomed, but the young, prefame Salinger would have given an arm to be either of them. *The Catcher in the Rye* was published in the summer of 1951 and was an instant hit. For two years Holden Caulfield stood, virtually alone, as the voice of postwar reason, truth, and youthful power.

By 1953 the fictional Holden Caulfield had competition: a young girl who had been dead for nearly a decade, her life snuffed out by hate and pestilence and the very hypocrisy and cruelty and general cruddiness that Salinger's narrator assails. Unlike Holden, she had actually existed. She was real. She lived, briefly, and then she perished of typhus, naked, bald, and covered with lice, in the Auschwitz death camps in Poland, convinced (incorrectly) that her entire family was also doomed. Anne Frank does not exist in our minds this way, of course. In books and plays and on concept albums she is a voice of honesty, reason, hope, wit, and sanity in a world that seems broken and insane. She goes on until she can no longer, but, even in the concentration camp, she persists.

It seems unfair and probably unwise to continue to compare the real Anne Frank to any fictional character, even though Holden seems so real and Anne has been so effectively dramatized over the years onstage and in film that she seems beyond flesh and blood and commands that seamless permanence of a great fictional character. I only mean to say that the idea and example of Anne is similar to that of Holden. Both ask, "Why can't things be different?" Her appearance (in the scant photos and one bit of film footage available) before the camps supports these thoughts of her. She is a darkly beautiful and precocious, very young woman with a mischievous, humorous gleam in her eye and a smile on her face. She is neatly, almost crisply attired, like the fastidious writer she aspired to be.

Like many Salinger characters, the real Anne came from privilege. Her father, Otto, was a German businessman who moved his family from Frankfurt to Holland when the Nazis first rose to power in the early 1930s, convinced, incorrectly, that Hitler would never invade there. Anne and her older sister Margot attempted to maintain a normal life, attending a Montessori school in Amsterdam and preserving a plucky, dreamy outlook even as the Nazis took over the Netherlands and, one by one, they lost the freedoms that meant everything to a teenager. Otto was all the while making provisions for an even worse fate, converting his office into a two-story secret annex where his family might wait out the war and avoid the fate of those rumored to have been carted off to the extermination camps in Poland and Germany. When Margot received a call-up letter to report to a transport camp, bound for hard labor or worse, the family acted. With the help of Miep Gies, a loyal employee, the Franks and their friends the van Daans moved behind a secret bookcase and hid there for nearly three years, waiting for their city to be liberated by the Allies. Anne, who would today be considered either a gifted or a problem child, altered her "spicy" personality not one bit during these horrid circumstances, and this makes her heroic—but what truly separates her is her life of the mind, recorded in the red cloth diary she received as a present on her thirteenth birthday, June 12, 1942.

It was almost as if her father had a premonition that she would need it, and it was quickly put to use. Anne would tell the diary, addressed as "Kitty" after a character in one of her favorite young-adult fiction series, things she could not say to anyone else, not even her older sister. She contemplated the idea of adulthood, she railed against the cruelty of the Nazi thugs, she confessed survivor's guilt—knowing that many of her Jewish schoolmates were now in camps—and, like most teenage girls, she complained about her mother. She also dreamed: of going to Switzerland, where Jews were still free, to skate, and perhaps on to America—to Hollywood to become a great journalist or writer. She wrote and rewrote the diary with an eye toward freedom while under the constant threat of discovery; every day until six P.M., the Franks, the van Daans, and their late-joining exile, the dentist Mr. Dussel, had to be silent. At night they were free to chat, listen to the radio, observe their holidays, and share hopes of liberation: what they missed, what they would do when permitted to leave. "I don't know if anything will ever feel normal again," Margot says in the theatrical version.

But there's normal teenage love. Anne Frank, thirteen when she entered the annex, developed feelings for the van Daans' teenage son, Peter. The Nazis could not deprive her of these feelings. Anne refused to be deprived of much, despite her circumstances, and even in the camps she fought, hanging on until one month before the British liberated them.

Gies, of course, saved the diary after the Nazis who discovered the annex looted it for anything superficially valuable. She never read it until she was sure of Anne's fate. After that she turned it over to Otto, the only annex dweller to survive the camps. Otto was not sure he should publish it, but by 1947, convinced his daughter was somehow alive inside the book, he began sharing it with publishers. By the early 1950s it was a best seller and a hit Broadway play, later adapted as an acclaimed film by director George Stevens. Anne's visage, the dark hair and eyes, the bangs, the neat dresses and eager, hopeful, clearly intelligent expressions, fostered a sense of survivor's guilt in boomers who were not even born during her lifetime. If you read Frank's diary, or reread it, it has little of the melodrama that the play and the film bring. Anne was a gifted writer, an observer and a brave confessor or self-confessor, not an actress. "My head is haunted by so many wishes and thoughts . . ." she wrote. "I'm really not as conceited as so many people seem to think. I know my own faults and shortcomings better than everyone . . ." There's a little bit of Anne Frank in every modern teenager, and vice versa. To do her justice pop culturally would require something equally raw and young. She did not live to see the dawn of rock and roll, only a few years away, but rock and roll would do right by her.

As with Elie Weisel's *Night* and Primo Levi's *Survival in Auschwitz*, *The Diary of a Young Girl* has been assigned reading to middle and high school students in America for decades. It is the kind of book that many did awkward and sometimes hasty reports on, as, let's face it, these books were downers. Academia and ten million obligatory book reports might have snuffed all the roiling youth and urgency of *The Diary of a Young Girl* if Anne had not been recontextualized as an Indie hero in 1998. Neutral Milk Hotel, the moniker that Louisianan Jeff Mangum and later his band had recorded and toured under since the mid-1990s, somehow returned real youthful emotion to *The Diary*. Overnight, Neutral Milk's second and final album *In the Aeroplane Over the Sea* seemed to remind us that this is a raw read. Loosely based on Mangum's readings of Frank's diary, it's the product of urgency and confusion, less a concept album than a kind of diffident yet primal scream. When Mangum opened his throat and bared his own emotions, channeling Frank, sometimes directly (in "Holland, 1945") and sometimes abstractly (in "Two-Headed Boy"), it was as if a few hundred thousand teenagers awoke from a teacher-cast trance. Mangum's rendering was so unadorned and nervy that it put off many "cool" listeners even as it fast became the favorite album of all time for others. "*Aeroplane* doesn't have the near-consensus of top-shelf 90s rock artifacts like, say, [My Bloody Valentine's] *Loveless*, [Radiohead's] *OK Computer*, or [Pavement's] *Slanted and Enchanted*. These records are varied, of course, different in many ways. But in one key respect *Aeroplane* stands apart: This album is not cool," *Pitchfork*'s Mark Richardson wrote when Domino Records reissued the by-then classic album in 2005. While it didn't chart in its initial run, like so many cult classics it has sold steadily toward gold certification and is now a routine figure on various best-ever lists, and even inspired an all-ukulele version (courtesy of Neutral Uke Hotel). In 2013 Neutral Milk reunited for a tour that proved to be an instant sellout, playing for plenty of fans who were not even born when the album first appeared in '98. It's a pre-Emo burst of undiluted (and again, unselfconsciously nonmasculine) emotion: pain, joy, and hope. Musically it's got both a vast and a handmade quality that would, a decade later, deeply influence improbable arena rockers like Arcade Fire and Mumford and Sons.

Aeroplane is an album about childhood made by childhood friends who remembered it. The band members began their semiprofessional career recording onto cassettes and decorating them by hand. Even with the attention, the process remained messy and the sound unruly, for all its stately bits with French horns, trumpets, and tubas. When you are a child, love is almost never in enough supply, and as you grow older, it's almost always unrequited at least once. *Aeroplane* captures this feeling so well, it becomes a kind of balm. Mangum is literally in love with a ghost resembling Frank (one, according to writer Kim

Cooper's 33 ⅓ series study of *Aeroplane,* that he actually saw while visiting the Musée Mécanique, a showroom full of vintage arcade and carnival contraptions on Fisherman's Wharf in San Francisco).

"The only girl I've ever loved," Mangum sings in "Holland, 1945," perhaps the most famous song on the iconic album, "was born with roses in her eyes . . . Now she's a little boy in Spain playing pianos filled with flames." It's whimsical and heartbreaking, dark and hopeful at once. Anne lives in the diary . . . and in Spain, and clearly in Mangum's too-open heart. "I love you, Jesus Christ," he wails over jarring power chords on the album's second track, "King of Carrot Flowers, Pts. 2–3." The album tackles fumbling teen sexuality and the mystery of existence itself ("How strange it is to be anything at all . . ."). Again and again, however, he returns to the ghost of Frank, as if straining to bring her back to life. Elsewhere he sings, "And she was born in a bottle rocket, 1929"—the year Anne Frank was born—"I know that she will live forever. She won't ever die."

Mangum has rarely given interviews, and his lost decade and a half after *Aeroplane* has only heightened his myth, giving him a kind of Syd Barrett–like holy hermit status. Gasps were audible when it was announced that he would perform a series of solo dates in 2011, leading up to the inevitable full Neutral Milk Hotel tour. His reluctance to deconstruct his own music might come down to a lack of conclusion. If any modern rock star seems like a vessel for a spirit, it's Mangum. "The songs sort of come out spontaneously and it'll take me awhile to figure out what exactly is happening lyrically, what kind of story I'm telling," he told *Pitchfork* in 2008.

Mangum's homage to *The Diary of a Young Girl* was not the only work in the Twee canon to explain the choking, almost unfathomable cruelty of the Holocaust to the young and the cool. More than a decade before that record, there was *Maus*. *The Diary* began what would become a half century's work in progress of explaining the Holocaust to children.

By the 1980s, comic books, so prized by the young, were transitioning to "graphic novels," tackling horror in a personal and respectful manner. Art Spiegelman's *Maus* and sequel *Maus II* were the results of the author's extensive personal and historical research of the Holocaust. "I had no interest in doing something like 'Captain America liberates Treblinka,'" Spiegelman has said. The child of survivors who sometimes woke up screaming, Spiegelman was never in Auschwitz himself, but it haunted him just the same. His family, after relocating to New York City, socialized with fellow survivors.

In the late 1970s and early '80s, Spiegelman found himself a key figure of the alternative comics movement as an editor of *RAW*, a paperback publication that would showcase the talents of other sophisticated but young "comix" artists like Gary Panter, Kaz, Lynda Barry, Bill Griffith, and Charles Burns and forever remove the art form from the category of easily dismissed juvenilia. An avid reader of Kafka, Spiegelman was not interested in the bawdiness and crudeness that marked many of the style's works. The teen-aimed *Heavy Metal* and the like, with giant-breasted women, and even the work of celebrated 1960s cartoonist R. Crumb seemed limited, despite their loyal fan bases. Why couldn't a comic book tackle a serious theme, like racism? Different animals as factions, sometimes violently opposed to each other, was something already hardwired into every child who ever sat in front of a *Tom and Jerry* cartoon. Using such a trope might be one of the only ways to make any sense of the attempted eradication of the European Jews. Spiegelman's mother committed suicide in the late '60s, but his father was still alive. Via a series of interviews, which are depicted in the books along with flashbacks to Nazi atrocities in Poland, Spiegelman accomplishes something that scholars and documentarians had sometimes failed to do: made the Holocaust something pop-culturally accessible.

His anthropomorphized mice (Jews), cats (Nazis), pigs (Poles), and dogs (American soldiers) are so complex and fully realized that when the author's father, Vladek, was shown the work, "he never noticed that I was using cats and mice." Although it employs comic-book panels, thought bubbles, and black-and-white artwork, *Maus* feels more like a film, with cinematic devices and a tension that's palpable as the Nazi cats rise to power. Readers who might not have ever read Elie Wiesel or even Anne Frank found themselves weeping over the image of a gasping or grimacing rodent.

America lost nearly half a million souls in World War II, but while Pearl Harbor was attacked, none of our cities were destroyed and our factories—ginned up by the war machine—were continuously booming. So were the babies. A new age of prosperity was upon us, but our kids were not all right.

At their most well-adjusted, 1950s kids, fictional and not, used fantasy and whimsy as a middle finger to often-absent parents struck dumb by the Depression and the war. Kay Thompson and Hilary Knight's Eloise is one of the feistier, more aggressive of these '50s kids, possibly due to her urban sophistication and privilege.

"Here's what I like to do," Eloise explains, "pretend. Sometimes I am a mother with 40 children. Sometimes I am a giant with fire coming out of my hair. Sometimes I get terribly sick and have to be waited on." Eloise's real parents are scarce: traveling, uninterested, aloof.

"I find that book to be tragically sad," says writer and actor John Hodgman. "It's about a daughter who's been abandoned by her mother and is being raised in a hotel. There is obviously something glamorous and enticing to any children's story when a child is sent out into the world on their own—children love to read about that—but there's something about Eloise's particular mania and verbosity. I feel like she's filling up time so that she doesn't stop and realize that her mommy abandoned her."

Eloise is a brat, and a braggart ("My mother knows Coco Chanel"), and possibly, as Hodgman suggests, secretly miserable, but she was also among the first to inspire rebellion in young girls of the modern era, in part because of the life of her mind, and in part because she is a latchkey kid . . . albeit with room service, making her the envy of latchkey kids in suburbs everywhere.

The late 1950s saw another oddball Twee heroine in the form of dark and dotty Holly Golightly. She was the creation of the precocious Truman Capote, himself a Twee touchstone.

Even as a child, Capote dressed like a small man in vests and ties and fancied himself a sort of exceptional creature, not straight, not gay, but simply unique. He is, of course, the model for Scout's best friend, Dill, in the classic *To Kill a Mockingbird*, written by Capote's great confidante Harper Lee. Capote began writing seriously at just eight, although he did poorly in his organized classes. As he grew up, Capote continued to affect a sort of untamable "prodigy chic," often portraying himself as much younger and more boyish than he actually was in an effort to inspire wonder over his already highly sophisticated and detailed writing. He also never let go of his Southern Gothic affectations, despite having left the south for the private schools of the northeast after his mother remarried a wealthy businessman, Joe Capote (Truman took his name). "When he was sixteen, he looked ten," Phoebe Pierce Vreeland later told Capote biographer George Plimpton. "When he was thirty, he looked eighteen." With his "butterscotch hair" and smooth cheeks; his high, amused, ambiguous speaking voice; and tiny stature, Capote was often referred to in superhuman terms: sometimes an angel, other times a troll. "Truman remained a child all his life," his onetime schoolmaster Clarence Bruner-Smith opined to Plimpton. It's as if a Seussian rascal had come to life; Capote was the cat in the hat.

His author photo, submitted for his first collection, the celebrated *Other Voices, Other Rooms,* is iconic, his bedroom eyes and jutting lower lip suggesting some kind of carnal or postcoital trance. He was just twenty-three when that book was published in 1948. The following year he was shot by famed artist and photographer Cecil Beaton midleap like a Peter Pan made flesh. Twee band the Smiths would later use that image on the sleeve of their 1986 single "The Boy with the Thorn in His Side." There's also an Irving Penn shot that depicts Capote wrapped in a tweed overcoat that seems several sizes too big and gives him even more of the air of a gifted, puckish man-child. By the 1950s he was a celebrated *New Yorker* contributor, all the while drinking and regaling in various salons and saloons with his socialites, the Swans. Capote's most iconic creation, however, was war scarred and haunted, just like Seymour Glass, despite answering to the buoyant moniker of her own choosing.

In the novella—but not in the more famous film, starring Audrey Hepburn and George Peppard—Holly is a "working girl," just eighteen and fled from an unhappy hillbilly marriage. In New York City she cuts her hair, adopts an elegant style (pearls, black dresses), and smokes cigarettes as "ugly old men" file conspicuously in and out of her Upper East Side brownstone (the keys to which she is frequently losing). Golightly confides that she is a frequent sufferer of an ailment she calls "the mean reds" (we later learn that much of this has to do with the combat death of her brother) and that the only place that can provide any relief for her is Tiffany and Co., the iconic jewelry store on Fifth Avenue in Manhattan.

"The mean reds are horrible," Holly says. "You're afraid and you sweat like hell but you don't know what you're afraid of." When she has the "mean reds" she gets into a cab and goes to the celebrated and expensive Tiffany and Co., not for the jewelry or the proximity to the soon-to-be-wedded or expecting parents, but rather for the "calm, the quiet and the proud look of it. If I could find a real life place that made me feel like Tiffany's then I'd buy some furniture and give the cat a name."

Holly calls her cat simply "Cat." She is also not who she claims to be; self-invented as "Holly Golightly," and her beauty and sadness and pluck in the face of urban decay have made her yet another Twee heroine of the postwar age.

Among the last great postwar and pre-rock Twee heroes, James Dean barely fought his mean reds at all. He just sort of gave in to them. Dean was, of course, a real-life lost farm boy out of Indiana, but as with Anne Frank, his time on earth (twenty-four years, thanks to a wrecked Porsche Spyder somewhere out on route 466 on September 30, 1955) was so short and has been so mythologized that it's easy to see him as a fictional character too—a sort of boy doll with his big ears, bed head, swollen lower lip, and sad dark and darting eyes.

In film, Dean did not wear leather à la Marlon Brando's Johnny in *The Wild One*. Brando was solid and slick, a hunk like Paul Newman,

Kirk Douglas, and the other major stars of the 1950s. Dean was androgynous and unsure, his sexuality a constant matter of debate (like Capote, he is a Smiths cover star and Morrissey obsession), and his relationship with both his real-life family and his surrogate city family of struggling actors (his mother died when he was nine; his father was aloof) amounted to one constant and fruitless search for love and acceptance.

Dean only comes into focus as a hero, like all Twee godheads, when confronted with bullies. Then and only then does he stiffen and shine.

"I thought only Punks fought with knives," he taunts the local hoods in *Rebel Without a Cause*. Both Natalie Wood and Sal Mineo adore him, but it's no solace.

The adults, who were put on alert by the work of Salinger and Seuss, are literally choked by Dean. Eloise retreated into a private dream world, Holly simply ran away, but Dean threw his body into it. He became the martyr for the new generation's dismissal of their parents' cowardice and shell shock.

"Stand up!" his character begs his father, played by Jim Backus. It's as if he's speaking to the entire World War II generation. But the parents are cowed, broken, and shattered. Dean can't find peace with that, so he must negate the adults, one by one. It is easy to see why Dean remains, to this day, a talisman.

This is where Dean and another great 1950s rebel hero cross over and meet in a world that is entirely youth-invented: the adults are literally voiceless. The only other rebel of the late '50s with the same power to express grief at the weakness, hypocrisy, and utter futility of the Eisenhower era in the manner of Dean is a boy named Charlie Brown.

Yes, I am drawing a comparison between James Dean and Charlie Brown, and if you think I'm crazy, I should point out that thousands of American college students did the same in the late 1950s. In that decade, the *Peanuts* antihero was the most popular character in college newspapers across the country; like Dean, Charlie became a sort of existential hero in an age of helplessness and horror, brokenhearted but still hopeful. He will try to kick the ball every time, just as Dean's Jim Stark will never give up his secret faith that people, especially his old man, have virtue in them. He will die trying to conjure it.

"I don't feel the way I'm supposed to feel," Charlie Brown sighs, and there's no cigarette-smoking French philosopher in a beret who could articulate it better. He is a Twee hero because he, like Dean, confronts a cold world with idealism. In a strip from the early '50s, as Dean is reinventing the matinee idol, Charlie says to Lucy, "You don't like me."

She replies, "Sure I do, Charlie Brown."

"Well, maybe you like me a little," he responds, "but you don't think I'm *perfect*."

Charlie Brown hates school, is puzzled by girls, and finds his dog, Snoopy, to be trouble. He is a new kind of loser: one who sees his fate as unjust and, in the age of analysis, is happy to kvetch. He doesn't hate himself, but rather quietly rages at the status quo that doesn't recognize his genius. He is Hannah Horvath, a half century beforehand; a model for Generation Y and, I suppose, even Z as he inhabits a postwar baby boomer realm.

"Look at those two, I bet they're talking about me," he mutters in another strip from the era while passing two chatting girls. "It always worries me when I know people are talking about me." (They are discussing a cowboy movie.)

He is Twee or proto-Twee because he is an aesthete, a perfectionist. He constructs, one winter, what he considers the perfect snowman, only to return to find Snoopy has eaten the carrot nose. Drawn simply by Schulz, like children's book characters, the Peanuts gang (Linus, Lucy, Schroeder, even Snoopy) are given blood and soul by weight of their neuroses. They're all messes. Linus can't go anywhere without his blanket and Schroeder can't even lift his head. Lucy, who tends unrequited love for the slumped pianist, is compulsive and type A while completely oblivious to her own psychic flaws. Pig Pen doesn't wash. Let's not even get into Peppermint Patty and Marcie.

When asked to name his favorite filmmakers, Wes Anderson included Bill Melendez, Peanuts creator Charles M. Schulz's chief animator and the man responsible for the perennial *A Charlie Brown Christmas*, which showcases in heart-shaking blues and wintry whites the character's wounded ennui during a time when most are spilling over with goodwill.

"Drats! Nobody sent me a Christmas card today," Charlie Brown complains. "I almost wish there wasn't a holiday season. I know nobody likes me. Why do we have to have a holiday season to emphasize it?" And yet he will check the mailbox again tomorrow. Like Disney and Dean and Seuss and even the cynical J. D. Salinger, he has not lost hope even as most around him have grown hard from their pain and fear.

Dozens of *Peanuts* homages lurk in Anderson's oeuvre, from the use of Vince Guaraldi's signature melancholy tinkling in both the *Bottle Rocket* short and *The Royal Tenenbaums* to the placement of a (doomed) beagle in the latter and making Max Fischer's father a barber, like Charlie Brown's, in *Rushmore*. "Chuck" finally got his long-belated due in the summer of 2013 when a Tumblr page by graphic artist Lauren Loprete called *This Charming Charlie* went viral. Combining *Peanuts* panels with well-chosen Morrissey lyrics, it was akin to Dangermouse's *Gray Album*, which synched Jay Z's *Black Album* perfectly with the Beatles' *White Album*. This connection seemed obvious, something that had been hanging in the zeitgeist forever, simply waiting to be brought together and shared. It was also subversive. One panel featured bespectacled Marcie staring longingly at Peppermint Patty and confessing, "I dreamt about you last night and I fell out of bed twice." Morrissey approved of the mash-up, at a time when the great man approved of very little. Shortly thereafter, a *Peanuts* reboot was announced, to be helmed by *Freaks and Geeks* creator Paul Feig.

Peanuts all but erased the generation that came before it in a way that Disney, Eames, Salinger, and any number of idealistic futurists could not, literally stripping them of their voice. In the animated television specials the sound of an adult speaking (or scolding) had no assonance or consonance. It was a muted and moot bleat: a blah-blah-blah.

The end of the postwar 1940s and the start of the modern era would see a different kind of Twee Tribe hero, one with a stronger, surer sense of his outsiderism. These heroes would wear their nerdiness and insecurity a bit more proudly and achieve great work not only in spite of it, but also, for the first time, because of it. Musically, chief among them was the great Buddy Holly. If Brando was the hard man to Dean's soft boy, Holly was the fastidious and ambitious workaholic to Elvis's loose and easy rockabilly cat. He looked like a school nerd, but he was as much a rebel as Brando's Johnny, willfully dispensing with gospel and country in favor of "race music." He was also as control freakish as Brian Wilson and the Beatles would later be, insisting on producing his own self-penned music and incorporating odd (for rock and roll) instruments like the glockenspiel (on "Everyday") for an unsuspecting teenybopper's aural enjoyment.

His influence on Wilson, the Beatles, the Rolling Stones, and the Kinks is singular.

He is also, like so many Twee heroes, forever young. Holly died in a small-plane crash over Iowa in the frigid early morning of February 3, 1959, at just twenty-two (along with tour mates the Big Bopper and Ritchie Valens). He left behind a dozen and a half perfect pop songs simultaneously tough ("That'll Be the Day," a line borrowed from John Wayne in *The Searchers* and stripped of just enough menace), lusty ("Peggy Sue"), and breathlessly romantic ("True Love Ways") but always, always, pure.

For all the genius of his music, Holly's greatest contribution may have been his style. He was the first hip nerd, riding motorcycles and, sartorially, inventing "geek chic" almost singlehandedly with his bow ties, slim suits, horn-rimmed glasses, neat hair, and toothy, eager smile. It's a look that David Byrne, Morrissey, the Feelies, and Weezer would appropriate, but not before the young, prefame Beatles and Stones.

"Normally [John] wore the horn-rim specs," Paul McCartney remembered of his late friend and partner, John Lennon, in a BBC documentary on Buddy Holly. "But he always took them off onstage. [After Holly] he was now able to put them on and see the world."

Chapter 2

Younger Than That Now

In which the eldest children of the modern world take off on their own, soar, crash, and then, once again, in the midst of a war, attempt to make something of all the broken parts. The 1960s, the quintessential Twee decade, begins, and a sense of whimsy is employed in everything from recording studios to the anti–Vietnam War protests.

Poor, poor Sylvia Plath. Today the Pulitzer Prize–winning poet and millions-selling novelist is both a literary and feminist icon and a too-easy punch line. Her outsize sadness and shakiness sometimes upstage her magnificent writing. Even those who have never read *Ariel* or *The Bell Jar* know she was a mess.

"Now I know why Sylvia Plath put her head in a *toaster*!," Julie Delpy groans midargument in Richard Linklater's *Before Midnight* (the final installment of his celebrated Sunrise Trilogy). Plath, of course, asphyxiated on gas from a proper English oven in February of 1963.

"You're hardly the authority on happiness, Sylvia," Patton Oswalt chides Charlize Theron in the script for Jason Reitman's 2011 black comedy *Young Adult*, penned by Diablo Cody.

In the film *Fight Club*, Brad Pitt's Tyler Durden quips, "In the Tibetan philosophy, Sylvia Plath sense of the word, I know we're *all* dying, but . . ."

In *Annie Hall*, Woody Allen browses Diane Keaton's bookshelf and plucks off a copy of *Ariel*. "Aha, Sylvia Plath," he muses. "Interesting poetess whose tragic suicide was misinterpreted as romantic by the college-girl mentality."

And yes, anyone who has read Plath's perfectly detailed and prolific journal knew that she was something of a Debbie Downer in her short life, but she also possessed a deep ambition, a sense of humor, and creative energy that surged with life. Life simply overwhelmed her, even as she never seemed to leave her private world and remained terrifically productive. "I fall on the bed, drugged, with this queer sickish greeny-vinous fatigue. Drugged, gugged, stogged and sludged with weariness. My life is a discipline, a prison: I live for my own work, without which I am nothing. My writing," she writes in her journal.

Plath too is a child of World War II and its horror; many of her poems allude to the Holocaust either directly or metaphorically, aligning her psychic suffering with that of an actual victim of Hitler's death camps, a device deemed controversial by some who saw only a relatively privileged and beautiful young woman, safely encased in academia. Still, Plath provides war-haunted voices for those who never served, and if anything enables a kind of suffering by proxy that is deeply empathetic and, yes, would be extremely tacky in less capable hands.

The Bell Jar, her masterpiece of prose, posthumously published in America on the twentieth anniversary of the original publication of *The Catcher in the Rye,* stands alongside that book and Anne Frank's diary in a kind of three-headed urtext of Twee. To call them bibles or designs for living would not be far off base. Like *Catcher, The Bell Jar* begins as a snapshot of New York City in the 1950s. Beautiful and ambitious Esther Greenwood seems, like Holden, within reach of success and opportunity, but she just can't stop ruminating or gird the raw nerves that cause her to obsess and eventually stop writing and break down. We, as readers, feel not only that these narrators (both are first person) live, as much as Anne Frank lived, but that their pain is our own, the key to any book one reads more than once and displays on subways or in cafeterias. They are books and they are prescriptions for a kind of temporary cure for pain.

Plath knew she had a gift. Like Salinger, she sent off poems to the key periodicals and journals of the day and was met with much rejection. "A day of misery," she writes in the spring of 1957, "*New Yorker* rejection." She is almost a Salinger character herself: beautiful, New York sophisticated (although she was born in Boston and studied at Cambridge, she knew the "jazz and push" of Manhattan), consumed with neuroses and a quiet, persistent suffering—Franny Glass made flesh. It's no accident that Gwyneth Paltrow was drawn to play her in the 2003 biopic after she adopted a crisp Plathian look as the fictional Margot Tenenbaum in Wes Anderson's *The Royal Tenenbaums.* Hardworking and determined as she was, there was something ghostly and unreal about Plath, a quality that loans itself to pastiche.

A wife (of eminent poet Ted Hughes) and a mother, Plath was not alone, of course, but that didn't spare her from feeling utterly isolated in life. "I have children but few friends," she wrote; a sort of call out from beyond to the lonely, bedroom-bound Twee Tribe member. Twees don't like their writers happy. It won't do.

Though the jokes about her make her seem humorless, Plath possessed wit, and the key Twee component: whimsy. "Then that red plush," she writes of accidentally slicing off the top of her thumb in "Cut." "Little pilgrim, / The Indian's axed your scalp. / Your turkey wattle."

When she took the gas in her London kitchen, Plath led a kind of march of the war-scarred into oblivion that would both seal her as a Twee heroine (tragic, beautiful, damned) and afford her followers a vacuum to fill. She was not alone in clearing this colorful, Seussian path. James Dean died in a car accident. Salinger disappeared into a New Hampshire bunker. Even the garrulous, attention-seeking Truman Capote walked away from writing—perhaps because he looked too deeply and clearly into the abyss with his chilling "nonfiction novel" *In Cold Blood,* about a random robbery and the murder of the Clutter family in Holcomb, Kansas on November 15, 1959. Following the publication of the book and a strange but intense intimacy with one of the two convicted killers, Perry Smith, Capote launched into one long celebration and avoided the hard thoughts he required to create. He was no longer boyish as he bloated and blurred into something of a tragedy himself. The middle-aged Capote was almost a specimen suggesting what a Dean or a Plath or a Holly might have become had they not died so young: a pure and raw-eyed creature battered and simply dragged around too long by life.

At this time, cinema moved once again to the forefront of a great cultural change where mischief and rebellion reigned (at least until the arrival of the Beatles and the Stones). The auteurs of what has come to be called the Nouvelle Vague—Godard, Truffaut, Chabrol, Malle, Rohmer (and the later auteur who would come to worship them, Wes Anderson)—were all students in one way or another. They weren't novices who happened to pick up a camera and swing it around. They studied film. Truffaut and Godard both contributed to the prestigious film quarterly *Cahiers du Cinéma*. They shared an admiration for the classics but also weariness with the establishment that wouldn't permit love of American pulp, especially the gangster films of the 1930s and '40s.

Truffaut's debut, 1959's *400 Blows*, is the story of a sad, queasy child, Antoine (Jean-Pierre Léaud, who would also play the character in a series of sequels), and his bickering, somewhat pathetic, Parisian working-class family. The success of this film enabled these new, cool cinema gods with their Gauloises and their dark sunglasses entry into institutions such as the Cannes Film Festival (where the film was nominated for the Palme d'Or). Antoine is beleaguered ("I just can't concentrate," he complains. "I want to quit school . . ."), but his main function is that of a Trojan horse sneaking a new kind of uncool-cool into the pop consciousness. Out of Truffaut's success we eventually get 1960's *Breathless*, which he championed and cowrote, and out of *Breathless* we get Jean-Paul Belmondo, who, gangly and swarthy, with the face of a sexy duck, looks nothing like the era's standard-issue leading men—but it doesn't matter. He acts all the more cocksure for it. Who knows what he sees when he looks in the mirror, but it's not what we see. Regardless, he's proud of the vision staring back. Preceding Dustin Hoffman in *The Graduate* by a good seven-plus years, Belmondo is, in his way, the first Twee leading man; godfather to everyone from Hoffman and Bud Cort to Zach Braff, Jason Schwartz-man, Michael Cera, and Jonah Hill.

The doomed Jean Seberg, the film's heroine, blond and beautiful, resembles all of the era's leading women, but in collaborating with Godard and Truffaut and in clinches with Belmondo (all cheekbones, nose, pursed lips, and tilted hat) she is given depth and strangeness, anger and frustration, that continue to speak to Indie culture. She is also given a haircut.

Seberg's wardrobe in Godard's *Breathless* is the big bang of fe-male Twee fashion—striped shirts, trousers, and Mary Janes with no socks—but it's the hair that is most atomic and eternal. From Mia Farrow in *Rosemary's Baby* to Isobel Campbell of Belle and Sebastian to Natalie Portman in *Hotel Chevalier* (the moody short that prefaces Anderson's *The Darjeeling Limited*) to the postfame Lena Dunham, Michelle Williams, Jennifer Lawrence, and even orange-skinned, '90s *Playboy* Playmate and B-movie actress Pamela Anderson, the Seberg cut, short on the sides and in back, a bit longer and boyishly parted in front, has become an icon and a sort of cultural signal for women. "I am a certain way. I read this type of book. I like these bands. I buy this handbag."

For all of her wholesome, Iowan beauty, Seberg the actress was something of a Dumbo figure herself when Godard and Truffaut (who cowrote the script) cast her as Patricia, an American in Paris selling the *New York Herald Tribune* (wearing a *Tribune* T-shirt that itself has become a fashion classic), living in a small apartment on the Left Bank and trying to decide if she is in love with her hoodlum boy-friend, Michel. The aging Hollywood director Otto Preminger had conducted a highly publicized cattle call of thousands of actors before settling on Seberg, who was just seventeen at the time, to play Joan of Arc in his epic *Saint Joan* in 1957. The film was the director's dream project and was intended to be Seberg's big break: Graham Greene wrote the script, and Sir John Gielgud was among the cast. And yet the critics savaged it, and Seberg, who had beaten out more than three thousand other actresses for the role, was cast aside. Ambitious and progressive, she left Hollywood for Europe, where she fell in with Godard, and together they made film history and built an archetype. That Seberg would later, like Plath and so many other Twee heroes, die by her own hand in good-bye-cruel-world fashion only strengthens her standing among the Twee. Indie culture has never taken its eye off her.

Today Seberg has become a fixture in the digital age. Her death at just forty (she was found in a parked car on a Paris street, overdosed on pills, on August 30, 1979) loans itself to conspiracy theory. Officially she was a suicide, but there have been books, websites, and multiple articles that claim the CIA was behind it, or drove her insane as payback for her opposition to the Vietnam War and being pro–Black Panthers. People have latched on to the tragedy as well as the image. Her second Preminger film, *Bonjour Tristesse,* was recently reissued on DVD. There are tribute videos all over YouTube. Kirsten Dunst (who played a doomed, Seberg-like figure in Sofia Coppola's *The Virgin Suicides*) expressed interest in starring in a biopic circa 2005. Had Seberg lived, she would be pushing eighty and surely wouldn't be the icon that she is now—the same probably goes for James Dean. An early death endears an artist to the Twee.

The British were enjoying a New Wave of their own as memories of German buzz bombs and rations slowly receded and a new kind of postwar prosperity began to rise. Suddenly there were jobs again for working-class kids, rebuilding bombed-out sites along with the British economy. Many of these newly employed spent their paychecks on Italian suits and scooters, as well as classic British sportswear designed by Fred Perry. The mods (or modernists), as this group was dubbed, felt a kinship with the American working class. They prized and collected speedy dance tracks out of Detroit and Memphis from the labels Motown and Stax, songs that would form the backbone of what would come to be known as northern soul. The young mods who listened to it formed their own bands, such as the Who; the style would blossom again amid the Punk and New Wave movement, catalyzed most notably by the Jam, whose 1980 album *Sound Affects* is a key recording for many a modern Twee. The Mod look—clean, tapered Italian suits, zip-up boots, bangs (for both men and women), and peacock-pattern scarves and ties—permeates British film of this time period and is just as key to the foundation of Twee as a carelessly exhaled French cigarette.

British modern film of this decade is also concerned with the young and beautiful misfits, but ebbs toward the melodramatic, as in "kitchen sink" dramas like *The L-Shaped Room*. In the film we see Jane, played by Leslie Caron, down on her luck, fleeing her past and newly checked into an infested boardinghouse in Notting Hill. Jane strolls the gutter, Wilde-style, with one eye on the stars and another on Toby, the chiseled and likewise "skint" or down-on-his-luck writer (played by the hunky Tom Bell) who lives across the hall. Together they nest and spruce, spraying cheap perfume over the acrid smell of bedbug spray. It's highly romantic stuff, and it introduces a beloved Twee cinema trope: two lovers kicking sweetly against the pricks (usually old pricks). Smooching on a blanket during a picnic in a public park, Jane and Toby are scoffed at by a matronly old woman. "Between her and the bomb, we don't stand a chance," he quips.

The war was over; the generation that fought it was giving way to a new one, but the threat of "the" bomb and the paranoia of the Cold War informed many of these sometimes-bleak romances. These films are largely about how lovers behave with death as a distinct possibility at any minute and the sweet, beautiful moments they steal amid the horrible gray English dread. In Tony Richardson's *A Taste of Honey*, Rita Tushingham plays the plucky, plain, but clever Helen, a cheeky working-class girl who may be pregnant with a black seaman's child. As she waits for her test results, she spends long afternoons dreaming of "a place of one's own" where she can not only fit in but celebrate her outsider status: "My usual self is very unusual," she announces. Her only support comes from another outcast, the homosexual Geoffrey, one of the few people in her world who doesn't cast judgment on her.

The Loneliness of the Long Distance Runner, based on a short story by Alan Sillitoe—and also beloved by Morrissey and, for good measure, name-checked in the song "The Loneliness of a Middle Distance Runner" by Twee heroes Belle and Sebastian—introduces a similarly unbreakable, tortured young English antihero in Tom Courtenay's Colin Smith. Colin's world is even more oppressive than Helen's. He clashes with his parents, then is banged up after a botched bakery robbery and sent off to reform school, where he's routinely beaten and bullied by the guards. Constantly scowling, he finds himself liberated when it comes to track and field. In a long scene we see Courtenay gliding, gazellelike, over the rocks and grass. He is graceful, clearly in his element, possessing something inviolate and pure. Exploited by a glory-minded warden, he is offered lenient treatment and even freedom if he competes and emerges victorious in an upcoming meet. He's easily fleet enough to crush any contenders, but just before he reaches the finish line . . . well, I won't spoil it.

Just as the Twee of today is drawn to old forms, whether it's canning and pickling cukes or plucking a ukulele, the dawn of rock's second and perhaps greatest wave in the early and mid-1960s was marked by an embrace of musical forms that had long been discarded as outré. The nascent Rolling Stones, Pink Floyd, and Yardbirds were record collectors, prizing forgotten blues B-sides out of Chicago. They played covers in clubs that featured "trad jazz," or faithful renditions of American Dixie swing.

"England has always been a country with a great interest in the past," says pop singer Ian Whitcomb, who would notch several hits during the British invasion, many of them like "You Turn Me On" and "Where Did Robinson Crusoe Go with Friday on Saturday Night?" featuring old-timey music hall piano and the instrument that would years later come to be a symbol of Twee: the ukulele. "As I child I knew all the music hall songs my parents knew. Same thing with the Beatles. They knew all the songs you sing in pubs. We treasure our pop culture and hang on to it." John Lennon, of course, led a group that played skiffle, a form of British folk often accompanied by a washtub bass. Upon kicking off their early songwriting partnership, Lennon and McCartney indeed did not throw out the book. Like Godard and Truffaut, they were students: they kept Cole Porter and Harold Arlen, Sammy Cahn and other composers of standards, and merely added Little Richard, Motown, and rockabilly touches the way Godard added jump cuts.

"The sixties and childishness both represent a simpler, happier, more genuine time. The sixties are seen as *rock*'s childhood, a moment of innocence before bloated middle age, before pop was overdetermined by criticism," Simon Reynolds wrote. "A time when the idea of youth was young."

The 1960s dream was heavily invested in keeping that youth spirit alive. Old men drank. Young men preferred to "Puff the Magic Dragon." That song was a massive hit for folk trio Peter, Paul and Mary in 1963, signaling a sort of pop changing of the guard, and, depending on whether you are Greg Focker ("Who would've thought it wasn't really about a dragon, huh?") or Jack Byrnes ("Puff's just the name of the boy's magical dragon"), deploying a sort of global treehouse culture of coded language designed to weed out the squares and the old folks.

As new as the world seemed, the Twee arcane styles—blues, folk, and country—were what informed the giddy first wave of British pop songwriting. Cowed by their headmasters into a kind of pathological shyness, many of these pioneering Brits were in love with Americana but could never be as openly expressive, sexual, or vulgar, so they embraced the abstract. A would-be poet like Donovan would not be able to convincingly channel the freewheelin' American writers he hero-worshipped: Kerouac, Ginsberg, Burroughs. The British were too buttoned-up and polite for that, but that desire for transcendence and kinetic freedom was run through the British schoolboy filter and ushered in a new kind of cool, beatnik-informed but shy and elegant. The Rolling Stones probably were as sexual and alpha as any swamp or city picker, but they were among the exceptions. A band that was never virtuosic when it came to true blues was now free to pivot from the faux-gruff, manly-man blues style embodied by Muddy Waters, Big Bill Broonzy, and Howlin' Wolf.

The Kinks a misfit quartet from London now prized as almost a holy combo by the Twee Tribe, were a beneficiary of this shift as well. "They were the worst blues band of the entire era," British music journalist Charles Shaar Murray has observed. "If they'd stayed a blues band they would have been in and out of the music business within their first record." Leader Ray Davies almost stumbled into a sort of uniquely urban but openhearted rock and roll style. "I thought I was making blues, and people said, 'Oh, you sound like Noël Coward,'" he has said. True, the grittier, thrumming early singles, like "All Day and All of the Night" and the immortal "You Really Got Me," notwithstanding, there is a sadness and a gentleness to many of the Kinks' singles, from "Tired of Waiting for You" to "See My Friends." Even their most iconic song, "Waterloo Sunset," is narrated by the lonely urban soul observing the world from afar. Davies is not the participant, not one of the two lovers meeting, but rather the kid watching "the world from my window." He looked great, dandy-clad, but at heart was a gap-toothed nerd with not one shred of faith in either rock stardom or the pomposity of English morality, which he shredded to bits in character studies like "A Well Respected Man" and "Dedicated Follower of Fashion." He was also unafraid of camp and sexual ambiguity, evidenced most famously on the hit single "Lola." Echoes of the Kinks can be heard in the Buzzcocks, the Raincoats, and even twenty-first-century bands with wit and vulnerability to go with their punch, like Franz Ferdinand, the Libertines, and Kaiser Chiefs, among many others.

"We realized there was no future in just copying the blues," says

Whitcomb. "We all wanted to speak our own minds and create our own sounds."

American bands, taking cues from Beatles songs like "Eleanor Rigby" and Rolling Stones ballads like "As Tears Go By" and "Lady Jane," started producing pop that could be called "future baroque." The Left Banke's bracing and heartbreaking "Walk Away Renée" and "Pretty Ballerina" singles easily vie with "Waterloo Sunset" for exquisiteness (both songs had a vast influence on Belle and Sebastian decades later). The Lovin' Spoonful (a fan of the old-timey conceits that Whitcomb was embracing overseas), Buffalo Springfield, even garagey Tommy James with "Crimson and Clover," picked up on the scene the Beatles and the Kinks set—a mad tea party of sorts. Cues were coming from England daily, with each former blues-rock outfit flowering into troubadours. Manfred Mann offered "Pretty Flamingo"; the Hollies, "Bus Stop"; the Small Faces, "Lazy Sunday" and the divine and dappled "Itchycoo Park": picture-postcard songs that seemed to defy their still standard running times and loan a sense of elegance to the middle-class and mundane.

There was nothing mundane (or middle-class) about the Beatles, relentlessly leading the charge into the future of fearless and thrilling pop. Their 1965 chart-topping singles "I Feel Fine" and "Eight Days a Week" signal an ethical reordering of sorts when it came to how a hit should or could sound. The former begins with a rubbery line of feedback from John Lennon's Rickenbacker guitar. "For electric guitarists, feedback is a hazard of amplification," the late rock critic Ian MacDonald observed in his classic Beatles-in-the-studio tome *Revolution in the Head*, "to either be avoided or incorporated into their sound in a controlled way." Like bored, gifted children, the four wealthy, world-traveled, and powerful Beatles embraced and used the anarchy. Lennon, McDonald says, was "inordinately proud" of it all. Similarly, "Eight Days a Week" begins with a fade-in, the chords growing louder and louder until the rapturous verse hits. The following year's "Rain," the B-side to the hit "Paperback Writer," finds the Beatles running the first verse backward as the track fades out. And this was before the acid period. By the time they followed with *Revolver,* which routinely tops the Best Album Ever lists the British music magazines seem to publish every year or two, they were intent on destroying not only the ego, as LSD gurus instructed, but also the studio, quite literally. Effects on the milestone "Tomorrow Never Knows" were achieved, according to McDonald, by breaking equipment as a child would after hours of enthustic play with a series of toys.

"Sending a voice track through the revolving speaker in a Leslie cabinet [was] a process which required physically breaking into the circuitry," the author marvels. Tracks like "Yellow Submarine" were grown-up music for both children and adults, made by adults who had the means and the gifts to hold on to their childhood.

After hearing their *Rubber Soul,* in 1965, Brian Wilson, America's greatest baroque futurist, joined in. By then Wilson was eating acid on an almost daily basis, smoking pot, and gorging on food, rejecting the path that destroyed Buddy Holly in favor of a controlled anarchy in his mansion or in the expensive studios that Capitol Records provided. He, like the Beatles, could do anything, indulge any whim on any schedule; the only pressure was to go farther and farther into the future, often by going backward. "I just wasn't made for these times," Wilson famously sang, and the flutes, strings, gongs, horns, bells, and lilting harmonies sounded like little else on the radio. Lyrically, Wilson was still writing about a California that didn't really exist, full of wholesome and loyal blondes, tasty waves, warming sun, and hot rods. Meanwhile, footage of the Vietnam War was featured on the evening news every night, and many clean-cut Beach Boys fans were being sent off to the jungles of Southeast Asia. "Wouldn't it be nice if we were older," Wilson sang at age twenty-four, well beyond the voting age. He was using his gifts, his prestige, and his fortune (and a pile of drugs) to "revolt into childhood," to borrow a phrase from Simon Reynolds. The very act was a middle finger to his more conservative band mates and his old-model music-biz-trained father, the domineering Murray Wilson. It's no wonder that soon Wilson turned to fellow visionary Van Dyke Parks, a former child star, for collaboration, scrambling reality (increasingly troubling as the war escalated) in favor of highly abstract lyrics that confounded and sometimes infuriated his fellow Beach Boys but delighted the whimsy-worshipping genius. The theremin on "Good Vibrations," the legendary sandbox constructed in the piano room (so he could feel the beach on his bare feet as he composed), even the sleeve of *Pet Sounds,* featuring the Beach Boys feeding a bunch of grateful goats, seem perfectly brilliant now that the album is revered, but at the time they were puzzling to both the label and the group's many fans. "Teenage symphonies to God?" What happened to surfing?

"Oh, but I was so much older then," the Byrds sang on "My Back Pages," another of their hits and a jangly Bob Dylan cover. "I'm younger than that now." The Byrds, out of Los Angeles, had both a Dylan connection (he was a friend and supplier of lucrative hits) and a Beatles connection (Derek Taylor, the Fab Four's elegant publicity chief, also worked with them). The quartet—Jim "Roger" McGuinn,

Gene Clark, David Crosby, Michael Clarke, and Chris Hillman—had a chic residency at Ciro's, a hot Hollywood nightclub, and dressed, as Godard's heroes did, like outlaws—in this case a combination of gangster and cowboy drag—while British rock stars seemed intent on dressing like nature-loving romantic poets. Many of the Byrds' songs were recorded in L.A., backed by the same studio perfectionists who played on first Phil Spector and then Brian Wilson's ambitious new compositions: the Wrecking Crew, as they came to be known. The Byrds had hits and style, and once Punk's first wave of earth scorchers lifted a ban on all things '60s, they emerged as heroes to the new post-Punk Indie school. Some of their members, like David Crosby, wore capes and did scads of drugs. They were soon singing songs like "Eight Miles High." Still, a sense of utopia reigned, and pop music grew limitless and seemed infinite. Orchestral works like the Moody Blues' *Days of Future Past*, the Pretty Things' *S.F. Sorrow*, the Zombies' *Odessey and Oracle*, and the caddish Serge Gainsbourg's *Histoire de Melody Nelson* swelled into the ear via headphones.

"I saw it as retrograde," says Whitcomb, who clung to the old-time style and stood as a classic Twee reactionary against a kind of zeitgeist overkill. "I didn't like it when they all went psychedelic and got pretentious. I like simple pop sounds. Pure, simple bread-and-butter music. Pop music involved girls and sunshine and beaches. It wasn't pretentious and serious. I liked the three-minute single. I like rock and roll, not 'rock.' There's a huge difference. 'Rock' died around 1965." Whitcomb continued to pluck his uke and became a cult figure for those who grew to love the tiny, Twee guitar. "It's easy to play and produces a very pleasingly plangent sound. A nice, novel sound," Whitcomb says.

For a blip it seemed as if the New Left, the leaders of the antiwar movement, might use whimsy as a potent weapon. The Youth International Party, or yippies—a nod to hippies and the cry of a child when he's having fun—nominated a pig for president in 1968. They burned legal tender as well as draft cards and would not let go the idea of a free society. "There is no ideology except that which each individual brings with him," Abbie Hoffman writes in *Revolution for the Hell of It*. "The role he plays in building the alternative society will shape in some ways its ideology." Fueled by this dream, the yippies (Jerry Rubin, Ed Sanders, and Paul Krasner were among the higher-profile members) embraced stunts and symbols over the kind of strategy that would require financing and endless meetings. When the Yippies did conspire, it was to determine how many people it would take to make a ring around the Pentagon so that it could be levitated and exorcised.

Needless to say, the building stayed put, but soon the hippies themselves started to jump out windows on LSD. Many of their leaders and heroes, such as Senator Robert Kennedy and Dr. Martin Luther King Jr., were, of course, assassinated (the childlike Andy Warhol nearly so as well). The war in Vietnam escalated. By the 1960s, death was already in the zeitgeist even as the "inner child" gained control. The Beatles classic "Tomorrow Never Knows," the "sound event" of the era, was based on *The Tibetan Book of the Dead*. The boomers had grown up on children's books, like Roald Dahl's *Charlie and the Chocolate Factory* and *The Witches* and Edward Gorey's macabre *The Gashlycrumb Tinies*, that were suffused with death: not make-believe death, but actual despair-causing death. In 1964's *Charlie and the Chocolate Factory*, Dahl depicts Violet Beauregarde's mother's horror as her daughter swells into a giant blueberry after ingesting something strange. She is but one of the horrible children who meet bizarre fates in Dahl's work. Only the pure and innocent—like Charlie—get out alive.

Gorey, who appeared as a bearded, cat-loving New Englander on the outside, was perhaps the most twisted author of this time. His 1957 book *The Doubtful Guest* was quietly terrifying, with a speechless creature—an upright-walking otter in a woolen scarf—that enters a family's home and stays for seventeen years without ever uttering a word. This guest is perhaps death, or the awareness of death itself.

Much of Gorey's output is told in a deceptively cheery rhyme. Perhaps his most famous book, 1963's *The Gashlycrumb Tinies*, is an alphabet of children and how they met their demises: *"N is for Neville who died of ennui."* There are more violent deaths included, by ax, by poisoning, et cetera. *The Gilded Bat*, from 1966, finds its characters sent to insane asylums and dealing with actual ennui, just the kind that did in poor Sylvia Plath. Maudie, Gorey's heroine in *The Gilded Bat*, becomes Mirella, a celebrated ballerina who perishes when a "great dark bird" flies into the propeller of her plane. *The Iron Tonic* (1969) returns to rhyme: "It is known the skating pond conceals / a family of enormous eels."

That same year, 1969, Dr. Elisabeth Kübler-Ross released the best seller *On Death and Dying*, which famously broke down the idea of accepting death into five stages: denial and isolation, anger, bargaining, depression, and acceptance. The mid-1960s seemed to be all about denial. The next three stages, by 1968, became a kind of tsunami of drugs and misty madness that would stun brave, astronaut-like man-child artists like Wilson, or Syd Barrett of Pink Floyd. The latter, a dark-eyed beauty in the throes of lysergic epiphany/meltdown, would eschew the expanses of his old band in favor of playful children's poetry, long walks in nature, and an embrace of a kind of pre-rock jug band aesthetic. A cult hero hermit, he would, at the height of Punk, inspire a classic "Whatever happened to . . ." essay by the great British journalist Nick Kent as well as an irresistible novelty song by the Television Personalities, "I Know Where Syd Barrett Lives," complete with very Twee sped-up vocals and bird calls.

Dr. Kübler-Ross's final stage, acceptance, saw music and film grow darker and more knowing toward the end of the decade too. Facing the darkness—and showing resolve against it—became vogue, the Stones' "Jumpin' Jack Flash" being a good example. There was also a postpsychedelic back-to-the-land movement, as evidenced by the Band's *Music from Big Pink* and the embrace of canyon living, organic farming, and earth tones. The Beatles broke up and John Lennon inevitably seized the last word concerning "the dream" on his early solo track "God": it was over. Decade-ending films like *Midnight Cowboy*, *Easy Rider*, and even Woody Allen's *Take the Money and Run* are shot through with a sort of cynicism that betrays a dashed spirit.

Dr. Kübler-Ross includes a caveat maintaining that throughout the stages of grieving, there is a sixth or perhaps a constant state that accompanies the cycle: hope, "the one thing that persists." Even in their death throes, the 1960s produced a few flowers that would be, as one generation turned to the next, as constant as hope. In this way the decade would never truly end, even as it died a rather ignoble and disappointing death.

Perhaps the most beautiful and childlike of all the era's natural-born stars was Nick Drake, the greatest proto-Twee icon to ever pick up a guitar and sing while staring at his worn-out shoes.

Drake was from a well-to-do family and attended Cambridge. He managed to perform at several concerts during the folk-rock boom of the late 1960s that produced Sandy Denny and Fairport Convention, but was reportedly so shy he could not look anyone in the eye or carry on much of a conversation. Listening to any of his three albums today—1969's *Five Leaves Left*, 1970's *Bryter Layter*, and 1972's *Pink Moon*—it's hard to imagine someone tongue-tied. Drake sings in a hushed, jazzy, and almost regal baritone, like a sort of terribly English Leonard Cohen, but even more haunted, if that's possible.

Built out of Drake's unmistakable voice, his acoustic guitar, and studio string arrangements, *Five Leaves Left* was woefully obscure when it was first released; according to legend, it sold only three thousand copies in its day. It was this sense of obscurity, however, that helped fortify the Drake myth, as, of course, would his death, via an overdose of antidepressants in 1974 at age twenty-six. But unlike icons like James Dean or even Ian Curtis, Drake's art won attention over his early demise. The music grabbed young fans first, a quarter century later, and the tragedy, discovered most likely via a Web search, only sealed them as devotees.

"Almost everyone I have ever talked to about Nick Drake says that they heard the music before they knew the story," says Joe Boyd, who discovered Drake and produced his first two albums. "It is the music and just the music. The story is tragically romantic for some, and that can enhance the effect, but it simply starts with his musical genius. The fact that he was handsome doesn't hurt, but it is a small part of the phenomenon."

Madison Avenue had been plundering youth movements since the end of World War II and continues to do so well into the twenty-first century; this odd up-from-the-streets-and-into-suburban-homes phenomenon is a continuum. In 1989 Barney Rubble, in dookie gold chain, shades, porkpie hat, and sneakers, busted a few rhymes in a Fruity Pebbles commercial. Fred Flintstone cut up some vinyl on a turntable supported by a green dinosaur. There was the notorious Subaru Impreza ad from 1992 that featured actor Jeremy Davies stating, "This car is like *Punk rock*. Just trust me. This is relevant. Remember when rock and roll was really boring and corporate? Well, Punk challenged all this and said, 'Hey, excuse me, but here's what's cool about music.' Remember? Now Subaru with its Impreza is challenging some car thinkin' . . ." Scary stuff.

Then there were the 1-800-Collect commercials with actor Calvert DeForest (David Letterman's Larry "Bud" Melman) dressed in full-flannel grunge regalia. Informed that he can save on his long-distance calls to, of course, Seattle, he turns around and shouts, "Thanks, phone dude!"

Drake's albums, according to Boyd, first received notoriety during the 1980s and '90s, when bands like R.E.M. and singer-songwriters like Elliott Smith began giving him shout-outs in zines and major music magazines. "It was word of mouth," Boyd insists.

Then came the "Milky Way" ad spot for Volkswagen, which made Nick Drake a supernova, something he strove for in life but never enjoyed, which certainly played a factor in his depression.

Volkswagen's Beetle and bus had long been embraced by young people for their affordability and practicality. Many an Indie-rock band toured the country in one of those VW buses. By the late '90s,

Volkswagen had reintroduced a modern version of the discontinued Beetle to capitalize on that generation's fervor for all things retro. The New Beetle made its debut in a stark ad tracked to Spiritualized's dreamy, druggy 1997 Britpop hit "Ladies and Gentlemen We Are Floating in Space." It was the right product synched up to the perfect song. No hard sell. The Cabriolet, however, did not have the same high level of cultural currency. The car company was on the verge of discontinuing its convertible in favor of a top-down edition of the New Beetle when it approached its ad agency for a low-impact retail spot designed, mostly, to unload the remaining stock.

The Boston-based Arnold Worldwide had done the successful New Beetle campaign, as well as the popular hatchback ad featuring German New Wave act Trio's "Da Da Da." "We sort of said, 'Maybe there's something more we can do with this,'" says Arnold's then co–creative director Alan Pafenbach. Pitching ideas with his partner Lance Jensen, Pafenbach came up with an angle. "We asked, 'What's interesting about convertibles?' Everybody usually associated convertibles with four blond girls on a sunny California day. Lance said, 'One of the things that's cool about a convertible is when you drive it around at night.'"

The presentation was simple. A full moon, a cruising convertible; a timid group of four kids pulls up on a house party, looks inside, sees a bunch of lunkheads getting drunk, and decides to blow it off in favor of more night driving. No pitchman. No info on price breaks or deals. "We created a kind of back story," says Pafenbach. "These were kids who all worked together at some summer job, and it was the last weekend of summer. They were all going to go out and celebrate." The drivers aren't dressed "young," but rather somber and Indie. Even the "California blonde" looks subdued. They are mixed gender, mixed race, but look as if they belong together. "We tried to cast something that looked more like an independent film," Pafenbach says.

Video-directing team Jonathan Dayton and Valerie Faris were hired after the ad team saw their video for the Smashing Pumpkins single "1979," which also features a crew of real-looking small-town kids joyriding. Dayton and Faris went on to direct *Little Miss Sunshine* years later, another milestone in the mainstreaming of Twee.

The Church's 1988 hit "Under the Milky Way" was earmarked for the soundtrack, but once in the editing bay, the team realized it didn't quite match the lilting feeling of the spot. "It was a little too Gothic," says Pafenbach. "And so we pulled out this Nick Drake cut and gave it to the editor. It just worked. It was more magical. It lent it an ambience."

There was nothing else on TV like it, a sort of blue-bathed grace moment of shyness and gentleness—used to sell a car. There was also an unusual sense of morality to the spot.

"The kids drive up to a drunken brawl and decide not to go drink their faces off," says Pafenbach. "They've apparently matured enough to realize the experience they're having with their friends is better than just being a drunken idiot."

The car company ran the hell out of "Pink Moon," and Nick Drake, who in his lifetime had failed at fame so mightily, was suddenly a star. In just over a minute, he was brought back to life, with people stopping to ask, "Who was *that*?"

Here was one of the first modern ads to assume its target was intelligent, emotionally sophisticated, and weary of the old hard sell. Nick

Drake, dead twenty-five years, killed the jingle and brought back the 1960s, and in a way, launched that second summer of love—that new digital '60s. Many a long-dead '60s troubadour found new life in advertising and on soundtracks starting in the 1990s, from Harry Nilsson to Phil Ochs to Karen Dalton to Tim Hardin.

If it was obscure, dark, and hailing from the '60s, it was not only fascinating: it was money. "His songs are very atmospheric, but there is no one mood—each song is different," says Boyd. "Nick never pushed himself at the listener, he lured them into the music, which can be effective when using a song as underscore."

Here were the heroes buried in the 1960s. They did not get out of there alive—but eventually the Twee would come to dig them out, and take to them with open hearts and open wallets.

Chapter 3

The Wild Things

1972–1977

In which Punk rises from the death of the 1960s dream and responds to chagrined hippies and a lack of opportunity by embracing nihilism and antifashion and consigning anything from the previous era to the great tar pit of irrelevance. Some older artists are right there with them. Others seem determined to neutralize their Stalinist approach and make the world safe for butterflies and ice cream men.

aurice Sendak's monsters and the Sex Pistols were both on the cover of *Rolling Stone,* less than one year apart, in 1976 and '77. One might say, "Well, that's a coincidence," and have a good point. The magazine also featured actress Louise Lasser and the Grateful Dead on its covers during those years. It is, however, the embrace of Sendak by the children of the 1970s, a decade of escalating war, supply shortages, freaky cults, cocaine culture, and deadening and repetitive progressive rock that is most interesting. It is also interesting that *Rolling Stone*—then, as it is now, the arbiter of zeitgeist—gave a children's book author the same real estate that it gave the poster children of early Punk.

Elvis was on the outs. He'd be dead by the end of the coming summer. Sendak, then in middle age, was a king of rock.

Sendak's work contained a sort of innate empathy for suffering and perseverance; most of his endings were happy, even in his darkest fare such as *Pierre*, from 1962's *Nutshell Library*, in which the protagonist is literally, albeit briefly, devoured by a lion (spoiler: Pierre is spit out). Sendak was born just a little more than a year before the Great Depression started, and as a child in Brooklyn he was one of those Ray Davies–like window watchers, observing and drawing his more socially outgoing neighbors. He was haunted first by the disappearance of the Lindbergh baby and next by the Holocaust, news of which filtered back to his family dinner table; suffering and death were never far from his mind. Sendak used the terror, distilling it into something selfless and palatable.

The story of Punk's advent has been told and retold to the point that it's tedious. But for the sake of context, and to align the genre with the bleakness of one of its unsung "Punk" voices—Sendak—it requires framing. In mid-1970s England there were miners' strikes, and therefore frequent blackouts because of a lack of coal. Garbage piled up. Kids left school with almost no hope of getting a job. Their rock and literary heroes didn't articulate much rage anymore. The Rolling Stones certainly didn't; Lennon, like Dylan before him, had disappeared into domesticity in the Dakota with Yoko. Into this void came a sense of, for a time, sincere nihilism. Johnny Rotten sang, on the Sex Pistols single "Pretty Vacant," "We're so pretty, oh so pretty . . . we're vacant . . . and we don't care!" echoing, eerily, little

Pierre, whose mantra is, until the lion devours him anyway, "I don't care!" Pierre shouts this repeatedly.

What is a Punk, anyway, but an idealist? Johnny Rotten sang "God Save the Queen" and "Anarchy in the UK" not because he wished to see England burn but because he wanted to save it. And while the band's image was that of a crew of drooglike thugs, they were all intellectually curious—even Sid Vicious, who read any book that David Bowie, his idol, happened to mention in the press.

Their managers, Malcolm McLaren and Vivienne Westwood, clothiers before entering the rock business, studied philosophy like situationism and existentialism and never saw the group as much more than an art project or prank—and certainly a way to take money from the wealthy, Merry Men style.

Sendak had his nihilistic side as well. When director Spike Jonze, who would later adapt *Where the Wild Things Are* into a dark, puzzling, and enchanting feature film, asked the author and artist, "Do you have any advice for young people?" he replied, "Quit this life as soon as possible." But Sendak was also, crucially, a mensch and an aesthete. *The Nutshell Library* is a perfect fetish item; beautifully illustrated little books that fit into a tiny case. He knew the power of the book as object.

"There's so much more to a book than just the reading," he has said. "I've seen children touch books, fondle books, smell books, and it's all the reason in the world why books should be beautifully produced."

Sendak's most famous story is, of course, *Where the Wild Things Are*—published in 1963, and by the mid-1970s already a children's classic, winner of multiple awards and a must-read. Unlike most children's books, which open on a high note, *Wild Things* opens with its hero, Max, frowning. He is in the midst of what would come to be known as "acting out," brandishing a hammer, chasing his poor dog, and dressed in a wolf costume. There's no father in the picture, and Mother cannot control him with her threats and scolds. Max is a Punk before there was a word for it, before Iggy Pop ever had the notion to join a band. The writer Dave Eggers penned a novelization of the Spike Jonze adaptation (for which he also wrote the screenplay) and surmises, "Max's dad lived in the city and phoned on Wednesdays and Sundays but sometimes did not."

Deprived of his supper, Max decides, like Johnny Rotten, to "use the enemy." He sails toward the unknown and the frightening, albeit in his imagination. Escape would mark a later Sendak book as well, the lesser-known but just as enchanting *Higglety Pigglety Pop!*, from 1967. There, a pampered dog, Jennie, wonders, "There must be more to life than having everything," and sets out on a journey. "I am discontented," the pooch complains. "I want something I do not have. There must be more to life."

Jennie encounters danger in the cold woods ("There must be more to life than having nothing!" she then says, shivering), and later great success, becoming a star at the Mother Goose Theater. Sendak seems to be introducing ideas of the search for utopia in many of his books. The cynical part of Sendak clearly knows it's another illusion, a pipe dream, but a vital one, especially given the cruel realities all around. As horrible as the real world is, we must never stop looking.

Like Jennie, Max looks for his own utopia. He escapes his bedroom via boat and finds himself on an island full of beasts who "roared their terrible roars and gnashed their terrible teeth." There he makes himself the wildest thing of all, much in the way the Punks did. (What is a shredded T-shirt, bondage trousers, Doc Marten stomping boots, or a safety pin through the face if not a form of wolf suit?) "Be still!" he demands, and these creatures obey, and a wild rumpus starts. Just like London in '76.

"Maurice Sendak understood what he was doing when he wrote that book," the writer/actor and expert on most things Twee, John Hodgman, says of *Wild Things*. "The boy loses his control, loses his temper, and he consequently loses his mother." Twee rebels don't want to destroy everything around them. Rather, they want to fix it. And if creativity requires a temporary destruction, as most agree it does, and a few tantrums must be thrown, so be it. Critics of Twee complain that this isn't rebellion at all, that one must be prepared to sacrifice everything and lose oneself forever in the darkness. The Punks seemed to be in this corner. Not so the Twees, which is why Max, who travels only so far before returning home to a (hopefully) better relationship with his mother, is such an archetype.

"Max goes into a world where his temper is at first rewarded, but then he realizes that it's going to consume him, and he wants to go home," Hodgman says. "Sendak understood that children are angry and hate the world around them in a way that very few children's books acknowledged, and most parents didn't acknowledge."

Max indeed returns home—he most likely never really left—and enjoys its comforts, whereas Sendak himself suffered for his vision for much of his career. Many of Sendak's books were banned, for decades even—the most obvious example being *In the Night Kitchen,* featuring a little boy in various states of utterly sexless undress and in the midst of a dream. Sendak was openly gay, and subject to all the suspicions and prejudices that went with that identity during his lifetime; whether this is a fair trade for his output's now permanent status as Twee talismans is anyone's guess. Most likely not worth the pain, but it's probable that the pain was part of what makes them so.

If Sendak had a predecessor, it's Norton Juster and Jules Feiffer's 1961 novel *The Phantom Tollbooth*. Its hero, Milo, is the prototype for Max, but his nihilism is even more refined. He "doesn't know what to do with himself, not just sometimes but always." Milo makes Holden Caulfield look like a Boy Scout, and, like all the other discontented princes, he heads out, this time to Dictionopolis, another over-the-rainbow locale and metaphor for a new, postwar utopia that the young and searching seemed to require. Oz, Dictionopolis, Shangri La (which the Kinks sang about, albeit ironically), Brigadoon, Atlantis (the subject of a great Donovan epic) . . . seldom is a Twee hero happy where he or she stands, especially if that place is a school or an unfeeling home.

And if Sendak had a female counterpart—the queen of Twee Tribe youth-lit to his king—it was Judy Blume. Blume's books were aimed at slightly older children, but her stories were filled with characters that did not have the option of fantasy flight. They remained in an almost prison cell of adolescence, reduced to having talks with God and their own bodies, which also seemed at times like prisons. Her books tackled the realities of being a lonely, disenfranchised, and above all angry teen. In 1970's *Are You There God? It's Me, Margaret*, Margaret, waiting for puberty to arrive, resorts to a kind of desperate prayer. ("Please help me grow God. You know where.") In 1975's *Forever . . .*, Blume, who looked more like a suburban housewife than a Punk, almost dared bookstores and libraries to attack her with the release of such a sexually frank and often hilarious tale (in which the male object of affection, Michael, has christened his penis "Ralph"). "There he was on top of me and I felt Ralph hard against my thigh," says the book's narrator, Katherine. In the 1970s, *Forever . . .* was a kind of *Tropic of Cancer* or *Lady Chatterley's Lover,* a paperback hidden in book bags, underlined (the sex parts, of course), and traded in shadows among preteens and teens.

These authors were both subversive and incredibly popular, selling millions of copies of their books. Sendak even paired with singer-songwriter Carole King, then a superstar, to collaborate on the hit album and TV special *Really Rosie,* another must-own for any pained '70s kid looking to be enchanted without being insulted.

"I'm Really Rosie," King sings on the soundtrack, "and I'm Rosie Real." These were not the bullshitters of the past. "You better believe me!" she sings, the same way Johnny Rotten added "We mean it, man!" to a verse of "God Save the Queen."

King's multimillion-selling *Tapestry* album (1971), accomplished and often achingly beautiful as it is, came, ironically, at the forefront of the era of big-rock and superstar-singer-songwriter music that virtually required a Sex Pistols reactionary attack on laid-back, unchallenging fashion and values.

"I remember believing very definitively that there needed to be a kind of rehaul by '76, '77," says the veteran music writer Paul Morley. "It was clear it was a racist and sexist—and narrow-minded—society, unartistic if you like, and there had to be a cleansing. But by '77, '78, a lot of these [Punk] characters seemed to have fallen by the wayside."

The thing about Punk was that, like Max's trip to the Island of the Wild Things, it didn't last very long. "Punk had lost an ideological battle," Morley says. Its principles were simply too rigid to sustain. There were those who did not want to dismiss everything that went before and be Stalinist about their music, their dress, and their culture. Some claimed 1977 was "year zero," while others secretly missed the Beatles and the Stones and mourned the death of the King that year.

"Let's say it's 1977," Nitsuh Abebe writes in his now classic *Pitchfork* essay "Twee as Fuck." "You live in London. And with Punk going full-steam—in this new scene that's abandoned sophistication and chops, this scene that insists *anyone* can start a band—you start thinking: Why not me? Only there's a problem. Punks act certain ways: They're loud and angry, or else they're arty and clever . . . You have a schoolboy voice and you'd feel stupid spiking your hair or pulling on bondage trousers . . . and you certainly don't see any reason to stop loving the Kinks . . . so what are you going to do?"

"People who don't buy into the ethos of cool that goes around Punk rock—the danger element or sex or swagger—the people for whom that's not really an important part, will always carve out another niche," Abebe says today.

Jonathan Richman and the Modern Lovers were revered by the original Punks of '76 and '77, but Richman wasn't buying it either. When the singer-songwriter first heard William Blake's "The Lamb," recited by a fellow guest during the taping of a British talk show in 1978, he was so overcome with emotion, he teared up on camera. The host asked Richman if being considered naïve or simplistic ever bothered him. "The Lamb" seemed to validate Richman's controversial and already semimythical retreat from the hard cynicism and greed of the newly massive music business of the Fleetwood Mac–Frampton 1970s. "If that makes me simplistic, then I'm one [of the simple people]," he said, gesturing toward the man off camera who'd just read the Blake. He ran a hand through his curly brown hair, shook his head, and wiped his long nose.

Raised like Theodor Geisel/Dr. Seuss in suburban Massachusetts ("See, I come from Boston," he sings in his autobiographical hit "New England"), Richman was just a teenager when he entered the rock scene. He had heard Lou Reed sing "Sunday Morning" and "Femme Fatale" on *The Velvet Underground and Nico,* and something about the tough-but-gentle, street-numb-but-vulnerable music convinced him that he had to stand as close as possible to this band and take in their energy. The Velvets were another should-have-been-huge act in their own time. They had the personality and the publicity (courtesy of "manager" and "producer" Andy Warhol), plus lyrics about S&M, heroin, and death. Instead they enjoyed "cult" success among students and hipsters, with a strong fan base among the hip Boston college crowd. When they played a residency at the rock club the Boston Tea Party in early '69, they all came out in their black turtlenecks. Richman was there.

The Tea Party's owner, Steve Sesnick, would soon replace Andy Warhol as the band's manager. He'd sign Richman as well, convinced that with a worthy student of the Velvets, he couldn't lose. Both acts, however, were tricky. The Velvets were in transition. Nico and then cofounder John Cale followed Warhol out the door, replaced by the handsome, sweet-voiced Doug Yule, who instantly vied with Reed as front man. Guitarist Sterling Morrison and tomboyish drummer Maureen "Mo" Tucker remained. Minus the classically trained Cale and the chilling Nico, the Velvets were free to be sweet and simple.

It's Tucker who sings the sweetest and the simplest of these new-direction songs, like "After Hours" and the Reed duet "I'm Sticking with You." Both songs are Twee classics. Nasal and off-key, Tucker sounded like a small boy skipping over dead bodies, the Blossom

Dearie of the gutter. According to legend, Tucker was so shy she had to sing the former track in a closed studio with only Reed for moral support. "The Velvets have changed considerably since they left Warhol's gang," the *Village Voice* wrote in 1970 while the band debuted its new lineup and sound at Max's Kansas City, still the nucleus of the hip downtown Warhol-centric art scene. "No more demonic assault on the audience. No more ear wrenching shrieks of art. No more esoterica."

The sweet side of this quintessentially tough, streetwise band was a revelation to the impressionable teenage Richman. He followed them to New York City, and for a short time he was one of the young, ambitious souls to hang around the Warhol Factory, running errands for Warhol's staff and hoping to get into their de facto clubhouse Max's Kansas City, just across from Union Square.

Returning to Boston, Richman spent his afternoons busking with his guitar, singing original songs for the Harvard, Cambridge, and MIT students who'd pass, waiting for his big break. A friend, percussionist Dave Robinson, would sometimes join him, and when they had a chance to play indoors, Harvard architecture student and keyboardist Jerry Harrison and bassist Ernie Brooks sat in. There was good band chemistry and a nifty garage-rock sound. Soon they were calling themselves the Modern Lovers as a kind of fuck-you to the old, womanizing lothario approach to rock stardom and its attendant womanizing. The Velvet Underground never sang about groupies; Reed filled his lyrics with portraits of genius junkie girls (and genius junkies who dressed like girls).

Soon, Richman's yearning singer-songwriter confessions were rocked up. The band played parties. They played recreation halls. They got tighter and they got taped. As with the Velvets, soon fans started sharing bootlegs as if it was their personal cause to make the Modern Lovers the biggest band since the Rolling Stones.

"In about 1971, Jonathan came to the attention of everyone. A number of people in the entertainment industry tried to woo and court him," says Matthew King Kaufman, founder of the Northern California–based independent label Berserkley Records and, soon, a key Richman supporter. Whenever the Modern Lovers performed a showcase, powerful executives like Columbia's Clive Davis, A&M's Jerry Moss, and Steve Paul, owner of the hip club the Scene and founder of Blue Sky Records, all came to check them out. Even John Cale, now ensconced behind a big desk in the A&R department of the newly expanding Warner Bros. record division, was interested. At the start of the big-rock era, wings of major media and entertainment companies like Warner Bros. were gobbling up the little mom-and-pop independent labels that had released many of the classic 1950s and '60s R&B, country, and garage-band hits, and subsequently placed themselves in the position of having to find one sensation after the other to impress shareholders and justify their very hugeness.

For all his apparent shyness, Richman was a natural showman on-stage, effortlessly able to connect with a crowd. He worked the mike like a game-show host, setting up each number and leading the band through them with an "All right, Modern Lovers . . ."

The songs were thrilling. There was "Pablo Picasso," an ode to confidence and vision over physical limitations, a Punk ethic if there ever was one. And then there was "Roadrunner," which took Bo Diddley's "Roadrunner" into the New England suburbs, placing a lonely hero on a starry night, young and moving fast, powered by the radio. "I'm in love with rock and roll, and I'll be out all night . . ." Richman had written the track when he was eleven and dreaming of having a car instead of a bike. There was no heavy metaphor here. It was a classic car song, as American and accessible as it got, and every one of those golden-eared idol-makers in the audience could tell it was the single.

Following one showcase, an A&R rep from Warner Bros. casually told Richman that he would have to sing "Roadrunner" at every show he played for the rest of his life. The teenager was horrified. "Jonathan couldn't believe they actually said that, and he was going to lose all his free will," says Kaufman.

John Cale, just shy of thirty, took a big-brotherly role with the star, which makes perfect sense when you consider how much Richman worshipped Cale's former band. It was clear that Warner Bros. was the Modern Lovers' first choice despite the bad juju Richman had gotten from one of their employees. Warner Bros. had absorbed smaller labels like an amoeba and had amassed a roster of superstar acts including Black Sabbath, America, Van Morrison, the Grateful Dead, the Doobie Brothers, and James Taylor. All involved expected the Modern Lovers to be next in this long line of massive stars.

The band flew out to Los Angeles to record with Cale for three days. Cale had produced the Stooges' 1969 debut and was, via work with Nico and avant-garde classical musician Terry Riley, on his way to establishing himself as someone who could take hip street energy and heady, student-beloved expansion and capture it all, pleasingly, on a marketable track. (In 1975, he would produce Patti Smith's debut, the Punk rock epic *Horses,* as well as Squeeze's self-titled debut in '77.)

Cale had a personal preference for Richman's voice when it had a bit of Dylan-esque sneer to it, as it did on "She Cracked." It fit nicely with Harrison's aggressive electric organ, which he pulled up in the mix. "Cale would be saying, 'Now, Jonathan, I want you to sing this in a mean way,'" Harrison has said. "And Jonathan would just look at him, you know, 'Mean? I won't sing mean. I don't feel mean!'"

The Cale tapes were electrifyingly raw, but in the pre-Punk era few at the label felt this was an asset. The sound was not dark and stoner-friendly à la Black Sabbath, or soft pop like America. It was not baroque and showy like Elton John. Hoping to push their acquisition into a more marketable direction, Kim Fowley, veteran hit maker and eccentric, self-styled rock and roll Frankenstein (best known for later assembling the proto-Punk girl group the Runaways) was also hired to fuss with the Modern Lovers. Warner Bros., once so intent on signing this sought-after band, now didn't know what to do with them.

"They couldn't market it," says Kaufman. Richman was trim, good-looking in a clean-cut way, but naturally strange: was he the new David Cassidy or the new Jim Morrison? Once their West Coast sessions and shows were completed, an excited Modern Lovers returned to Boston and waited . . . and waited . . . for word from the label. Ultimately, Warner Bros. did what many giant companies do when faced with what seemed like an insurmountable and time-sucking dilemma: they ignored it. The tapes were placed on the shelf, and Richman and the band were left to wonder, "What just happened?"

This lasted eighteen months. When the label eventually informed the band that they were being dropped, it was almost a relief. Matthew King Kaufman, still a believer, was allowed to purchase the Cale tapes at a bargain-bin rate. "About ten cents on the dollar," he says. As the band slowly came apart, Kaufman began assembling what would come to be universally known as the Modern Lovers' self-titled debut.

Today that record is regarded as a pre-Punk classic, easily as influential as anything by the Velvet Underground. Its purple-and-gray color scheme and the band's logo are T-shirt- and sticker-worthy icons. But it was never an "album" in the classic sense. It was essentially a demo. That's how good this band was. Paul Nelson, the legendary music writer from *Rolling Stone,* provided Kaufman with a copy of the crucial track "Hospital."

"I go to bakeries all day long," Richman sings on that ballad, a pledge of unconditional love for a troubled scene queen. "There's a lack of sweetness in my life."

These bootleg Modern Lovers tapes slowly transformed Richman into the star that the industry could never make: a word-of-mouth legend. His absence only fed into the burgeoning myth. Where was Richman? Where did he go after being dropped? Bermuda? Israel?

"Jonathan changed radically during that period," Kaufman says. "This was around the time when he was starting to want to write and sing only happy songs," Harrison recalled to a journalist years later.

The major labels had moved on to the next big thing, but out in Berkeley, Matthew King Kaufman was inspired by the contained excitement for the band among the brighter music writers. When Kaufman invited Richman out to California for a visit in 1975, it had been nearly four years since the band had been signed by Warner Bros. Back in New York City, there were half a dozen bands starting to coalesce around CBGB, a small, grubby club on the Bowery. Harrison had relocated to Manhattan and joined one of them. They were called Talking Heads, and their lead singer, David Byrne, was as puzzling and singular and unlikely a rock star as Richman had been, a sort of nerd with the stage presence of David Bowie or Bryan Ferry. The Ramones, Television, and Blondie were all raised on the kind of garage rock that Richman had taken and turned on its ear. Here were young bands presenting the same elemental, teen-friendly, cathartic noise as Richman. But when there's half a dozen of them, they call it a movement. When it's only one, it's "unmarketable."

Over in England, in '75, the nascent London Punk scene was forming around McLaren and Westwood's bondage-wear shop in the King's Road. The store, called Sex, had an old-style 1950s jukebox in the back and a few dozen original rock and roll hits: Little Richard, Eddie Cochran, Jerry Lee Lewis, Chuck Berry, Gene Vincent. Aghast by the bloat of the music industry and the pretensions of artists like Emerson, Lake & Palmer and Yes (with all their elaborate concerts on ice), the kids who'd convene there turned to the birth of rock and roll for inspiration.

"We went back to what came before that," says Pistols bassist Glen Matlock. "More rockin'. More concise." Sixties Mod tracks from the Who and the Small Faces were acceptable. If anything from the 1970s fit in, it was the occasional Iggy or New York Dolls track, until one day the aforementioned Nick Kent, a journalist for *New Musical Express* (*N.M.E.*) and a famous rock writer in an era when rock writers had a lot of power, showed up at the store with one of the Modern Lovers cassettes from America.

"The Modern Lovers were kind of this call back," Kent says of the band's neat fit into the back-to-basics context that so bewitched these English kids. "At the time, Richman was very much out on his own." McLaren's assembled players, who would soon be christened the Sex Pistols, had no idea what Richman looked like or even what he was singing about half the time ("Put down your cigarette and drop out of B.U.!," he sang on "Modern World." *What's B.U.?*, they must have wondered), but the Kent tape quickly became something they could all agree on. It was tough, but there were melodies and that sneer that had so bewitched Cale. Matlock was an unashamed fan of the Kinks and girl groups like the Shirelles and the Ronettes. He clashed with the group's new lead singer, Johnny Rotten, who only allowed hardcore dub, select prog rock like Van Der Graaf Generator, and yet another proto-Punk icon, Captain Beefheart and his Magic Band, into the mix. But "Roadrunner" passed the test with both, and it was easy enough to learn: a few chords and a chorus that was basically the title repeated and repeated. "We didn't know what it meant," Matlock says. "Some kind of car? It just sounded different." The Pistols still managed to screw it up. And yet "Roadrunner" stood out as one of the few romantic notions in the band's set: the idea of driving with the top down didn't exactly jibe with songs like "Bodies" and "Holidays in the Sun." The band had dismissed such sentiment as hedonistic and socially irresponsible given the urban decay and day-to-day peril of life in late-'70s London. Somehow Richman's sweetness made it through, and the song—the one that Richman was warned would dog him his entire career—was about to show up in his life again. With an insurgency he was unwittingly helping to fuel now under way, Richman himself was out in Santa Monica making street music with a bunch of winos.

"He actually wanted to record with the winos playing with rolled-up newspapers, beating on the ground. I told him he was a little far afield," Kaufman says.

Richman soon headed north and moved into the Berserkley of-fices, where a "comeback" plan was proposed. Richman had continued to write songs in the intervening years, but when he played them for Kaufman and his small staff, it was a shock. The melodies were sweet street-corner doo-wop and bare-bones-folk inspired and spare, produced so the listener could hear every strum. His lyrics were no longer about girls or hip boys in cities: Richman sang instead of creatures from outer space ("Here Come the Martian Martians") and what kind of ice cream they liked.

But Richman had not lost his mind like Pink Floyd's founder Syd Barrett. This wasn't outsider art, like Frank Zappa's deranged protégé Wild Man Fischer. Here was, the songwriter insisted, his true, musical self at work. The puzzlement only seemed to strengthen Richman's resolve. "I know he comes off as an extremist," Kaufman says, "but he's more of a contrarian. If you tell him the world is round, he'll find the flat spot." Richman signed to Berserkley and was promised autonomy. As a gesture of gratitude, perhaps, he agreed to record a new version of "Roadrunner" as a showcase single for the label. It was the obvious track to introduce him to the world—always had been.

Kaufman was in London for a record-industry convention in 1976 when he first realized that the old Modern Lovers were being embraced by a new generation of Punk kids despite the album never having been officially released. "I was sick and asleep in the hotel and there were messages being pushed under the door about the number of orders." The new "Roadrunner" single, slower and thicker than the original but still a rush, had become a radio hit and was on its way into the British pop Top Ten, just as the Sex Pistols were routinely starting to make the front pages of the UK tabloids.

"Nothing even resembled 'Roadrunner' on the radio," Kaufman says. "It appealed to the disenfranchised. When I met Johnny Rotten he told me the Modern Lovers was the only record he listened to. He recited the lyrics to me. I was impressed."

Richman and his new Modern Lovers played a show to promote the release of his album at New York City's prestigious Town Hall, which drew and instantly perplexed the city's rock elite who'd so prided themselves on being hip to the unreleased Warner Bros. album. "The older, dippier Richman seemed to have succumbed to terminal cutesy poo," the legendary Lester Bangs groaned in his review for the *N.M.E.* The *New York Rocker*'s Lisa Persky mused, "His unpretentiousness is almost a pretension." The warning out of New York was completely unheeded in London. There, after nearly a half decade, Richman was finally a rock star, completely on his own terms.

Richman never said much. He didn't dress flashy. He wore his brown, curly hair neatly trimmed. He never once attempted to increase his standing with the worshipful Punks by donning a bondage bracelet or spiking his hair. You'd never imagine that across the ocean, the kids in London (and Manchester and Liverpool) who were "inventing" Punk rock were enthralled with this man.

Richman and the new Lovers recorded (in quick, no-frills DIY style with Richman at the controls) a second album for Berserkley, this one entitled, with equal simplicity, *Rock n' Roll with the Modern Lovers*. When released in '77, it yielded an even bigger British chart single, the instrumental "Egyptian Reggae": a typically spare, strummed riff, a clip-clop beat, and an occasional gong hit for panache. A full tour was booked, with stays in luxury hotels and high-end travel—and, as expected, the Punks queued up to buy tickets. But they had no idea what they were in for.

As the Euro tour began to roll out, once the house lights dimmed, the crowds braced, as they always did at Punk shows, for volume, and lots of it. But the Modern Lovers played softly. "I was playing a B-15 amp, probably turned up to like three," bassist Asa Brebner says. "It was more like going to see a play."

Richman's stage costume consisted of a white shirt knotted at the front, dark trousers, curly hair, and a pencil-thin, Little Richard–style mustache. He looked odd. And before long, like sharks in bloody water, the hecklers came, emboldened, sometimes challenged, by Richman's obstinate refusal to signal to the crowd with a wink that this was a joke. He couldn't, because it wasn't. Still, he had not lost his ability as master of ceremonies, and even when it was contentious, the star engaged directly. "There were definitely people in the audience who were more than ready to say fuck-you to this shit," the bassist recalls. "People were expecting to hear that first album. We got stuff thrown at us. It was really scary."

Brebner recalls, "This one guy started screaming and Jonathan looked at him and said, 'You're very angry for such a young man. Did your mommy forget to change you?' The guy just shut the fuck up."

"Halfway through the gig, he won that audience over," journalist Kent says.

Richman is a Twee Tribe saint because he opened up the clenched Punk rock heart, and by example demonstrated that it was okay to be both tender and appreciative of the sound of the "Old World"— whether it was the 1960s or even earlier, well beyond the jug band and ukulele ditties and the skiffle and Chicago blues favored by that decade's troubadours. He said what he meant (whether people believed it or not), and did not follow fashion at the time that "anti-fashion" itself was in vogue. Take the example of Shane MacGowan, himself a legend now, but at the time a dentally challeged, scrawny follower of the Punk movement and erstwhile leader of a couple of also-ran bands like the Nipple Erectors—the Nips for short—and the Chainsaws. Bored with Punk's limitations, he remembered the songs he heard as a child, the powerful Irish ballads, dirges, and celebratory sing-alongs, and determined that they were even more pure than the three chords every Punk kid in London now knew too well. "What I wanted to do was go back beyond rock and roll, before rock and roll," he writes in *A Drink with Shane MacGowan,* a sort of interview as memoir, "and do Irish music but do it for a pop audience because I think Irish music is very like rock and roll, it's one of the musics that influenced rock and roll, it's one of the musics that makes up rock and roll. A lot of Irish songs are rock and roll songs." One didn't have to be Van Morrison to embrace the Celtic in a post-Richman world. The perennial and the emotional were now up for grabs.

In the Midwest of America, the teen Punks who would form the indispensable Twee Tribe combo the Violent Femmes in the 1980s were feeling the same Punk fatigue. "[Femmes drummer] Victor [De-Lorenzo] and I were playing a lot of other stuff," says bassist Brian Ritchie. "Jazz, folk, what is now called 'world music,' and we loved the freedom and mobility of acoustic music and busking." Later, both the Pogues and the Femmes would plug in, but both essential bands began quiet, the volume coming from the heart like the "new" Jonathan Richman. As these teens turned twenty and began forming bands, an entire world would open up—musically, culturally, and politically. Some call it post-Punk, but what it really stood for was the freedom to be you.

Chapter 4

Sixteen Again

1977–1981

In which the sweaty, angry, nervous kids in glasses and too-tight neck ties, clash with the sneering, snarling Punks in bondage leather and metal studs . . . and win! The underdogs free the young and studious pop fans to come out of the closet and declare a love for ABBA, disco, and books (if not Thatcher) and a distaste for the pogo.

That Williamsburg, Brooklyn, as we've established, the epicenter of Twee, would ultimately provide a home for the quintessential Indie record shop, Rough Trade, is, depending on whom you ask, either antithetical or perfect. The nine-thousand-square-foot superstore, a repurposed industrial space on once-desolate North Ninth Street still boasting metal staircases, high ceilings, and concrete floors, is a triumph in that it's one of the few large and ambitious record stores remaining on the planet; the West Coast's Amoeba stores also come to mind. The first Rough Trade record shop, which opened on Kensington Park Road in West London in the winter of 1976, was originally stocked in part with albums thrifted from bins by a soft-spoken space rock fan named Geoff Travis. On a trip to Canada (to visit a girlfriend in Montreal) and America (with lengthier stops in Chicago and San Francisco in '75) Travis amassed the first bit of Rough Trade stock, mostly in U.S. thrift stores.

A homey sense of love and care can still be found in the Rough Trade Brooklyn bins, with their markered labels ('60s, '70s, '80s, Jazz, Country, Psychedelic, Reggae), but there are other elements that may vex the purist. There's a sense of utter completism. You won't miss anything here, and you won't have to dig in crates. It's all there, every classic "must-have" album, everything educational and indispensable. Yes, much of it is vinyl, but it still has that one-click feel to it. Where there were once zines at the London shop in the '70s, the literary section is now lined with expensive coffee-table books. And it's branded up the wazoo, with turntable covers, lapel badges, canvas totes, and tees. Rough Trade, the store and the record label that sprang from it, has earned the right to sell a tote bag or two: simply signing the Fall or the Smiths or the Strokes before anyone knew who they were would justify a lifelong pass to cash in one's cred, but there's something icky about the utter lack of politics—icky and very new Brooklyn. "We're a partner," says Travis over coffee during a visit to New York in the winter of 2013. "I'm thrilled it's happening. My main concern is that it be good. That it's a place that will turn people on to great music that they don't know about. And I hope it's not too expensive." Travis seems well aware of the disconnect between the store's humble roots and the kind of hyperbranding and mass clientele who would now not seem out of place at a bustling HMV.

Rough Trade's name seems ironic. These are gentle, diffident, record collecting souls. Still, it's a name that came to prominence when there were riots and strikes in London. Was it all simply a means to selling a Lee Hazlewood or Palace Brothers album to a trust funder? The young Joe Strummer would probably throw a Molotov through the window, but would he be right in doing so? He himself was a part-time Punk, after all, and quickly dropped the conceits of the movement once it ceased to be fresh. In a post-hip universe, all, not just the kids with the right gear, seem to be welcome to the Island of Misfit Toys, with its luxury hotels like the Wythe instead of squats, but first there had to be a battle, with pioneers and sacrifices.

Travis was among those in the cultural foxhole back in the day, challenging, along with his original staff (including future Swell Maps founders Niki Sudden and Epic Soundtracks), Punk's binary nature with a crucial sense of hippie-age, utopian accessibility, its doors always open no matter what kind of trousers (or flares) one was wearing, its model being the studiously stocked but user-friendly City Lights (the legendary San Francisco literary haven founded by beat poet Lawrence Ferlinghetti). One didn't need to be a beatnik to shop at City Lights, and its very stock of inspiring texts (as opposed to LPs in Rough Trade's case) could bring numbers to the cause. The original Rough Trade was located in Ladbroke Grove, long a bastion for the counterculture. The Pink Fairies and Mick Farren's subversive Deviants played there. There were West Indian families and heldover hippies. *Performance* was shot nearby in Powis Square. Jimi Hendrix breathed his last nearby as well.

"I was never a hard liner," Travis says, explaining how his shop became a haven to the proto-Twees who could not kick with the Stalinist Punks. "I have a wide net. I thought it was really amusing that the Punks had all these laws. I was just concerned that I move things that

I see as good into a bigger arena." Among the things he saw as good were artists like Tim Buckley, Jesse Winchester, Bobby Charles, and tons of the disco and reggae that Travis DJ'd at the local club Dingwalls. "We only sold things in the shop that we liked, which was a pretty strange, noncommercial decision." But Rough Trade was not anti-Punk, either. "Plenty of people came in wearing bondage pants," Travis recalls. They were simply not *only* Punk, at a time when the Punks were intent on smashing down all remnants of the past.

The staff was thrilled when the first Talking Heads single arrived from New York. They stocked zines like *Search and Destroy* out of San Francisco, as well as *ZigZag* and the *New York Rocker*. If one could stomach the volume (two massive Jamaican-style sound system speakers blared music all day, mostly reggae like Gregory Isaacs and Big Youth) you were welcome. "Basically, we opened a refuge from the real world and a place to listen to good music. Gradually people drifted in and never went away. People started coming for the things we had that nobody else had. The Velvet Underground EP with 'I'm Sticking with You.' The Iggy Pop bootleg—*Metallic K.O.* Bowie's *Live at Santa Monica Civic*, the Flamin' Groovies's first LP."

That lack of judgment, born from Travis's hippie-era beginnings, has carried on for four decades. Twee Tribers and Indie kids today adore a great rap single, whether it's from Lil Wayne, Kanye West, Azealia Banks, or Jay-Z. Over the course of its history, Indie has evolved a sophisticated filtration system and can appreciate a groove while dismissing an offending lyric. There's no Twee Triber I know, for example, who did not respond in the summer of 2013 to Robin Thicke's "Blurred Lines." They are, at heart, and often in spite of themselves, pop fans (the aforementioned Real Housewives and Kardashians are guilty pleasures as well as sources of horror). They rarely slag off or feel personally threatened by popular art just because normal people, even their haters, like it too. Lena Dunham, for example, tweets constantly about hit network series like *Scandal* even while her own HBO show is considered high television art. One of the more iconic scenes in the first season of *Girls* depicts Dunham as she gavottes to Robyn's Swedish pop-candy kernel "Dancing on My Own." Twees also love reality TV, cooking shows, and the Harry Potter books—not only love them, but see the hidden depth therein. Other times, most recently in the case of Taylor Swift, some Twee can rub off on a mainstream superstar for the better.

Pop is joyful, and Punks were obliged to be older before their time because the world around them was oppressive. Take away the oppression, and what do you have?

Rough Trade, Williamsburg.

But you also have, or had, as Punk drew its last breath, a world safe for pop kids who like loud, fast, and, yes, joyful music. Post-Punk provided a kind of waterslide back toward adolescence, eventually leading to Twee pop as we would come to know it. "Bands like the Buzzcocks were absolutely vital to this," says journalist Paul Morley.

It was Rough Trade that distributed the Buzzcocks' legendary debut EP, *Spiral Scratch*, in 1978. The shop had evolved into a sophisticated distribution system, taking on these new beyond-Punk artists on consignment and exposing them to a larger audience while protecting them from the major label system.

"What was missing in the marketplace was a proper distribution system [for the Indie world]. That was our major contribution. The major labels were a different world," says Travis, "nothing to do with us. The Clash? Why sign to [major] CBS? That was pathetic. That was our attitude. We still loved them but . . . politically we felt their managers were old-school." The first consignment release, from a band called the Desperate Bicycles, featured the excellent post-Punk singles "Smokescreen" and "Handlebars." Released in the summer of 1977, great as it was, it was more powerful perhaps as an example of DIY can-do than as a commercial concern; more business model than sonic influence. *Spiral Scratch*, the four-song Buzzcocks EP anchored by the anthem "Boredom," was on another level, a truly scorching collection that placed both the Buzzcocks and Rough Trade into a realm outside of Britain, gained influence in America, and introduced a gentler, smarter, unashamedly pop-loving strain of Punk or early post-Punk into the water supply. "The *Spiral Scratch* EP was hugely important," Travis says.

The Buzzcocks were not anti-Punk or remotely Punk fearing. They coordinated the Sex Pistols' famous show at Manchester's Lesser Free Trade Hall on June 4, 1976 (a scene re-created in Michael Winterbottom's *24 Hour Party People*). They simply weren't *only* Punk. They knew what few people would say out loud: that the Sex Pistols wrote great pop songs.

The Buzzcocks possessed a gift for marrying sweet backing vocals to leads that were at turns raw and sincere à la Richman (a key influence) and camp as a row of tents, as they say. Take the later single "Love You More," one of their two dozen perfect three-minute pop songs. "After this love, there'll be no other," promises Pete Shelley, the band's cofounder and the song's composer, pale, weak-chinned, weedy but somehow romantic. He adds, "until the razor cuts." Count Plath as godmother here too.

Steve Diggle, the alien-looking Howard Devoto, and teen drummer John Maher quickly sped beyond their heroes musically by marrying a boldly lovelorn, sweet, and unapologetically camp approach to standard Punk. The way Twee culture dominates, they are today the far more influential band, even if their name is not as well-known as the more firebrand Clash and the Sex Pistols. Every "pop-Punk" outfit with a sense of wit and romance, from Green Day to Fall Out Boy, owes them a tax.

By the start of the 1980s, Rough Trade was its own Indie label as well, signing undeniable acts like the Fall, the Young Marble Giants; the Normal's seminal "T.V.O.D." single, and Crass (and eventually the Smiths); artists who, like the Buzzcocks, were too odd, sensitive, grumpy, and strange to pass as Punks proper (while still maintaining an unmistakable Punk energy). Rough Trade also established an ethic that would inform the Indie publishing and distribution world of the '80s. "The only thing we turned down were things we felt were sexist or racist," Travis says. Jonathan Richman might have been the shock of the new (or the old, as it were), but Geoff Travis picked up the mantle and institutionalized a kind of complex, somewhat softer Punk culture; one where complicated, rumpled, shy, sweaty, oddball, proto-Twee heroes could have careers and have their say.

"Everything around Punk had expired and become its own cliché—bands sounding the same, zines looking the same," says former Buzzcocks manager Richard Boon, founder of the Indie label New Hormones, who released *Spiral Scratch* in late January 1977 (before it was picked up by Rough Trade in London). Only one thousand copies were printed, a method later employed by Belle and Sebastian with their debut, *Tigermilk*—the whole less-is-more, "Can we find it in the shops?" strategy. If people know they can't get something, they want it even more.

The Buzzcocks could not have come from London in the same way that Richman and Kaufman could not have been bred in New York City. A distance from the center of the action provides a different perspective. "There's the cliché in England that 'people are friendlier in the north,'" Boon says. "My maxim, as it were, was to make the place one happens to be living the place one wants to be living. In the inspirational fallout of seeing the Pistols in January '76, we wanted to spread the virus and make something happen—in Manchester. With no real venues, there was no choice but to do things ourselves."

The Buzzcocks, also like Richman and even Andy Kaufman, were Punks without wearing the Punk drag, which had already become a dreary uniform. You could see them lingering in the crowd before their shows. They were available and inimitable, sartorially anyway, years before the Smiths and later Nirvana made this seem revolutionary. "Pete would be approached for autographs," Boon recalls, "so he took to carrying an autograph book himself, collecting the signatures of those asking for his." This bred a fierce loyalty among the group's fan club, dubbed the Secret Public, their logo borrowed from the post-horn graphic in Thomas Pynchon's *The Crying of Lot 49*.

"There was something about the blankness of their clothing and artwork and two-note guitar solos," Paul Morley says. "They were more important than the Pistols or the Clash or any of the London bands. They also brought with them a philosophical attitude as to *why* they made their music—what it was about, how it wanted to appear and grow up—and therefore now they have a much bigger influence on the Brooklynization thing, the Indie thing."

As scenes developed in Manchester, with Joy Division emerging soon after the Buzzcocks, as well as in Sheffield, Leeds, and Liverpool, down in the capital the rigidity of Punk was relaxing, like a Mohawk falling into unruly cowlicks. Well-read bands like the Raincoats, Marine Girls, and Young Marble Giants prized their 1960s Kinks and Herman's Hermits 45s, shopped in thrift stores, and cultivated a soon-to-be highly influential "art school" aesthetic. The original Rough Trade record shop became a hub for defiantly Twee vinyl connoisseurs from all corners of the Isles.

"There was a shift in consciousness," says Gina Birch of the Raincoats. "We didn't dress up. We weren't leather girls. We wore weird spotty dresses, big Madeira boots, and jumpers with holes in them. We didn't brush our hair. We looked like we just got out of bed." But the spiky, smart music they made earned them the respect of the "Rough Trade Brigade," as well as powerful BBC DJ John Peel, who threw his back into supporting these new, oddly modest Indie bands, allowing them to have actual hit singles.

Being smart and shy was no longer a liability, and screaming had ceased to be a requirement: even Johnny Rotten had gotten murky and dubby with his post-Pistols band, Public Image. Then there was XTC, a four-piece from unfashionable suburban Swindon. Chief songwriters Andy Partridge and Colin Moulding weren't toughs and couldn't pretend that they were unclever or crude. They wrote pleasingly cathartic thrashes you could sing along to ("This Is Pop!") and stinging satire ("Respectable Street" and, most famously, "Making Plans for Nigel"), but they also couldn't pretend that they didn't know the Kinks had gotten there first. They were Punk's precocious and gifted children.

"XTC, Squeeze, Elvis Costello, even the Police, these were people who were clearly not droogs. They were sort of student-ish," says journalist Morley. "They understood the ideological action that was happening around them and changed their hair and clothing and graphic design and presentation so they could look like they were part of the revolution without being part of the revolution."

The violence at these shows was no longer kneejerk but became instead a sort of overgrown teen tantrum. The relatively dainty (when compared to Johnny Rotten) Pete Shelley famously hated being "gobbed at"—spat upon—by fans from the floor. He didn't do the pogo, the hopping dance invented by Punk's tragic cartoon Sid Vicious.

"You know I don't like dancin'—and I don't like to bop. Too much movement's exertion makes me wish that I could drop," he sneered on the early track "Sixteen," from their debut LP, *Another Music in a Different Kitchen*. Released early in '78, it would be one of two Buzzcocks tracks that celebrated being sweet sixteen. The other was "Sixteen Again."

If the Buzzcocks were gleefully camp, Elvis Costello, the angry young man who didn't wear the leather motorcycle jacket, did not seem to trust glee at all. "The main thing that came across when I first saw Elvis Costello," says They Might Be Giants cofounder and future Twee culture hero John Flansburgh, who traveled overseas from his native New England as a teenager and caught a very early Elvis Costello show at the Nashville Rooms, "were not his Buddy Holly glasses but the fierceness of the vitriol. It was the internal violence of his songs." Costello had no Malcolm McLaren or Vivienne Westwood to kit him out, either. He dressed like the computer puncher he was. "And he didn't try to present himself as a particularly attractive person," Flansburgh recalls. "He was very sweaty. The street-level quality of that new era was one of the most winning things about it."

Rock now seemed to be a place where the angry nerd, previously bound to his or her bedroom, could be a star, and this began to manifest itself in post-Punk lyrics as well. Take Dexys Midnight Runners' "There, There, My Dear," from their incredible debut *Searching for the Young Soul Rebels* (if you only know "Come on Eileen," for shame!): "If you're so anti-fashion, why not wear flares instead of dressing down all the same," front man Kevin Rowland asks. Flares, like long hair, were longtime Punk targets, cultural signals that one was living in the past.

Devo, who barely fit in with post-Punk, much less Punk (much less the human race), sang "We're through being cool" on their 1981 single of the same name. The Violent Femmes, discovered by late Pretenders guitarist James Honeyman-Scott while the Pretenders were on tour in Wisconsin, took their very name from slang for the American high school *fag* or *femme,* although this one was not to be pushed around. This one was "angry," as lead singer Gordon Gano threatened in "Add It Up." During the late 1970s and early '80s, all of these misfits were signed to and had to reckon with Punk labels (in America the Femmes were on Slash, home to X and the Germs, and in the UK they were on Rough Trade). They filled their sets with not only acoustic but furious teenage blues. "The songs were instantly appealing and so was the sound," says Ritchie. "Still, many people at the time refused to think of us as Punk or any kind of rock music at all, because we were not electric. Of course, they were ignorant slobs who had never heard Gene Vincent or early Elvis Presley. We had a few female supporters amongst the Slash staff who played our demo and the first album tape so much that the head honchos said, 'All right, we'll sign them if you stop playing that shit in the office!' We got no advance. And they always treated us like a band that didn't deserve an advance. And we were always an enigma in England."

And yet, once *The Violent Femmes* was released in the spring of 1983, it seemed to ride a mainline into the lonely, horny, frustrated teenage psyche, the part of the brain that looked out at the world through a boxlike bedroom and said, "Why can't I join in? Why can't people see that I am beautiful and I see beauty?" It was, and remains, rock and roll's *Catcher in the Rye*.

To continue the literary metaphors, with the uncaging of the Punk-fed student bands, geeks with guitars, it was as if Piggy from *The Lord of the Flies* triumphed in the end. XTC's Andy Partridge is even described by Nick Kent in an early feature as "a grown up version of Piggy." But as lumpen and student-ish as all these bands are (with the exception, of course, of the Police's Adonis-like Sting), all these stars are still somehow beautiful. Most likely it comes down to the genuine innocence they wielded so powerfully in their songs. "I don't know how to put it without boasting," Partridge told Morley in a 1980 interview, "but I think I'm quite mature and intelligent. At the same time, I've kept the things I appreciated as a kid in my head. I think a lot of people lose that. And they lose a big part of their personality. I still love toys." To be young in rock and roll, you had to be griping: the archetypal angry young man. Suddenly, one was able to express displeasure, frustration (sexual and otherwise), and disaffection in a more personal and honest way, as if the diary—not agitprop—became the new wellspring overnight.

Chapter 5

I'm a Loner, Dottie, a Rebel

1982–1987

In which the Angry Young Nerds of Hollywood (inspired by those of the New Wave rock and roll) evolve into new leading men and women, and their sensitive, shy, idealistic tendencies become, with the help of rock and roll and a horrible plague, somehow preferable to those of the swaggering jock or the shrugging tramp.

Cinematically, something would began to shift in the 1980s that would result in our modern strain of box-office heroes and heroines. Back then, they were called *quirky* or *offbeat*, and many of them were relegated to the "best friend" role. Today they are simply accepted as cinema stars, and most of them play the lead.

Beginning with the very early days of the AIDS crisis, Hollywood seemed to presciently churn out more and more teen-angst- or teen-confusion-based entertainment, featuring sex-terrified boys (Tom Cruise in *Risky Business*) on the cusp of manhood and confused girls (Jennifer Jason Leigh in *Fast Times at Ridgemont High*) on the cusp of womanhood. These characters became the surrogates for a new generation of teens who were experiencing similar emotions in their real lives.

It's as if the times forced films into frankness. New Wave music, which featured on many of these film soundtracks, was a step ahead (Sparks' "Angst in My Pants," the Gleaming Spires "Are You Ready for the Sex Girls?"), but by mid-decade, the screen stars were all Devo. Nerds were ready for their close-up.

That's not to say that AIDS, thought of as a death sentence at this point, had any bearing on what screenwriters were churning out circa '82, '83 and '84—only that some bad moon was rising; it would be confirmed in 1985 with the death of former conventional heartthrob leading man Rock Hudson and the rise of anxiety-stoking AIDS tests. Slob comedies were on the wane and openhearted sob comedies full of the new Twee princes and princesses were about to become de rigueur.

On MTV, the sexy librarian wasn't sexy until she let her hair down, took off the glasses, and kicked it with ZZ Top or Van Halen. But in film, the librarians were slowly winning out.

Part of the reason 1982's *Fast Times at Ridgemont High* remains, three decades on, the most transformative teen film ever made is that it highlights this shift in sexual power. This is embodied by the dynamic between Robert Romanus's slick, strutting, fast-talking Mike Damone and Brian Backer's molelike Mark Ratner, the hapless, virginal movie-theater usher. "Rat" is the only one who gets the girl in the end, even if they still don't go all the way. Meanwhile Judge Reinhold's Brad, a "single successful guy," loses his job, and, in the film's most famous scene, is sexually humiliated by Phoebe Cates when she walks in on him pleasuring himself. And Damone, as Cates's Linda scrawls on his locker for all to see, is just a "little prick."

Rolling Stone journalist turned filmmaker Cameron Crowe, then not too long out of his teens himself, went undercover at a real Southern California high school to deliver the book *Fast Times at Ridgemont*

High, then later adapted the screenplay for Universal Studios. Bronx-bred director Amy Heckerling turned Crowe's script into a teen comic and a Twee milestone that would inform every other teen film that came later, from *Risky Business* to the John Hughes oeuvre. Jocks were out. Geeks and proto-Twees were in.

"Cameron Crowe's book set the tone," says Eric Stoltz, who appears along with future *Revenge of the Nerds* star Anthony Edwards as one of Jeff Spicoli's shirtless surfer buds, refused service at All American Burger ("No shirt, no shoes . . . no dice"). "It was rooted in the reality of the characters and situations. We were lucky enough to have Cameron on set every day, and he and Amy Heckerling were intent on making something true to life, rather than formulaic."

"It's no huge thing, it's just sex," Linda reassures Stacy as she prepares to lose her virginity, but everyone, even Linda (with her mysterious, off-camera, and possibly imaginary boyfriend), knows this is a lie. Hormones drive the film. Sean Penn's Spicoli has ripped-out *Playboy* centerfolds taped to his bedroom wall; the film's resident Buddha, zinc on his nose, has lust in his heart. Like the work of Seuss and Sendak, *Fast Times* is both sweet and, even with its occasionally broad, sketchy humor, painfully real. "If this film has a theme," the powerful *New Yorker* magazine film critic Pauline Kael wrote, "it's sexual embarrassment."

"I can't help doing what feels right to me [even] if it came out as awkward or sweet," Heckerling says. "It wouldn't occur to me to make those kinds of moments wacky."

Many found the fumbling dangerous. Pre–wide release, *Fast Times* was rewarded for its groundbreaking content with an X rating and had to be recut. "I don't believe it was entirely because of the nudity," Stoltz says. "It was [also] one of the first teen films to deal with abortion."

Fast Times could also be considered the first feminist teen film.

The sex scene between Damone and Stacy originally featured Robert Romanus's full frontal nudity, and not his partner's. Heckerling's options were to take a trip to Washington to fight the rating or cut the scene. She eventually folded. "The Reagan moral majority was in full swing," she says. "That was the beginning of the just-say-no era."

Heckerling's power was limited—for instance, she wanted much more New Wave and less Jackson Browne on the soundtrack—but she was too young to have any fear or timidity when it came to fighting with the studio to keep the film honest. She was also too close to the characters to betray them, not that any of this brave behavior seemed unnatural.

"I was a young person—I was just happy to be making a movie," she says today. "I wasn't somebody that knew all the formulas and the inner thoughts of people running Hollywood—I wasn't that savvy."

As with most future Twee films, from *Heathers* to Heckerling's later foray into the world of unusually sensitive teens, *Clueless*, the adult characters are ridiculous. This is a very common Twee trope. In *Fast Times*, there's Mr. Hand (Ray Walston), who greets people with "Aloha," and is convinced that half his student body is "on dope." There's Mr. Vargas, who digs lustily into cadavers and has just switched to Sanka. There are coaches, absent parents, obnoxious patrons at fast-food joints.

"I wasn't thinking I wasn't going to do a movie that was different than all other youth movies or anything like that," Heckerling says. "I can only do what I come up with or feel." It's really the "youth" that Heckerling mentions that make *Fast Times* different, the literal freshness of Crowe and Heckerling and their game cast of future superstars.

"*Fast Times* tested horribly," Heckerling recalls of the advance previews major studios routinely do before releasing a film. "I showed the movie in Orange County, and it was unanimous. On all the cards, they said we were horrible Hollywood people making teenagers into sluts and druggies. And this is from young people—there were teenagers telling me this!"

Risky Business, which came a year later, in '83, covered similar ground—AIDS-age sexual terror and a good measure of values questioning: "Doesn't anyone want to accomplish anything, or do we just want to make money?" This is the question that still baby-faced Tom Cruise's Joel Goodsen, a suburban Illinois virgin bound for the Ivy League (or so he hopes), asks. "Make a lot of money," comes the answer. Ironically, *Risky Business* is much artier and darker than *Fast Times*, with a moody Tangerine Dream track, a surplus of fantasy sequences, and public sex (on a real train with the sultry Rebecca De Mornay), but it met with none of the grief that Heckerling's film did. It became the surprise box-office smash of that year.

De Mornay's call girl, Lana, can be seen as filling the same role as the Cat in Dr. Seuss's beloved tale. Like the Cat, she creates havoc when the parents are away, jars a man-child out of his torpor, and exits just in time to leave everything safe and sound by the time the adults return.

Risky Business is also noteworthy for introducing an enduring Twee icon: the cool loser. John Belushi was dead by March of '82. Slob comedies were yielding fewer and fewer box office dividends and suddenly you had to actually be Ivy League bound, with your stellar book and record collection packed, in order to fill the sizable antihero void he left behind. Perhaps the greatest of these winning losers was Curtis Armstrong, who created a kind of icon of the form over the course of three seminal '80s films, all of them Twee touchstones. "Sometimes you just gotta say 'What the fuck,'" Armstrong's Miles instructs Cruise's Joel in the first, *Risky Business*. "What the fuck gives you freedom. Freedom brings opportunity. Opportunity makes your future." Here was a situationist credo uttered by a teen (though Curtis Armstrong was pushing thirty when he made the movie)—and not only a "teen," but also one with the same haircut that Bob Dylan wore on the cover of *Blonde on Blonde*. His character gets into Harvard, while Joel's is still sweating Princeton. This archetype of the loser who comes out on top would prove such a revelation to filmmakers, many of whom started out as nerds and geeks themselves, that Armstrong was typecast in the "Miles" role in two subsequent films and is probably singlehandedly responsible for Jack Black's character in *High Fidelity*.

"It started with *Risky Business*," Armstrong says. "Because *Risky Business* was so admired by other filmmakers, I was offered the Booger part in *Revenge of the Nerds*. The character of Booger didn't really exist on the page."

If Mark Ratner's locker-room fight with Damone (defending Stacy Hamilton-Jennifer Jason Leigh's honor, of course) was the first shot in this transition from jock hero to Twee hero, *Revenge of the Nerds* was the riot. On the surface it's a campus comedy, raunchy à la the bygone *Animal House* and the current *Porky's* (one of the few franchises of the neo-slob comedy affairs), but at heart it's a morality play with a cast of fine character actors (John Goodman, James Cromwell, *Fast Times* vet Anthony Edwards, Robert Carradine, and Ted McGinley) addressing major issues of civil rights. The titular nerds are turned away from every frat house on campus and forced to sleep in the gym because of the way they look and their interests (chess, computers, computers, chess). It is no coincidence that the only frat that will have them is Triple Lambda, a largely African-American fraternity "open to people of all races and creeds."

"There's a nerd sign burning on the lawn," Armstrong points out, an echo of KKK burning crosses, "and all this dialogue about how nobody is free until nerds are free. If you go through the movie thinking about it in those terms, it's clear what the writers were talking about—but because it's an exploitative movie and because it's got a lot of broad humor in it, people sometimes miss the subject of the film, which is about bigotry, acceptance, and tolerance." Continuing his proto-Twee rock-god throw-down, Armstrong appears in the final musical sequence in full Vegas Elvis garb with Anthony Edwards and Robert Carradine paying tribute to Devo. "We have news for the beautiful people," Edwards's character, Gilbert, says in his big monologue toward the film's conclusion. "There are a lot more of us than there are of you." In the 1980s, with Indie culture fast on the rise, this appeared to be coming true.

Writer, director, and mix-tape creator John Hughes graduated Glenbrook North High School in suburban Illinois in the tumultuous spring of 1968. In 1984, he was already a Hollywood success, having parlayed a staff position at the then culturally significant publication *National Lampoon* into a pair of produced screenplays, *Class Reunion* and the first *National Lampoon's Vacation* film, based on a short story he'd written for the magazine. Hughes should not have remembered what it was really like for teenagers to walk those tricky halls and hang out in those polarized parking lots two decades away from his high school days, especially during the glossy 1980s, the idealistic flip side to the radical late '60s. But, rightfully so, Hughes suspected that the dynamic was more or less the same now as it had been then.

"John Hughes *was* a young person. I found him to be the youngest, most awkward guy on the set, and I always felt he was writing different versions of himself," Eric Stoltz, the star of Hughes's *Some Kind of Wonderful*, recalls.

Hughes's genius was not necessarily the films themselves; the writing in *Sixteen Candles* can be hacky, and at times politically incorrect (Long Duk Dong, anyone?). The beauty of his work was its long overdue exploration of just "why" the binary nature of high school existed, why cool vs. uncool was so immovable. Cameron Crowe presented the "how" of things by laying out his undercover data for a sense of verisimilitude. Hughes suggested a powerfully attractive alternative and began to ask "why," without an eye toward or a care for the "real" teenager of the 1980s, or even his own 1960s.

Adults, again, are idiots in Hughes's movies, with toilet paper hanging out of the back of their pants. They see every kid as binary, good or bad, and the good kids need to be rewarded and the bad kids need to be punished—until, that is, one Saturday in late March when a weird mix of both wind up in detention. Hughes's biggest contribution to pop may be the notion that the cool kids are just as fragile and fucked up (and terrified) as the geeks.

"You see us as a brain, an athlete, a basket case, a princess, and a criminal—that's the way we saw each other at seven this morning. We were brainwashed," Anthony Michael Hall says in voice-over at the film's feel-good conclusion. Judd Nelson's Bender is the Socratic Punk instigator who brings everything to an explosive boil, but once it bubbles over, there's a huge sigh, among both the cast and the audience. Suddenly everything seems different. Perhaps Monday they will all go back to their own cultural corners, but in real life, that didn't seem to happen. In the wake of the new 1980s Hollywood, teens seemed to want truth, not just cheap release; they needed answers.

"Are we gonna be like our parents?" Ally Sheedy's misfit asks in *The Breakfast Club*.

"Not me, never," Emilio Estevez's star wrestler swears.

"It's unavoidable. It just happens. When you grow up, your heart dies," Sheedy responds. Teenage Twees of the 1980s, now in middle age like the Brat Pack actors themselves, seemingly never forgot those words.

The summer of '85, in addition to hosting the *Breakfast Club* revolution, was also the summer of the 1980s' greatest man-child, the eternally, sometimes uncomfortably youthful Pee-wee Herman. Like all great Twee figures, Pee-wee divided the room. Some thought he was simply perfect with his retro kitsch irony and anarchy. Others found it rather creepy that a man in his thirties would smear his face with rouge and lipstick, don a too-short suit and large shoes, and cavort like a young boy in a universe of his own making that *Rolling Stone* would later describe as "the collision of the Cabinet of Dr. Caligari with a raspberry-and-lime Jell-O mold constructed by Disney technicians recovering from the Taiwan flu." Pee-wee was like a Seuss character made flesh, all hyperkinetic energy and mischief but with a gentle soul.

Paul Reubens had been around for years by the time *The Pee-wee Herman Show* premiered at the Groundlings Theater in 1981 and moved to the Roxy nightclub a year later. Reubens attended Cal Arts and studied improv with the famed Groundlings improv group, but it was clear his career was moving fast. Simply put, there was nothing else like him onstage or in the small parts he landed onscreen. He stole the spotlight, for example, from Cheech and Chong in a bizarre Chinese-restaurant scene in *Cheech and Chong's Nice Dreams*. Reubens played Howie the Hamburger Man, a coked-up New Waver who utters the immortal lines, "You wanna know about the future of rock and roll? Bruce Springsteen's fuckin' it all up. New Wave. *Neeeeeeew Wave!*" If you've never seen this, all I can say is that this scene alone is better than most comedies, heck, most big-budget theater today. Howie should have been given his own feature-length film immediately, but it would be Pee-wee who would unite actual children and adults still in touch with their childhood. Pee-wee would mainstream Twee as much as any figure who came before or since.

Reubens's stage act was honed at the Groundlings theater at a time when performance art, irony, and a love of retro kitsch were in vogue in Hollywood: rockabilly was L.A.'s big post-Punk movement, for example. Punk designer Gary Panter (who did logos for local acts like the Screamers and drew the *Jimbo* comic strip) designed the stage set. *The Pee-wee Herman Show* was a critical and commercial hit locally, and was later filmed as a nationally televised HBO comedy special. A wry, knowing, and affectionate take on Disney's *Mickey Mouse Club*, *Howdy Doody*, and pre-Beatles '60s pop culture tropes, it was live-action contained chaos. Pee-wee was prankish: shoe mirrors for looking up ladies' dresses are employed, as is fake poo and a "Naked Gumby." He was also wistful; his greatest dream was to be able to fly like Pterri the Pterodactyl, one of his myriad misfit visitors. Others include Hammy, who is in love with eating ham; Captain Carl (played by Hartman, a cowriter), who's been too long at sea; and a pair of hippies who stage a musical salute to Sly and the Family Stone complete with pink flamingo-shaped guitar. Punkish as Pee-wee was, the '60s were not off-limits but rather once again holy. Pee-wee screened vintage cartoons and public service reels ("Only Mr. Bungle would run in the lunchroom") to the delight of a knowing, increasingly postmodernist crowd who gobbled up the naughty humor and winking kitsch love like it was button candy. Reubens could do prop comedy, work in an ensemble, and hold the stage solo (or with Dr. Mongo, his ventriloquist dummy). He was a marvel or a psycho, depending on whom you asked. A veteran of Chuck Barris's unstable *The Gong Show,* he became a favored guest of the legendary early days of *Late Night with David Letterman* as well.

The buzz led to Reubens's feature-film debut based around the character. Eccentric visual artist and animator-turned-director Tim Burton signed on to direct. Danny Elfman would provide the madcap score, which became essential to the film's opening sequence, in which Pee-wee wakes up in his kitsch-strewn house and makes breakfast for himself and his Chihuahua, Speck, via an ingenious Rube Goldberg contraption. Reubens plays Pee-wee as both dirty-minded and chaste. He knows about sex, but he doesn't seem to be interested in it. His true love is his prized bright red bike, a vintage beauty in true Twee fashion.

When Dottie, the pretty blond employee at the local bike shop, asks him if he wants to go out, he hilariously warns her: "You don't wanna get mixed up with a guy like me. I'm a loner, Dottie. A rebel." But as he leaves the bike shop, he's giggling, amazed that he's managed to pull off a line like that at all. Here Reubens is no different from Dustin Hoffman when he dons dark glasses to take Elaine out on a date in *The Graduate,* or Mark Ratner playing Led Zeppelin in his car as he drives Stacy out for a large German meal in *Fast Times at Ridgemont High:* the geeks, Punks, freaks, and, in Pee-wee's case, ninety-eight-pound weaklings simply cannot believe that they are inheriting the earth. With Pee-wee, Reubens, like Walt Disney before him, built a world of his own, designed and suited to his Twee vision of retro safety and permachildhood, and almost by force of charisma and will alone, it became not only palatable but vital and attractive to other lonely, frightened souls. Dottie is not sexually drawn to Pee-wee so much as she's enchanted by the man, or man-child, who goes it alone, against the flow. Pee-wee, like James Dean, actually *is* a loner and a rebel. There's little irony in the actuality of the observation, even if the delivery is deadpan.

The Reubens saga, of course, would take a few unhappy turns. The success of *Pee-wee's Big Adventure* paid off for both him and Burton, whose next film was the hit *Beetlejuice*. Reubens then brought Pee-wee and his gang (a beatnik puppet band, a genie, a talking globe and chair, a family of dinosaurs that lived in a mouse hole) to Saturday-morning television in 1986, and after a slow start (as Pee-wee had to wait for people to get it) *Pee-wee's Playhouse* became a smash, landing him on the cover of *Rolling Stone* and winning him an Emmy. But the big-screen sequel *Big Top Pee-wee*, a circus-themed meander, flopped, and we all know what happened next. Reubens became another one of those soul-sinking mug shots that remind us that nothing ever stays completely pure.

It took years for Reubens to revitalize his image and launch a comeback, first as a character actor and, in recent years, as Pee-wee himself. Still svelte and manic, the middle-aged Pee-wee is kind of like the Peter Pan that Michael Jackson aspired to be, a real-life Twee hero for the hybrid generation, singlehandedly responsible for phenomena like *Yo Gabba Gabba!*, the kiddie hit of the '00s. Pee-wee can now be taken seriously by critics. Reubens as Pee-wee had a hit Broadway show in 2012, and a new Pee-wee movie is currently in development with the new king of arrested adolescence, Judd Apatow. One can almost hear Pee-wee's vengeful cackle off in the distance now: "I know you are, but what am I? Infinity!" Only vengeance was never Pee-wee's thing. He was crucially a kind character. He didn't condescend. The sweetness, the very Twee-ness was what both put him over the top and took him down. Always destined to be a kind of cult, he flirted with superstardom during a very strange time in popular culture and it nearly destroyed him. Today, the world seems ready for him again. He fits with the unfolding Twee age like a clip-on red bow tie on a pin-down white collar.

Chapter 6

Blue Boys

*Glasgow becomes the epicenter for the first consolidated Twee cul-
ture boom that the media (read: London) acknowledges, and, to its
own horror, the Glasgow School paves the way for acts that will
rule the second half of the decade.*

*I*t is clear how the shy boys and anti–femme fatales took over
Hollywood, but let us travel backward a bit, as we are about
to chart the course of how the Twee trend in music became
massive and arena filling. It begins not in Los Angeles, New York,
or, more crucially, London, but rather in the port city of Glasgow,
Scotland. Glasgow was not the easiest place to grow up. Here middle-
class kids and arts-college students often found themselves navigating
the same urban basins as drunk, working-class football fans carrying
knives. Sometimes just turning the wrong corner at the wrong time
(read: after a football match) could get you "glassed" (slashed in the
face with a broken pint glass). "It was a city that had an edge to it—
certainly—and you could provoke a reaction by the way you behaved,"

says Stephen McRobbie, also known as Stephen Pastel, leader of the beloved Glasgow band the Pastels.

In the late 1970s, with the United Kingdom still emerging from economic decline, a clear uneasiness seemed to run through this otherwise beautiful city, with its centuries-old, spire-topped buildings; slate-blue lakes; and verdant highlands. Glasgow was old country. Few in London, especially Punks still fighting to stay relevant, paid it any mind. Only Rod Stewart sang mistily of Scotland. The Bay City Rollers, Gerry "Baker Street" Rafferty, and the oft-maligned Ian Anderson of Jethro Tull were Glasgow's favorite rock and roll sons. Nobody would have expected that here, Punk's DIY spirit would be kept alive well into the 1980s. But it was far easier for a teen from Glasgow, Liverpool, Leeds, or Dublin, with only a tenuous connection to London via *N.M.E.*, *Melody Maker, Sounds,* and the *Mirror,* to drop Punk and move on. Punk wasn't so pervasive in these far-flung towns, away from the epicenter. Teenagers are like that. It's not infidelity: it's part and parcel of their bone deep, electrified search to belong.

"Nothing from that period can be separated completely from Punk," says singer-songwriter Lloyd Cole, who moved to Glasgow to study and by the early '80s led one of the city's breakout bands, the Commotions. "We'd long stopped dressing that way. But even when it became a laughingstock, we hadn't forgotten what great Punk records there were. 'Complete Control' by the Clash and the Sex Pistols singles. They were all fantastic pop songs."

"The better things of the Indie era are always going to be seen and heard through a Punk and post-Punk filter," music critic Paul Morley agrees. Megabands such as U2, the Police, R.E.M., the

Smiths, Depeche Mode, and the Cure have very close Punk proximity, no matter how massive their sound, stagecraft, and success became.

Why Scotland is important in the inevitable popularization of Twee is the groove. Glasgow was funky. Set against the stark realities of the Thatcher era's austerity and perceived lack of compassion for the poor, it was a task of the musicians of the time to preserve a sense of humor and hedonism. Even more important was creating a sense of optimism and idealism—which is the backbone of any great pop song. Does it make you dance? Does it pick you up when you are low? Does it even make you glad to be sad? Such were the new rules of thumb for young musicians as Punk fragmented into a half dozen subgenres at the end of the '70s, and there seemed to be a surplus of the subgenres in Glasgow. Elsewhere in the British Isles, Goth, industrial, neo-psychedelic, and new Mod all proved worthy new genres, but it was the music of Glasgow and later Edinburgh that made you want to dance the pain away. This was disco . . . through the Punk filter.

The Punk era had filmmakers like Derek Jarman, Penelope Spheeris, Don Letts, and Lech Kowalski; the "Glasgow School" also had its cinematic compatriots. Their films didn't reflect the nihilism of old, but rather a die-hard cheer and romance in the face of bleakness. Any scene requires the documentarian, so to speak. The New York No Wave movement, for example, had a young Jim Jarmusch. Glasgow had William Forsyth. Like many in the city during those early Thatcher years, the aspiring film director was broke but unbowed, possessed to make a film and fueled by natural pluck and ingenuity. Already in his mid-thirties, Forsyth was old enough to have devoured the first run of Nouvelle Vague films in the '60s. He'd idolized Truffaut and Godard and also amassed a wide and diverse personal library of other films he loved. Tall, shy, bearded but boyish, he was a quick study and managed to talk himself into a job at the commercial Thames and Clyde film-production company, where he learned basic filmmaking skills when not lugging heavy equipment. Inspired by the resolve and humor he saw every day in Glasgow despite the poverty and violence, Forsyth penned his first script, a black-comedy heist entitled *That Sinking Feeling*.

Nearly two decades before Danny Boyle's *Trainspotting*, Forsyth's film concerns a gang of similarly broke but resilient young Scotsmen who spend their days musing about the best ways to commit suicide (never acting, of course, just musing). With nothing to lose, the gang, led by the gawky, toothy Robert Buchanan, conspires to rob a warehouse full of porcelain sinks (hence the almost too-cheeky title).

Buchanan and much of the cast worked for nearly nothing. The cast was drafted by the desperate director out of the local Glasgow Youth Theatre, a part of the city's effort to keep young Scots out of trouble. Under Thatcher, such programs were eventually slashed.

"It was an Arts Council–funded program for teenagers," says John Gordon Sinclair, who briefly appears in *That Sinking Feeling* but would be the star of Forsyth's most iconic movie, *Gregory's Girl*. "It was my after-school and weekends thing. We would meet and do acting classes. We'd also rehearse scenes from plays. Then go on tour and do shows around Scotland. Church halls. Other community centers."

Early in preproduction for *That Sinking Feeling*, Forsyth realized that he had no money for casting. "Bill wanted to make a movie but couldn't get the finance for it," Sinclair says. "But he knew we were a bunch of kids interested in acting. I think he was also a bit scared of working with real actors." Forsyth found himself strengthened and inspired by the kids' enthusiasm.

That Sinking Feeling, released in 1979, was a critical hit, but only in the UK. Still, it provided Forsyth with the credentials he needed to secure funding for the production of his next script, this time set in the middle-class suburbs of Glasgow.

Plot-wise, *Gregory's Girl* is a picnic compared to *That Sinking Feeling*'s twenty-minute lunch break. Sinclair's young hero Gregory Underwood, pale, skinny, and sensitive, must decide how to respond to the realization that he's finally fallen in love with a new arrival, football star Dorothy, played by Dee Hepburn.

Where the film shines is not in its structure or its acting, but in how it shattered a decades-old formula for films about young people. Blond and beautiful Dorothy immediately proves to be the "jock" in the mix. The male lead is, in contrast, sensitive and insecure, and vocally so. "I bruise like a peach!" he frets loudly at one point. And yet Forsyth doesn't feminize Gregory or make Dorothy mannish. She is still the object of desire. Only their roles in moving the story forward are completely reversed. "It's a tricky time for me," Gregory worries. "I'm doing a lot of growing." And so is teen cinema.

Forsyth doesn't pretend that certain realities in coming-of-age tales can be ignored. The teens in *Gregory's Girl* are just as horny and hormonal as the teens that ran wild in *Fast Times*. Virginity and sweetness are things to be quickly unloaded, but in the right way. These thoughtful characters don't deny their hormones. They are simply smarter—and more honest and deliberate—in verbalizing what they are going through, similar to the kids in all of John Hughes's films. And yet for all the sophistication, they still sound like kids.

"Bill certainly had the idea in his head—didn't want it to just be a film, he wanted it to say something," Sinclair says. "But for a lot of people it was also the first time they saw their lives reflected in a movie. It kind of defined that period between adulthood and being a kid, and the madness that takes hold. I think it captures that very well. It's something that everyone goes through, something that everyone experiences."

In the U.S., during an age when Indie film was not routinely a box-office concern, *Gregory's Girl* sold tickets and drew critical raves for offering its open-minded, unabashedly affectionate take on classic teenage dilemmas and desires. Today, thanks in part to its impossibly sweet sequence near the end (in which Clare Grogan and Sinclair lie in the grass on their backs at sunset and "dance," pinned by gravity and cheerfully oblivious to the bicyclists and passersby—"Don't stop dancing, you'll fall off," he warns her), its place in both the Twee canon and the hearts of fans of smart British cinema remains. Sinclair and Forsyth even revisited the character for a sequel, *Gregory's Two Girls*, which did little to tarnish the original's legacy but fared not nearly as well upon release two decades later. Frankly, it was jarring to see the perfectly Twee Gregory as a middle-aged man.

Gregory's Girl intersected directly with the city's new independent pop scene, with which it shared its spirit, in the form of the pixie-ish Clare Grogan. Grogan was then the eighteen-year-old leader of a local band called Altered Images, who played sprightly New Wave with smart lyrics about Warholian popscapes. Driven along by Grogan's schoolgirl voice, the group's danceable songs shimmered like the best British post-Punk, a quality that would later put a pair of MTV perennials on the board: "I Could Be Happy" and "Happy Birthday."

Their exuberance was half ironic and half sincere to a fault. They wrote songs like "Dead Pop Stars," but often they sounded like a three-day children's birthday party.

Grogan was a Catholic-school student and a Punk-obsessive when she was cast in *Gregory's Girl*. When she wasn't rehearsing with the band and honing what would become a signature sound, she was waitressing at a local eatery called the Spaghetti Factory. It was there that Forsyth discovered her, Lana Turner style, and cast her as Susan, Gregory's true soul mate.

Of the close-knit *Gregory's Girl* cast, Grogan in her black turtle-necks, chunky jewelry, and granny dresses with Doc Martens was the most stylish. She knew all about the look of Nouvelle Vague stars like Anna Karina and Jean Seberg. She was also an avid record collector. "I became a bit of a geek about pop music," she says.

A music scene was forming around Nico's, a bar near the Glasgow School of Art. "It was very art-school driven. That's how it was perceived from where I was," says Garbage singer Shirley Manson, then a teenage Adam Ant fan in Edinburgh. "That kind of elitism felt very intimidating. They were very stylish. They all looked like sixties movie stars from Paris."

"There was a feeling in this bar that if you weren't trying to be a writer or a pop star or a painter or a sculptor, there was no way you were going to get a girlfriend," says Lloyd Cole. "If you wanted to be a part of the scene, you couldn't just be a hanger-on. You had to be doing something."

Before any London-based music journalist labeled them the next big thing, a group of hugely talented "pop geeks," first called the Nu-Sonics and then Orange Juice, were about to put the Glasgow scene on the pop-cultural map. "Growing up in Glasgow, we didn't have a huge pool of homegrown pop stars to admire and emulate, so for me I was interested to find out that they existed," Clare Grogan says of Orange Juice. Ironically, it was "Don't You (Forget About Me)," the theme to John Hughes's *The Breakfast Club* in 1985, that really delivered attention on Scotland's music in the '80s. Simple Minds had a number-one hit and became the biggest-ever Scottish pop act.

Orange Juice was fated to always be cooler and smaller than Simple Minds. The quartet's original lineup—drummer Steven Daly, guitarist James Kirk, bassist David McClymont, and singer-songwriter-guitarist Edwyn Collins—had all been in love with Punk in earlier years.

"We saw every Punk show," says Daly, now a writer with *Vanity Fair* and the coauthor of *The Rock Snob's Dictionary*. "It was year zero—we didn't believe in people who took drugs or had a thing about guitars."

Edwyn Collins owned a copy of *The Catcher in the Rye* and loaned it out to those who met with his favor. "I hadn't read it," Daly says. "It wasn't as much a part of the culture in Britain then as it was in America. [But] Edwyn was very Yank-o-centric, as was I."

Ian Curtis, the enigmatic lead singer of Joy Division, had been anointed as the new hero of post-Punk Britain. When he died, he left a void. The field was wide open for a figure as charismatic and as handsome as Collins to attract attention. He looked like a boyish Bowie with a great swoop of draping hair. He wrote great songs and dressed uniquely in flannel shirts, New Wave sport coats, and tapered trousers, like a cross between Joy Division, the Byrds, and Creedence Clearwater Revival.

The first Orange Juice singles, "Falling and Laughing" and "Blue

Boy," were driven by Chic-style grooves played without Chic-level skill. The aesthetic of their records was similarly sharp but shambolic, put out by a tiny label known as Postcard Records. Alan Horne ran the outfit out of his bedroom turned office. The Postcard logo featured a quizzical-looking cat holding a pair of drum mallets above the label name and the careful and proud: "Of Scotland."

"Postcard was an anomaly," the Pastels' McRobbie says. "They were actually quite snobbish and elitist, but they did it with a sense of humor. Their label had such a strong identity, they seemed more comfortable with a slightly Twee Scottishness—which was very much a middle finger up to London."

Orange Juice's "Blue Boy" appeared on *N.M.E.*'s first cassette giveaway, now known as *C81*, along with Postcard label mate Aztec Camera's "We Could Send Letters," a breezy pop song about pen-palling. The influential weekly music paper had finally twigged to the Glasgow scene after investing whole hog in Manchester, only to be heartbroken by the death of Ian Curtis. In the wake of *C81,* the Glasgow school was courted by the majors, but only Altered Images ended up signing, recording their debut, *Pinky Blue*, for Epic. Orange Juice held out, intent on preserving a tether to their faux naïveté, to kick against the corporate pricks and keep the band's upstart soul. "It was contrived amateurism," Collins would later tell a journalist.

Horne held his ground and London indeed had come to him, but at what cost? And how long could Postcard resist the fruits of its own wildly exciting and sharp pop vision? *Ambition* remained a dirty word. Simple Minds, some believed, was an aptly named act, but the "Sound of Young Scotland" and its key faces would soon be on television with Altered Images, joining Duran Duran, Bow Wow Wow, and Adam

Ant as some of the first New Wave video stars on America's newly launched MTV.

With the heightened scrutiny of media adoration, however, came an almost inevitable backlash. It proved a jarring blow to the more isolated, openhearted Scottish stars. When Clare Grogan performed, she did so in the persona of a wildly precocious girly girl, and *N.M.E.* dubbed her Tallulah Gosh in a notorious profile (the name comes from Jodie Foster's character in the aforementioned *Bugsy Malone*). In America, where the band's first single from *Pinky Blue* was taking off, *Creem* magazine described her voice as "itsy little boop de boop."

"I was playing a role a wee bit. I used to literally walk around with a book of *Lolita* with me," Grogan now says. With press and pressure, it was suddenly possible to be too smart, too much a sum of all the right influences, and just too sweet. "I did become aware of the criticism and was slightly horrified and embarrassed and hurt," says Grogan. Soon the overhead would crush the two biggest Postcard bands. Orange Juice signed to Polydor, and Aztec Camera to Seymour Stein's Sire Records in America, with their single "Oblivious" joining Altered Images' "I Could Be Happy" on MTV. Aztec Camera's full-length debut, *High Land, Hard Rain,* is the kind of record that can still make a pop geek rave with glassy-eyed nostalgia, but at the time it seemed somehow predoomed, the subtleties of the band's sound destined to be drowned out by the pounding drum machines and blinding flash pots all around them.

Perversely, Aztec Camera's biggest American hit would be a cover of Van Halen's 1984 smash "Jump." Orange Juice's lone UK Top 40 hit was the suave anthem "Rip It Up and Start Again," which took them to *Top of the Pops,* but just the once.

"They definitely lost a bit of momentum," McRobbie says. Their obstinacy ran counter to the rigidity and impersonal touch of the big British record industry of the era. Orange Juice could have only ever seen them as square.

"Still, when they went on *Top of the Pops,* that was a huge deal," recalls Shirley Manson. "It was heroic. Because the Scottish boys had made no concessions."

Postcard Records's roster was cherry picked by the more powerful majors and, while it may have been torn asunder by its own rigidity and closeted ambition, the label continued to function, and has been afforded an immaculate myth by the passing years as well. Today, after the rise and fall of Nirvana and the ultimate collapse of the music industry, its bedroom-run operation seems both prescient and romantic. While they never enjoyed long careers or sold millions of records, Orange Juice, Aztec Camera, and other Postcard bands carry a certain cachet.

"Nobody could have imagined at that point just the kind of influence Postcard would have," says Clare Grogan, speaking of current artists like Franz Ferdinand, James Murphy of LCD Soundsystem, the Rapture, and even late-era Arcade Fire, who've adopted the dance-floor-ready post-Punk of the early-'80s Scottish scene. "I look back and I love just about every act they signed."

Chapter 7

Meet the Tweetles

1983–1988

In which the Smiths, R.E.M., and a surprise third contender become genuine rock and roll attractions and cultural powerhouses by retrofitting the bedroom aesthetic for a mass audience and wrestle with established MTV stars as well as their own sense of purity and integrity as Twee bands in the throes of unprecedented, fatal fame.

I think the Smiths were shit," says Orange Juice's Steven Daly, expressing what can safely be called, in 2014, a minority opinion. "They were prosaic and they were awful, but what they did was put certain things together in a package that appealed to what I called 'thick plus.'" In other words, the band took the coy and fey archness of the Postcard bands and other extra-London scene habitués and made it palatable not only for London but for arenas all over the world. "Morrissey dressed all of these quite elevated ideas up for the thick-plus crowd—and so they became very big." The Smiths and their American contemporaries R.E.M. indeed married the Twee bedroom aesthetic to sporty, loud, and increasingly stonking guitars and a tight, danceable, ultra-capable rhythm section. Their choruses grew anthemic and their box office expanded in kind. Both bands offered an alternative to 1980s fashion, politics, social interaction, and general style as well as a list of personal heroes to share and various reading and screening assignments. They were beyond bands—they were lifestyles for the offering, almost clubs or cults to join.

"Geoff Travis played us the first Smiths album before it was released," recalls Brian Ritchie of the Violent Femmes, "when we were there on our first tour and said he thought they were doing the same thing as us. [But] there are few wordsmiths of Morrissey's caliber, and the music Johnny Marr put behind it was very spiritual."

Never before had something that appeared so marginal on the surface, self-marginalizing even, seemed so ready to market; so appealing to the masses. "The Smiths and R.E.M. had come to light at roughly the same time," Morrissey writes in his 2013 memoir, *Autobiography,* "and as a Sire Records executive had remarked, 'It's just a question of which of the two will explode in America first.'" R.E.M. won that battle, but at what cost?

As crazy as it seems to those of a certain age, there may be a time in the near future when teenagers won't know who R.E.M. was. It's like that old joke where the kid asks his father if Paul McCartney was in a band before Wings. Even though they sold seventy million records, played stadiums, were inducted into the Rock and Roll Hall of Fame in 2007—their first eligible year—and were generally regarded in their time as the best band in America, R.E.M. no longer automatically speaks to and for every outsider teen. That isn't to say the quartet will soon be forgotten by anybody who ever owned a copy of *Murmur,*

Reckoning, or even *Green*. It's merely to suggest that sometimes a band can help define the very culture that leaves it behind.

The Smiths, however, are as alive in the hearts and on the digital devices of even more sad, smart, self-styled misfits than they were in 1987, the last time all four founding members spent any time together in a room that wasn't a courtroom. (Drummer Mike Joyce sued Morrissey and Marr for back royalties in 1996.)

"R.E.M. are more has-beeny," Paul Morley says of the great but now very late (as opposed to immortal) R.E.M. "They seem more fixed in time." R.E.M. may be the better band, but for the Twee race of faux underdogs now, the culture of the Smiths is a better fit. In life, the Smiths grew from a four-piece to a loud, stonking five-piece, topped the British charts, and crashed the American Top 40. They got big enough to fill amphitheaters in the States and were heading toward the same level of fame as their peers who feel so irrelevant today. Then they split. The Smiths, as a group, are dead, and in death they are James Dean perfect, never too far from the bedroom where they began. They are a band with a creation myth and a death cult. Combine that with a few dozen absolutely perfect songs that, as Morrissey astutely if not humbly points out, were only growing in stature at the time. Even today, wealthy, world traveled, and well into his fifties, he is the eternal flame for every lonely teen. One cannot say that about either Elvis (Presley or Costello) or even the Smiths-worshipping Emo stars of the last decade like Chris Carrabba of Dashboard Confessional. You don't outgrow the Smiths any more than you outgrow your vital organs. They are unrenounceable, and as long as they never reunite (to date they are one of the few bands to decline the fortunes of festival-headlining slots and the nostalgia industry), they remain saintly and pure, innocent, uncorrupted: qualities the Twee values over all.

Their invention seems miraculous given the Dickensian world that Morrissey describes in his memoir: the cheerlessness and isolation of Manchester. That four predominantly Irish Catholic Northern England youths with almost nothing in common would find one another amid this urban industrial wasteland where "birds refuse to sing" is fable making. If Twee has a religion, it is Smiths worship. They are the last quarter century's only truly holy concern when it comes to rock and roll.

"I had a very small bedroom," Morrissey has said, "and I remember going through periods when I was eighteen and nineteen where I literally would not leave it for three to four weeks. I would be in there day after day, the sun would be blazingly hot and I'd have the curtains drawn. I'd be sitting there in near darkness alone with the typewriter and surrounded by masses of paper. The walls were totally bespattered with James Dean, almost to the point of claustrophobia, and I remember little bits of paper pinned everywhere with profound comments," adding, "everything I am was conceived in this room."

When the teenage Morrissey, living with his mother and working clerical jobs in the Salford section of Manchester to pay for his record collection, engaged with the outside world, he did so via letters, many written to the famous Nick Kent at *N.M.E.*, one of the few similarly music-obsessed pen pals that he could find. "Certainly when I was younger than I am now it was very unusual to come across any other living human who actually heard the records that you heard and it was very unusual to discuss lyrics with somebody," he has said. Sometimes he would leave his house and walk the streets alone, from the outside a kind of dour, killjoy presence, but in actuality a young man hiding a secret capacity to be jubilant and to spread joy. "My parents got divorced when I was seventeen though they were working towards it for many years," he has said. "Realizing that your parents aren't compatible, I think gives you a premature sense of wisdom that life isn't easy and it isn't simple to be happy—happiness is something you're very lucky to find."

In his hometown, Morrissey was the subject of mockery within the cool Indie scene, dominated by bands like Joy Division and the Fall. Most treated him like a village idiot. His closest friend who wasn't a cat (named Tibby) was the artist and musician Linder Sterling, who fronted the post-Punk band Ludus and designed the iconic sleeve for the Buzzcocks single "Orgasm Addict." They'd hang out in graveyards.

The younger Johnny Marr, by contrast, hung out in a cool clothing store called X. He was a flashy, record-collecting teenager who could kick with the cool crowd and didn't need the protection of a little room. But he needed words.

Marr, then only eighteen, had met Morrissey (four years older) once briefly at a Patti Smith show in Manchester years earlier. He materialized with an unannounced knock on a May afternoon in 1982 at the doorstep of Morrissey's home on 384 Stretford Street. Smiths obsessives even know the time of day—around one in the afternoon.

Marr had recently viewed a documentary about the great 1950s songwriting team Jerry Leiber and Mike Stoller ("Poison Ivy," "Hound Dog," "Stand by Me," "Is That All There Is?") in which Leiber relates a story about a similarly unannounced introduction to his partner. Marr and Morrissey had each already done time in two failed bands,

Marr in White Dice and Freak Party (where he'd played with future Smiths bassist Andy Rourke) and Morrissey in Ed Banger and the Nosebleeds and Slaughter and the Dogs. A mutual friend, Billy Duffy (who went on to cofound the Cult), had praised the quality of Morrissey's writing to Marr, and this stuck in the younger man's mind. He was well on his way to becoming a shockingly original guitarist, but he didn't write many lyrics. And so he asked another mutual acquaintance, Steven Pomfret, to bring him to meet Morrissey. He had a precedent and an outsize confidence. He was cool as an Otter Pop. Morrissey—not so much. There was no guarantee they would even get along, much less spark creatively in what has since been described as a more or less immediate way. "Nothing ever failed, nothing ever stumbled," Morrissey writes.

There are plenty of worthy books that chronicle what happened next: the rise, the fall, the analysis of every single and B-side and album track. It's an industry now, Smiths deconstruction. I only strain to examine why the band finds such favor among the young each year, and how they became, essentially, the Twee Beatles. Their very Twee intolerance of bullying is surely important to their stature. Within hours of being born, the Smiths were already attacking bullies head-on and giving voice to the world's assailed innocents, something Morrissey's lyrics would continue to do for the remainder of his career. "Fame is a kind of revenge," he had said, and in part it's retribution meted out on those in society who prey upon the weak.

Through his words and Marr's music, Morrissey is delivered from countless childhood nightmares, and bullies everywhere are put on notice. The songs connected with the rich and the poor and the not very rich and the very poor. "I sing out to the youth of the slums,"

Morrissey writes. There are bands that are merely young men and women who play instruments and sing together, and they are fine and worthy. And then there are bands who become heroes, defenders, catchers in the rye.

"People get picked on because there's a perceived otherness and a perceived weakness," says *The Perks of Being a Wallflower* author and director Stephen Chbosky (both the book and movie versions feature the Smiths song "Asleep"). "I think it's a chicken-or-the-egg thing. If you loved John Waters's *Pink Flamingos*, the Smiths' *Louder Than Bombs*, and going to *The Rocky Horror Picture Show* on a Saturday night, you're not automatically picked on as a cause and effect. But if you're the kid who gets picked on, you will find yourself loving *Pink Flamingos*, *Louder Than Bombs*, and going to *Rocky Horror* on a Saturday night. And it's hugely empowering. You feel like you aren't alone anymore."

The Smiths' "This Charming Man" single, issued by Rough Trade, crashed the Top 30 and led to a now legendary appearance on *Top of the Pops* in which Morrissey, open-chested like Robert Plant but ringed with matronly beads, twirls a bouquet of flowers the way Roger Daltrey of the Who used to twirl his microphone cord. In an instant, the Smiths combated the notion of front-man masculinity. "When I saw the Smiths on *Top of the Pops*, I thought, There's a rock star being not very Punk at all," says Shirley Manson. "He's being very girlie, and that seemed exciting."

You didn't even have to be human to have an ally in the Smiths. They topped the British charts with an album called *Meat Is Murder*, and, once given the floor, Morrissey started assailing all those who fed on flesh and never stopped. Even today when he performs the songs, he shows footage of chickens being debeaked and cattle being pummeled by unscrupulous and sadistic workers. The Smiths, like the Clash before them, seemed to be fueled by injustice.

"There were lots and lots of people ready to identify with what I was feeling," Morrissey said. "Hatred. Hating everything, but not being offensively hateful. It was like hate from quite gentle people."

By the time one of their final singles was released, "Stop Me if You Think You've Heard This One Before," complete with a video that featured a few dozen young Brits dressed in his classic cardigan sweater, Morrissey was already an icon. Early on, the Smiths offered a sense of being a part of something massive while still feeling like a minority. But soon, they too began to skirt the clichés of rock and roll. Drugs? Check. (Bassist Andy Rourke briefly struggled with heroin addiction.) Creative differences? Check. (Marr was determined to play with other bands, to Morrissey's chagrin.) Management and financial issues? Check. Ego? Check. Check. Check.

Morrissey sold papers. Once journalists began asking him questions, he had a satchel of quips at the ready; his way with the "pull quote" helped to solidify his rock and roll character, an outsize version of his actual pained, shy, sexually ambiguous self.

"Who last saw you in your natural state?" a reporter from the fashion monthly *The Face* asked in the summer of '84. "Almost certainly the doctor who brought me into this cruel world," Morrissey replied. Nobody before or since has been as clever, self-deprecating, playful, and manipulative with a rock journo. "I can get very erotic about blotting paper," he confessed to another.

Unlike R.E.M.'s albums following the departure of linchpin drummer Bill Berry, nothing that Morrissey (or Marr) has done as a solo artist has tarnished his legacy or the Smiths as gospel. Musically, he has released fine solo material that never really acknowledged a quarter century's worth of sonic trend. You've never caught him out on the arm of a supermodel, male or female. He's never been snapped by a TMZ reporter at the drive-through of an In-N-Out Burger. And one could imagine him fitting nicely back into the "box bedroom" he describes in his book, whereas it's hard to imagine Michael Stipe, after the late 1980s, spending much time alone at all. He was producing movies, hanging around with models, wearing message tees, signing what was then the biggest recording contract in history with Warner Bros., and, by 1990, R.E.M. was recording rap-rock songs with KRS-One, all but erasing memories of a college rock band that covered Roger Miller and the Clique and sampled old Japanese monster movies.

Like Samson, once Stipe lost his hair, his cool seemed to go as well. A last gasp of Twee friendliness came in 1992 with the release of *Automatic for the People*, gorgeous from end to end and name-checking both Dr. Seuss and Andy Kaufman in various lyrics, but R.E.M. then seemed to abdicate their Twee throne, and it's just as well. There's only room for one king anyway, and Moz sits, probably forever, upon it. Ironically, Morrissey well knew that with the unstoppable (and still desirable to concert promoters who plead for reunions) power of the Smiths, micro-Twee would never be the same again. "Never again would a band like the Raincoats be entertained by Rough Trade," Morrissey writes in *Autobiography*. And yet, even as he killed off a kind of micro-Twee in favor of world beating, he is less the villain or the sellout, the joke as it were, than Stipe, Bono, Robert Smith, Depeche Mode or any other soon-to-be-huge peers. They seem to age, and age poorly, while Morrissey exists—like Sinatra, Liz Taylor,

Mick Jagger, and to an extent Michael Jackson—in the public eye in a kind of perma-youth, his young, handsome image gracing record sleeves even as he edges toward sixty.

"He's still the same bedroom boy, baffled by life and rattled by death and not sure how to breathe or eat or negotiate the pavement, except he's got fame and wealth and adoration, which helps him be a little more human," Morley wrote of Mozzer years ago. Today Morley is a bit more reverent. "Whatever people think of what he's done, it does nothing to contradict the idea that the Smiths were the Beatles of this zone. Their ideological power has taken thirty years to dribble into the mainstream."

If there's any Twee Stones to the Smiths' Twee Beatles, it's no longer R.E.M. but rather another American band that got its start in the early-'80s alternative scene and has now managed to enchant one generation after another while remaining fiercely Indie minded, mocking of fashion, and relentlessly clever. Can you guess? I'll give you a hint: you may know that Istanbul is no longer called Constantinople thanks to them. And nobody will ever offer this band millions of dollars to play festivals, because they've never gone away. "It's a larger phenomenon in the culture that I've come to realize is completely real," says John Flansburgh, cofounder of They Might Be Giants. Always a medium-popular band with a small but devout following, culture has simply bent their way and enabled them to continue to sell out international tours well into their members' fifties: it wasn't planned. "In many ways we might have been at the start of something and were a full beat ahead of something," Flansburgh says, "but part of me on a very core level profoundly does not get nerd culture."

Flansburgh and his partner John Linnell skewed nerdier in their early years on New York's East Village performance-art and No Wave scenes (which nurtured Sonic Youth, DNA, and others). "We were in awe of the No Wave people," Flansburgh says. He and Linnell, who transplanted to Brooklyn from the Boston area (where they worked in record stores and toiled in bands), wore leather jackets and dressed like sad vampires. Hardcore was going on at the same time, with its thrashing, violent tempos and extreme, often anti-Reagan lyrics. "We thought about putting together a hardcore set just to play this one club, 7A," Flansburgh says. "We wrote a short series of songs that would help us fit in. The titles make us blush to this day." He refuses to reveal one.

"We kind of trimmed our sails for stormy weather—the only other examples we knew didn't have much to show for their effort."

The feeling of not belonging stiffened their spines. Like the Smiths, They Might Be Giants had a strong sense of "here we are, a band in the record industry, writing and recording." They seemed to present, and frequently removed, the fourth wall: "Here are the songs." And the songs were wonderful.

"And now the song is over now, and now the song is over now," they observed on the very first track on their debut ("Everything Right Is Wrong Again"). Another song, "Older," observes, "You're older than you ever were and now you're even older . . . and now you're even older." They could harmonize sweetly, make skronk, play country, crack wise, or just jam (frequently with accordion) without ever losing this sense of scrap and humor.

These were, mind you, the dangerous days of Brooklyn, or at least the desolate ones. TMBG have impeccable Brooklandia cred, and it's in no small way a reason they are now a supergroup. The world came to Brooklyn, and, by extension, Brooklyn came to them. Toiling in then-desolate Park Slope and Fort Greene took decades to pay off but finally did. "We were in a big apartment," Flansburgh recalls. "Very cheap and very large. It didn't matter if we played the drums there." They wrote hundreds of songs, so many that when Linnell injured his wrist while working as a bike messenger, they had a backlog. Soon Dial-A-Song was born. Fans could literally call in to an answering machine in their apartment, triggering a cassette of a newly released song. The format was based on the then-popular Dial-A-Joke service in which you could trade a toll call for a usually bad punch line. It was at once both a novelty and a genuinely practical, alternative means of distribution, and the band continued to offer it to fans even after they started releasing albums again, on Indie label Bar/None.

"It was a glorious thing," Flansburgh says. It was also rebellious in its own way. "Phone machines were an emerging technology. AT&T owned your phone equipment at the time. You were no more allowed to put a phone machine on your phone than you were to climb up onto a telephone pole and move the wires around—to take that phone and manipulate it and change the wires on your phone, to take a privately held, publicly recognized monopoly and manipulate it. My biggest fear was I would instantly have my phone line cut and I wouldn't have a phone." Some of TMBG's most beloved songs first found life on Dial-A-Song, including their signature Twee anthem "Birdhouse in Your Soul," a love song to a blue canary-shaped night-light (as a metaphor, of course, for holding on to kindness and youth). Later they would move from the Indies to the majors without anyone crying foul and sell over a million copies of a truly oddball collection called *Flood* based largely on a re-recorded version of that same song; they would also crash MTV's heavy rotation with the homemade video for their

"Don't Let's Start" single a half decade before Nirvana and Pearl Jam arrived. WLIR in New York and KROQ in L.A, the two most powerful modern rock stations of the day, played it constantly.

"We could not have had the career at MTV and alternative radio without Dial-A-Song," says Flansburgh, "but I don't think we'd still be here as a band without it." It was an old contraption, a soon-to-be-out-of-date answering machine, that, in very Twee fashion, kept them fresh and original.

TMBG continued to tour, and, by middle age, their fans began to share their They Might Be Giants records with their children. Noticing this hand-me-down phenomenon, TMBG began cutting out the middleman and composing songs directly for the children, Wu Tang–like.

"For some reason, They Might Be Giants rarely show up alongside U2, the Rolling Stones and Los Lobos on lists of great bands that have managed to stay together over a long period of time," the music writer Steve Knopper wrote in the *Chicago Tribune* recently, observing that the slight might be down to the fact that "the duo have had a sort of novelty reputation . . . the Johns' nasal voices often sound as if they're singing children's songs, even when they're not actually singing children's songs; and they pack so many sounds and ideas into each song that their albums seem like rock circuses."

And still they go on, twenty-five-plus years after the dissolution of the Smiths, with the patina of the underdog. In theaters and clubs one can now hear both past and future Twee kids screaming for their favorites. But with regard to both bands, if three generations know your songs by heart and attend your concerts (or, in the Smiths' case, the solo shows) together, you are the Beatles and the Stones, no matter how square.

Chapter 8

Slings at the Corporate Ogre

1983–1989

In which a small group of socially and politically conscious entrepreneurs stick to their guns and their values and reject the Big Eighties temptations in favor of small business models and a defiantly amateurish, pure, and childlike aesthetic—which is promptly co-opted anyway.

*P*unk's do-it-yourself ethic, which gained real cultural power in the late 1970s and early '80s, goes hand in hand with the phenomenon of green or "ecological" marketing. It's rare to put the two together, but there were some thinkers, slightly ahead of the game, in the late '70s who saw no difference between signing and distributing a local garage band and growing tomatoes and selling them to their friends. As long as it cut out the middleman and took money out of the hands of greedy corporations with their political connections and lax morals and watchdogging, then it was the same political act: recording and rocking, growing and eating.

Every Portland, Brooklyn, or L.A. food truck, owned and run by a person and not a conglomerate, cooking with sourceable ingredients, is, for all the mockery and kvetching about the occasionally higher prices or exclusivity, a Punk rock enterprise. As Twee as the presentation becomes or as precious or proud the operators may seem about their product, they are, at heart, rebels.

This was commonplace in the Pacific Northwest when most New York Punks were still subsisting on dirty-water hot dogs, potato chips, and drugs. The back-to-the-earth hippies got run through the "Punk filter," as Paul Morley described. Maybe growing a wonderful tomato was a natural offshoot of figuring out ways to concoct the best strain of hydroponic bud. It's all gardening. To this day, the area is a bastion of "correct" living, eating, and rocking, with a rigidity that polarizes but, with collectives and food banks continuing to thrive, aligns some of its key figures—and has for decades now—with the Twee-food movement.

The whole of the Pacific Northwest's nascent Twee culture reminds me a little bit of Crockett Johnson's classic children's book *Harold and the Purple Crayon,* published in 1955. You've got Harold, and he's just young enough to look at the world around him and say, "Fuck this." And he's got this crayon that enables him to draw and create whatever he imagines, and it becomes real (purple, but real). There's no moon in the sky, and he thinks a moon would be nice, so he creates one. There's no forest on a blank white patch of land, so he makes one. The forest is decidedly small. It's really just one quaint little tree that he sits and admires. And once the tree bears fruit, Harold realizes it's an apple tree. "The apples would be very tasty, Harold thought, when they got red," the author writes. But Harold gets worried. What if people come around and try to mess with his tiny tree with its prized fruit? And so Harold creates a dragon to protect it. But the dragon is so frightening that it scares Harold off as well. What good is growing the best, most organic apples if they are unattainable, unmarketable, and incapable of being simply enjoyed? Such is the dilemma of "cred," and in the 1980s, as the Smiths, R.E.M., and their contemporaries in film, literature, and TV slowly ceded their cred, others operated on an almost ascetic level and made peace with the dragon.

"There's no morality involved. It just makes sense if I like local farmers, I should support them with my dollars—so they will continue to make a living and offer me their tomatoes, because I want tomatoes grown within ten miles of me," says Calvin Johnson, a central figure for one of the most sustainable—and Twee—DIY scenes in America, centered around the label he cofounded, K Records.

Today Whole Foods, the expensive and politically polarizing emporium founded by conservative John Mackey, is about as close as we will get to is about as close as we will get to the conscious and, most crucially, intimate or interpersonal food shopping that is so common to the Pacific Northwest. As a nation, we will probably never turn en masse to the street markets with their buckets and crates, wildflowers, canned jams, and compost collection anytime soon. The air-conditioned supermarket and the obese shopper are still the norm, but increasingly the idea of an alternative is getting around, and people are gradually coming around to the notion that farm-to-table consumption is not something elitist. Some teenage Punks have been all over it, intent on eliminating the middlemen and profiteers since the 1970s.

In 1977, a fifteen-year-old Calvin Johnson began shifting as a disc jockey on KAOS out of Olympia, Washington, southwest of Seattle. KAOS, founded four years earlier at Evergreen State College, a small liberal-arts university surrounded by a small section of bars and stores, was intended as a community station for local students and residents. You couldn't see Punk bands in Olympia in '77.

"There weren't any bands that were identifying as Punk and New Wave that were active in town," Johnson says of the time period. Punk and early New Wave music was broadcast through the woods, the rain, and the cold via the Indie airwaves. The station's call letters were in tribute to the evil organization in Mel Brooks and Buck Henry's 1960s spy farce *Get Smart*, then in syndicated reruns. DJs like Johnson and KAOS founder Dean Katz, as well as local figures like John Foster (who started the highly regarded zine *OP*, launched to give a forum to Indie musicians in Washington State and beyond), were, like Maxwell Smart and Agent 99, aligned against an evil empire. Johnson saw the major labels of the 1970s as merely an arm of a conglomerate of conscience-free fat cats and decided that it was as good a place as any to begin an insurgency. KAOS had already implemented a guideline that at least 80 percent of its playlist would be sourced from independent labels. "John Foster and some of the other people that were involved at the time, they thought it was a logical extension of the concept of community radio," says Johnson, "to apply the same ideas to the music programming. A lot of what community radio is about is reaching out to disenfranchised groups. People underserved by traditional radio and traditional media. So by extending that to the music programming, they said, 'We should play local music, and we should play music that doesn't get airplay on other stations.'" Johnson didn't shop at chain stores for music or food. He was eating locally farmed tomatoes before it became commonplace, and conducted himself with a monklike sense of clarity with regard to what could and could not be done to further the "cause." It would become part of his personal myth, and before long, the Punk rock community that was slowly growing in Olympia made it a go-to destination for Pacific Northwest bands.

"KAOS was one of the first, if not *the* first college radio station in the country, to declare 'no major label music'—stationwide. Nothing but Indie music was the policy," remembers Slim Moon, an Evergreen student who would later found Kill Rock Stars, one of the most important American Indie labels, which would sign Sleater-Kinney, Elliott Smith, the Decemberists, and the Gossip, among many others. "By the time I got there in '86, Olympia had been an early, early flag bearer," says Moon.

Johnson had what Leonard Cohen called "the gift of a golden voice." Like Cohen's or Sinatra's, it was deep and rich and made for radio. Over the airwaves it took on a performer's sense of nuance and humor, although Johnson kept his self-consciousness in check as he played his Jam and X-Ray Spex singles on his Friday-night radio show, which he called Boy Meets Girl. "I always operated under the assumption that no one was listening," he says. "If someone was listening, that was gravy."

In 1982, with his teenage years now behind him, Johnson cofounded a label, K Records, as an extension of his DJ show and general Indie philosophy. To him it was an art project, no more or less creative than painting a canvas. The first band to sign to K was Supreme Cool Beings, featuring Heather Lewis, an Evergreen student, on drums and vocals and Doug Monaghan and Gary Allen on guitars. Their *Survival of the Coolest* album, recorded during an in-the-studio performance on Boy Meets Girl, was released as a mail-order cassette only.

"I started K to be a part of the decentralizing [of corporate labels]," Johnson now says. "That's what my life is all about since I was fifteen. The idea of battling with corporate control of our lives overall—food, music, movies—it's not just culture, it's about everyday life. One of the ideas of Punk was you could control your own media. You could do a fanzine, you could have a radio show, you could put on shows, you can have a label—when Punk started, that was part of it all. All those things were the same thing as being in a band. They were all on equal levels."

Despite his unique voice, Johnson was never in the school choir, did not grow up singing, and had no ambition to be a front man. He found himself a lead singer as a sort of logical extension of his activity at KAOS, and now as a label head inspired by the artists he was supporting. "I feel like the music was visionary," he says. "Whatever genre, the theme of K was that the artist had a very personal vision that they were trying to achieve. It wasn't about any particular style of music or graphic design—just the artist going over their own ideal."

Lewis joined Johnson's band along with Laura Carter, another Olympia musician, and for a short while they were known simply as Laura, Heather and Calvin. Soon they became Beat Happening. Before they even rehearsed, Beat Happening was playing college parties. "We didn't really want to have anything to be too worked out," says Johnson. "We were relying on a good deal of improvisation." There was quite a bit of feedback, some pounding, primal drums, and Johnson's basso profundo trading lead vocals with Lewis's flat, girly phrasing. It was as elemental as rock and roll got. "I always felt if it ain't broke, don't fix it—the music I liked was very simple, and I aspired to create music as beautiful."

"Beat Happening had no bass player," says Moon. "[Future K signees] Mecca Normal had no drums. The outside world's perception of Olympia was that no band in Olympia was really a rock band. They never had the classic lineup of two guitar players, a bass player, and a drummer. When Olympia bands would go play in Seattle, the audience would boo them. That felt revolutionary."

Like Jonathan Richman and Andy Kaufman, Beat Happening was deadly serious about their stance, even if to some outsiders it might have appeared a prank. Those waiting for the wink never got one. Here was a great band, but one that was certainly an acquired taste, and those who got it became fans and probably still are. Those who came to the shows to heckle or looky-loo were given what would come to be something of a community-wide glare.

"That scene had a really high standard," says Moon. "It expected you to be productive. And we were kind of mean if people just wanted to show up and consume. We thought, We can do it all and make much more meaningful music and much more meaningful community than what was being given to us by MTV."

K's slogan said it all: "Exploding the teenage underground into passionate revolt against the corporate ogre since '82."

This pose wasn't faux naïveté but rather a fierce, almost harsh, dragonlike guardianship of the Indie ethic that everyone knew was under assault. They were fighting against the shoulder-pads-and-coke 1980s zeitgeist.

Still, as the legend of Beat Happening and K Records grew, the question arose again and again, especially about Calvin Johnson: "Can anyone be *that* pure?"

"There was a built-in backlash to Olympia in Seattle," says Sean

Nelson, future front man for Harvey Danger and now a writer, actor, and solo artist. "That Olympia world was hipster in the old sense. People dressed in a combination of Mod vintage suits and pajamas and had an inherent sense of judgment. There was a high-art element to it, not knowing how to play your instruments. In Seattle people felt like [Olympia] was really moralistic."

"It took me five years to figure out that Calvin wasn't pulling my leg," Moon says. "It's a total devotion to a worldview. A lot have trouble [believing] that he really is the guy he is appearing to be, but he is."

By the mid-'80s, the purity-via-simplicity ethos was something of a shared and international cause. One of Beat Happening's first major acts as a band was to travel across the Pacific to perform a series of shows in Tokyo, where a few dozen Indie-rock hubs had been established. There Japanese teenagers read imported British music weeklies and derived their own aesthetic too, just as the teenagers in Glasgow or Morrissey in Manchester had. They looked great and had a hunger for basic, unadorned, no-synths, no-drum-machines rock and roll. Some were entrenched in the burgeoning "cutie" or Kawaii culture, most famously exemplified by Sanrio's series of Disney-like characters, Hello Kitty the most iconic of them all. With no mouth, a blank expression, and a bow in her hair, Kitty was a sort of postmodern Mickey Mouse figure onto which any emotion could be projected. By the 1990s, that face would be the very emblem of postmodernism, a Warholian blankness staring out from coffee cups and guitars, jet airplanes and candy tins. It would also spark a social argument that would reemerge in the early 2010s: feminists argued that the strange cat character and "cutie" culture in general inspired women to remain permanently girlish and immature, while others simply appreciated the kitsch value. There were even those who saw Hello Kitty as a vital response to the increasingly modern and cold world. "Surrounding yourself with cute things could offset that a little," Ken Belson and Brian Bremner write in their history of Sanrio and its empire, now worth billions, "bringing some whimsy and comfort into one's life, lending a subjective quality to otherwise sterilized products like a vacuum cleaner, microwave ovens or rice cookers." In this way, Hello Kitty was rebellious, Punk rock even.

"It seemed like a new frontier," Johnson says of 1980s Tokyo. "No one we knew had anything to do with Japan. No bands even thought about going to Japan."

Despite their limitations, intentional or not, Beat Happening were beginning to write incredible songs and develop a sort of hybrid style of a piece with tough but funny predecessors like the Cramps. The most powerful songs of their oeuvre combine an elemental, Punk rock arrangement with lyrics about wearing pajamas, going on picnics, climbing trees, and having crushes.

Beat Happening's willful childlike stance—or antimacho pose—remained ridiculously Twee to some, but like a secret weapon against the soul-sucking '80s to others.

The DIY movement had like-minded souls all over America and in Europe as well as the Far East. In the pre-Internet age, cassette-sharing culture and zine trading held these factions together and fortified what seemed like a shared cause.

"Fanzines fed off each other," says Clare Wadd, who started the Bristol, England–based zine *Kvatch*. "I see massive parallels with the blogosphere and all of social media of today—that desire to reach out and connect with other people with similar interests, particularly for teenagers and young people who can feel quite isolated, maybe in small towns or whatever, and to build your own virtual community rather than just deal with the one you live in."

Fanzine productions separated the men from the boys (and the women from the girls). It was hard work: you had to really be committed, so if you had one, you were given the benefit of the doubt by your potential allies, a sort of instant respect, since they too knew what went into the creation. "I guess one of the hardest things to get across to people who've grown up in the era of the Internet and computer design is the sheer physical effort involved in producing an actual solid object, and then trying to market and distribute it . . . not to mention the cost," says Matt Haynes, who wrote the zine *Are You Scared to Get Happy?*, also out of Bristol. "But at least, in theory, that meant anyone who produced a fanzine was totally committed and had a vested interest in actually selling the finished product, otherwise they'd lose money."

Wadd recalls the arduous step-by-step. "We had to make paste-ups, with the text and pictures glued onto them and the edges held down with white poster paint so you didn't get shadow lines on your printing," she says. "Then you would get your fanzine back from the printers and have to collate them and staple them and fold them. And then you would have the whole mail-order side, and sending them off to other fanzines to review."

The impassioned zine hawker was quickly becoming a familiar sight at Indie-rock shows. "We'd sell them at gigs," Haynes recalls, "not at a stall—just by walking up to people and saying, 'Do you want to buy a fanzine?' Getting drunk and belligerent helped. But you picked your gigs carefully, and there were often two or three fanzine sellers doing the same thing, so people were used to this."

Copies were also given out to Indie record stores in hopes that customers would get hooked and become regular readers. The most organized zine writers included an address and instructions on where and how to subscribe, the best way to tape coins to a piece of cardboard to cover postage costs, et cetera. It was such a detail-oriented operation that, after a point, it didn't seem that much of a stretch to run a record label.

Sub Pop, which grew out of music writer and DJ Bruce Pavitt's KAOS radio show, Subterranean Pop, was such a zine-to-label phenomenon. Pavitt and Johnson were friends, and when Johnson briefly moved to the D.C. area (which had its own organic and somewhat rigid Punk scene, centered on Dischord Records and the Bad Brains), Pavitt took over Johnson's Boy Meets Girl slot. Pavitt later moved to Seattle and continued the brand, now shortened to Sub Pop, as both a zine and a monthly column in the city's local paper *The Rocket*.

Many zines, like the soon-to-explode *Sub Pop* and *Touch and Go*, out of East Lansing, Michigan, occasionally included a flexi disc, thus making their evolution into actual labels that much more natural. The better fanzines, ones that offered these song giveaways, had little trouble gaining the respect of record distributors. Soon UK zinesters Matt Haynes and Clare Wadd were teaming up and launching a label called Sarah Records.

Once a young writer, music fan, and politically sound zine publisher became an actual label head, he or she usually established a series of ground rules so as to avoid being corrupted by Calvin Johnson's "corporate ogre." These weren't manifestos à la Riot Grrrl, but were usually the product of a careful conversation. "The rules were pretty much that we both had to really like the record, the songs—not just the band, but the actual songs that we were releasing. We had to love it or it didn't come out," says Wadd.

Often there was a political agenda too. Zines were started to telegraph what you loved. Labels had the power to tear down what you hated. "These were quite militant times," says Phil Johnson of the June Brides, one of this period's biggest cult bands. "Several of the major labels had such a wide spread on investments and subcompanies that many people would not want to get involved with them for political reasons, us included. The independent labels offered a place where you could go and maintain your self-righteousness."

In the wake of Band Aid, Live Aid, and Farm Aid, pop stars were obliged to become political on a grand scale, making statements and recording saccharine anthems (while of course meaning well), then resuming a lifestyle that did nothing to support anything ecological or ideological. It was puffery orchestrated by major-label publicists, and it made the Indie scene seem like worker ants by comparison— but also a lot more admirable. Theirs was a lifestyle, not a statement; a ceaseless rebellion against greed, sexism, the screwing of artists, and the callous rescinding of social programs, not to mention the ravaging of the planet.

Ian MacKaye, leader of Washington, D.C., hardcore band Minor Threat, one of the major acts on the D.C. scene, started a new band, Fugazi, in 1987. MacKaye was already famous in the community as the most prominent "straight-edge" Punk, extolling a policy of no drinking, no smoking, no drugs. As Fugazi began to tour, they set about improving the conditions of the Punk rock show itself. They kept ticket prices to five dollars by eliminating what they regarded as the kind of excesses that resulted in the screwing of fans. They sold no T-shirts and rented out alternative venues. The shows themselves were marked by a lack of violent moshing or stage diving, with MacKaye willing to stop a song to hector a particularly brutal fan in the pit.

The year 1988, when Fugazi released their self-titled debut EP (known as *Seven Songs* to fans), was the era of music videos featuring scantily clad women grinding on top of cars. Sunset Strip hedonism, misogynistic lyrics, and the general notion that women had no place in rock and roll outside of drummer's girlfriend was being challenged by the voices out of Indie. A highlight of the Fugazi EP was "Suggestion," in which MacKaye gave voice to a female exasperated by unwanted cat calls: "Why can't I walk down a street, free of suggestion," he asks, aligning himself instantly with the likes of Wadd and Haynes, who were personally aghast at the casual use of the beautiful woman as a marketing tool, even among some so-called Indie bands.

"Taking on gender bias was very key to us," says Wadd. "We had a strict rule about not using women as decorative art on record covers, no cute sixties chicks." Lyrics that compared women to cars, long a standard in rock and roll, were out as well. Even the label's name was a sort of fuck-you to the sexist rock establishment. "We'd deliberately chosen it because we knew it would be confrontational," says Haynes. "Most music journalists couldn't bring themselves to treat a label with a girl's name seriously, and that said a lot about the sexism of the music industry and the world in general at the time. Most women in bands were just the singer or the tambourine player, and no women were in positions of power at any record labels. When Clare answered the phone, people would often assume she was my secretary. We wanted to challenge all this. "

The movement had key supporters among conventional media

outlets of the day. Just about every new offering from Sarah was welcomed enthusiastically by the still essential BBC DJ John Peel, but in the UK press, some jaded rock scribes felt there was a sort of holier-than-thou attitude that needed to be taken down a peg or two.

It helped that many of these bands were truly stellar; their singles modest masterpieces, among them the Field Mice's "Let's Kiss and Make Up" and the doleful "Emma's House." Each song sounded different, but like Beat Happening, they suggested first kisses and last kisses, and sonically felt shivery and warm at the same time, like your first bite of an ice cube and the sensation as it melts in your throat.

The Field Mice's Annemari Davies looked 1960s perfect as well in her sweaters, striped shirts, and vintage sunglasses that would not be out of place in Jean Seberg's or Anna Karina's purse. "Happy All the Time" by the Flatmates (signed to another Bristol-based independent label, the Subway Organization), "You Should Be Murdered" by Another Sunny Day (name-checked in a song by Belle and Sebastian), and "I've Got a Habit" by the Orchids were other milestone singles. Non-Sarah releases by Loop, Strawberry Switchblade, Spacemen 3, and the Dentists also contributed to the new Indie intrigue.

"We had excellent press for some of the early releases," says Wadd, "and perhaps more press than we could have expected, really, looking back. But then the people who hated us and despised us became more irritable as we persisted and succeeded."

In a post-Smiths age, even the most hardened rock writer knew Indie was both good business and the new style; *N.M.E.* and *Melody Maker* could take credit for "breaking" these bands and pad their reputation as cutting-edge news outlets. Readership was in decline—these publications needed a new bandwagon to jump on.

One possible turn was toward the Hip-Hop coming out of America. The rise of Hip-Hop superstars, especially Run-DMC and Public Enemy, polarized the staffs of these magazines. Some were thrilled with *Yo! Bum Rush the Show,* Public Enemy's 1987 debut. Others worried about practical matters: they couldn't sell issues by putting rappers on the cover. The Detroit techno and acid house artists that most kids were dancing to in clubs didn't even have faces to put on the covers in the first place: many of their record sleeves were plain white paper. Indie, with its sweet-faced, fringed, scrawny white kids, seemed the perfect compromise: it was political, progressive, but didn't frighten anyone by quoting Malcolm X and Minister Louis Farrakhan.

"Indie became a marketing device and genre rather than an ethos," Clare Wadd now says. In late '86, *N.M.E.*, under new editor in chief Ian Pye, rallied around "Indie" and quickly recast it to suit its purposes, dispensing with much of the political claptrap and focusing on the fashion and trappings.

A cassette giveaway was offered that collected all the Indie sounds. Promoted by the weekly, *C86* (for "cassette 1986") colored the next half decade of English style, right up until the ascent of Nirvana in 1991. C86 would be a sound (jangly pop, sweet vocals, dreamy lyrics with a 1960s bent), but it was also a certain type of haircut (the Jean Seberg, of course, for women; the David Crosby Byrds fringe for men), T-shirt (Warhol Factory–style striped), outerwear (motorcycle jacket anorak). It was a little bit Punk, a little bit Mod, with almost no overt political stance to be detected. Unlike the *C81* tape, which featured ska, pop, Punk, and electronic acts, *C86* was far less eclectic, with predominantly Anglo, literary-minded pop from the Pastels, the Soup Dragons, the Shop Assistants, Close Lobsters, the Wedding Present, and an early incarnation of Primal Scream. The bands who were not typical of the then-in-vogue "Indie" sound and look are now lost to history. "It's subsequently taken on a weird life of its own, which I don't fully understand! Several bands who were actually on the cassette would not be considered *C86* bands stylistically!" Phil Wilson of June Brides says.

Stephen McRobbie of the Pastels appears on *C86* and found the inclusion a double-edged sword. "There was a spectacular display of weeds all over the place, and it felt like the *N.M.E.* was trying to put them in a neat little garden. We had mixed feelings from the start."

Thus diluted of its ethic by the corporate ogres, "Indie" required nothing from its adherents and, as a result, multiplied a hundredfold. Today, *Indie* is a junk word, like *Mod* or *hippie*, used to inaccurately describe an item for sale on eBay.

"For us, it was very much the *N.M.E.* jumping on a scene two years too late and slightly missing the point," says Matt Haynes. The term also became a tool for some rock writers to politely but unmistakably dismiss a band as not rock enough, a little girly. "Even by the time it was released, *C86* was being treated as a term of abuse, and most of the writers [at *N.M.E.*] were embarrassed by it. These days, people tend to think of it as a landmark moment, but . . . I think that's a slight rewriting of history."

The biggest liability the *C86*-era Indie bands faced was the assumption that they couldn't really play. As with Beat Happening, there seemed to be a thread of self-limiting amateurism running through, with the rhythms a little off and the playing less than virtuoso. *Shambolic* was the term, affectionately coined by John Peel and adopted by the British press to express varying levels of admiration or dismissal by a million rock writers afterward. That some bands, like Fuzzbox and the early Jesus and Mary Chain, wore a love of ear-splitting distortion on their woolly, mohair sleeves only served to mask, some assumed, a lack of skill. Nobody expected the titanic masterworks that would come as the 1980s drew to a close and the 1990s began. A stew of economic shifting, brand-new drugs like Ecstasy, and the massive hype that Indie drew bestowed a confidence on these once-fringed and retiring front men, and suddenly, overnight, there was a new wave of Brian Wilsons and Serge Gainsbourgs and Beatles, each attempting to use as many newly available studio tracks as possible with noise, noise, noise, sometimes funky, sometimes pummeling, sometimes both at once, always with the swing of cocksure youth. Here is where you get your *Loveless,* your Stone Roses' self-titled debut, your *Screamadelica,* albums that changed lives, defined their times, and inspired new bands to form (and top them) after only a few listens (the unibrowed world beaters in Oasis among them). It was ironic that Hip-Hop divided the *N.M.E.* staff so much, as the same thing was going on in studios in New York City: hugely ambitious and bold albums like Public Enemy's *It Takes a Nation of Millions to Hold Us Back* and De La Soul's *Three Feet High and Rising* and A Tribe Called Quest's *The Low End Theory* were just as innovative and vast.

Primal Scream, the *C86* vets, quickly distanced themselves from that movement and led their once staunchly independent label, Creation, into a point-by-point re-creation of late '60s–early '70s Rolling Stones–like debauchery and largesse, complete with an image that suggested the ingestion of harder drugs, a laissez-faire attitude toward groupies, and a fondness for tons of money. It was all very rock and roll but not very Indie, and it made those like Haynes and Wadd of Sarah Records cringe. One step forward, they worried, and two decades back as far as social progress went; any notion of Twee righteousness frozen out by that old time rock and roll.

Those still operating as conscientious Indie outfits could only scratch their heads as they watched. "I used to be a huge Creation fan," says Matt Haynes. "And still have their first twenty singles and wouldn't part with them for anything, because they were so much a part of my life, and Sarah wouldn't have existed without them, but . . . when Primal Scream started wearing leather trousers and pretending to be the Rolling Stones, talking about sex and drugs and rock and roll and groupies and generally being a bit pathetic, I was just so disappointed."

Still, while the older UK Indie scene was becoming compromised, in part by its own popularity and media attention, the Indie scene in the Pacific Northwest was at its strongest. Beat Happening's 1988 release, *Jamboree,* was an international critical hit (issued in the UK on Rough Trade, the Smiths' label) and one of the biggest crossover successes of its day, pivoting from menace ("Hangman") to lust ("Bewitched") to pristine and virtuous child pop ("Indian Summer"). Kurt Cobain called it his favorite album.

Chapter 9

"You're in High School Again"

1988–1995

This chapter is about Nirvana. In addition to being many other important things, Nirvana was Twee. When Kurt Cobain was alive, he often went out of his way to prove this, so when you say to yourself, "Wait, Nirvana wasn't Twee, not at all," think of Kurt and how he would feel if he overheard you.

Everybody loved Nirvana," says Sean Nelson, the former Harvey Danger front man who relocated to the Seattle area in the late 1980s. "And everybody's reaction to Nirvana grew to be, 'Nobody else understands them like I do. Everybody loves Nirvana, but those people are assholes, and *I* really get it.' They were the first band where the best way to express your fandom was to *not* wear their T-shirt." For a brilliant band, Nirvana had pretty shitty merchandise: their signature shirt was an oversize black tee with a big, yellow, crooked-smile happy face. Who would wear that anyway, if you were a cool and righteous Indie Punk? "It's part of the Olympian strain of simply not participating in mass culture," Nelson continues.

"It was an easy act to cop: 'Oh, mass culture and MTV doesn't represent me in any way. I don't recognize myself in it. I don't know who the Gin Blossoms are.' Of course you know who the Gin Blossoms are. You've been in a supermarket! Kurt was just swaddled with shame for having any mainstream success and he went out of his way to shit on that world."

Nirvana often gets credit for taking the fundamentally intimate and manageable aesthetic of Indie or Twee and, depending on whom you ask, either triumphing over its limitations of reach and appeal or ruining it forever. But at the end of the 1980s, this shift was already under way in music with the audience expansion enjoyed by the Smiths, R.E.M., and the Cure (who had their Twee moments with singles like "The Love Cats" and "The Caterpillar"). John Hughes primed the mainstream for a sometimes reluctant acceptance of the shy, the clever, the vintage clad. The Hughes trilogy of *Sixteen Candles, The Breakfast Club,* and *Pretty in Pink*—and the bands that gibed with his vision, the Smiths among them—was a kind of Trojan horse for Indie; these were, after all, Hollywood films designed to reach mass audiences and make millions of dollars, suffused with a sensibility intended to self-limit. In the wake of Hughes and Pee-wee Herman came a sort of new mainstream: one with edge.

The era had its superstars—Prince, Madonna, Cyndi Lauper, Whitney Houston, and the King of Pop, Michael Jackson—and it had its cult heroes—the Cure, Depeche Mode, R.E.M., and the Smiths. At the start of the decade there seemed to be some kind of commercial moat between the two. As the '80s wore on, that divide dried up and a growing hunger for smarter, shyer, sadder pop stars who reflected real teenage emotion, anger, and confusion increased

wildly. While Nirvana was still trying to emulate the Melvins, *edge*—
that catchall word for anything left of center—was already becoming
big business, and by decade's end consumers wanted even more of it.
Hughes would come to seem tame. The Smiths would flame out, but
the Cure, R.E.M., and Depeche Mode started selling out arenas.

"I felt like Hughes was trying to coddle teenagers and almost
suck up to them—idealize them," says Daniel Waters, screenwriter of
1989's hilarious and brutal *Heathers*. "I was more of a terrorist coming
after John Hughes. What drove me nuts about the Hughes movies—
the third act was always something to do with how bad the parents
are and how bad the adults are and when you grow up your heart dies.
Hey, your heart dies when you're twelve!"

Heathers is also almost a throwback to 1960s and '70s films like *If,
Harold and Maude,* and the more rebellious Kubrick movies prized by
the Criterion-collecting Twee Tribe—quicker-witted than most teen
films, and saturated with long-bygone things like croquet and pâté
and Doris Day ("Que Sera Sera" opens the film). While a black fantasy, it also has the economy and elegance that defined the Nouvelle
Vague and *Breakfast at Tiffany's*. It's suburban but strangely urban and
sophisticated, as much as any Whit Stillman or midperiod Woody
Allen film, or, years later, the TV series *Gilmore Girls*.

"There were also Easter eggs for the smart teen," Waters admits.
"The high school is named after Paul Westerberg. We couldn't actually afford a soundtrack so it was kind of a mental soundtrack I made,
putting these keystones into the script. It would further embed you
into the sensibility of the movie. I was a kid coming out of college.
Basically my theory was, let's write something: when I open up the
newspaper, what am I not seeing? And I always wanted to see more of
a *Dr. Strangelove* version of teen films."

Heathers has no interest in the verisimilitude that Amy Heckerling and Cameron Crowe tried to achieve in *Fast Times*, either. Real-life kids in the 1980s and '90s didn't talk like the kids at Westerberg High. The dialogue is super stylized and self-consciously barbed.

"I had this poor girl," Waters says. "I was her camp counselor and she would always say, 'What's your damage?' and I completely stole it—I feel there's a poor girl walking around going, 'That was mine.' I was not trying to re-create the high school experience. I was jealous of Shakespeare. I wanted to write about kings and queens too. High school is the last universal experience we all have, and there are kings and queens." High school soap and social drama is merely another Trojan horse. "Bring in the cliché, because you can use it as a way to get crazy," Waters says. Though a commercial flop in its day, *Heathers* is now one of those rare films that can be quoted verbatim both by those who saw it in its theatrical run and those who own it. Like so many Twee Tribe films, its cultural penetration transcends its original performance commercially.

Tim Burton's Trojan horse would be a comic-book hero. In the 1960s, *Batman* was camp. The hero himself, portrayed by Adam West, seemed winded, even lazy, and the television show a place for C-list stars to earn some rent money. Burton's *Batman,* released the summer after *Heathers*'s 1989 spring offensive, announced yet another new sheriff in town. Burton (who had gothed out *Heathers* star Winona Ryder the previous summer in *Beetlejuice*) turned to artist Frank Miller's stark and intense rebooting of the DC comic-book hero for a template. Miller converted Batman from a prancing caped crusader to the Dark Knight, a twisted vigilante haunted by the death of his parents. Gotham City was now a gleaming, sleek black Gothic hellscape with touches of F. W. Murnau, Todd Browning, and the Swiss painter H. R. Giger (who'd designed the monster in *Alien* as well as controversial album sleeves for Debbie Harry and the Dead Kennedys). Burton's Batman probably listened to the Cure's *Pornography* in that cave when Alfred wasn't around. Jack Nicholson's Joker, unlike Cesar Romero, who played the hero's nemesis on television, looked like a real killer. With a budget approaching $50 million, unheard of in '89, *Batman* could have buried the franchise and done some serious shaking up at the Warner Bros. film division. They basically gave the world's second most iconic character (next to Superman) to the guy who made Pee-wee Herman do the big shoe dance, a guy who looked like he could have been one of the gawkier side members of the Jesus and Mary Chain.

Also pre-Nirvana, Katherine Dunn's *Geek Love* married the Goth of Todd Browning's *Freaks* with trash-culture satire and produced a literary smash for smart people—fucked-up smart people. Similarly, the popularity of *Weetzie Bat*, a Trojan horse for young-adult fiction, was another product of the '89 pop revolution and frightened some parents thanks to its unapologetic sexual frankness, its realistic portrayal of drinking, smoking, pogoing Hollywood teens, and its tackling of the AIDS crisis when even members of Congress were pretending it wasn't there. A "dark fairy tale," according to its author, Francesca Lia Block, *Weetzie* was yet another blockbuster.

Love was a dangerous angel indeed.

Even network television was no longer whitewashed of all its kinks and jagged edges. In the spring of 1990, ABC, then still one of the "big three" networks, debuted David Lynch and Mark Frost's *Twin Peaks* (Trojan horse: a high school murder mystery set in a small, insular, Pacific Northwest logging and mill town). Homecoming queen

Laura Palmer's body turned up, blue and "wrapped in plastic," and with it came an entirely new prime-time aesthetic. From the unpredictable pacing and earnest, almost camp performances (anchored by Kyle MacLachlan's special agent Dale Cooper) to Angelo Badalamenti's at times histrionic, other times beatnik score to the unapologetic quirk of its locals (no faceless extras here) to the implication that behind the varsity and club-lounge facade lay a horrible and secret darkness, *Twin Peaks* took elements of storytelling that were usually the province of cult films (like Lynch's *Blue Velvet*) to the mainstream.

"It was the first time I had the experience of being totally speechless while watching a television show," writer-director Alan Ball told me in 2010. "It really influenced me. There'd be no *Six Feet Under* or *True Blood* without it, I would say. And the fact that they got it onto a major network is still an amazing feat."

So there was no longer a question of when the Big Twee aesthetic was going to blow up. It already had. It took Nirvana to let the world know that the damage was already done.

Kurt Cobain grew up loving the Beatles, Led Zeppelin, Aerosmith, Kiss, and Black Sabbath. As with the Smiths, there are a multitude of worthy Nirvana histories, including excellent ones by Michael Azerrad and former *Rocket* editor in chief Charles R. Cross. I won't condense the saga here. It is worth absorbing it in full on your own. I am here to demonstrate how someone with a working knowledge of Punk and an appreciation of power chords became a Twee Tribe icon.

"Kurt Cobain came to town loving Scratch Acid and the Melvins, and discovered Leadbelly and the Vaselines by becoming a participant in the Olympia scene," says Slim Moon, a friend and neighbor of Cobain's in Olympia when Nirvana left Aberdeen for good in 1988.

Hailing from Edinburgh, the Vaselines were a duo (Eugene Kelly and Frances McKee) who married the Buzzcocks' simple, fast, pure pop with an even more arch sense of camp. (One of their most popular tracks was a cover of three-hundred-pound drag queen Divine's disco novelty song "You Think You're a Man.")

"It was part of what happens in a scene like that," Moon says. "Everybody plays each other music they love. There is a thing of community standards. You sort of lean on people: 'Well, if you don't like this, you're not cool.' Mostly it's joyful and organic. People just hang around and make mix tapes for each other. 'Oh, you have to hear this.'"

A romance with another Olympia resident, Tobi Vail—bandmate of Calvin Johnson in one of his many offshoot bands, the Go Team— set Cobain even farther apart from his Aberdeeners. Vail would go on to cowrite *The Riot Grrrl Manifesto,* a declaration of independence from the sexism and limitations of established and corporation-fortified culture. Proto–Riot Grrrl made Cobain feel guilty not simply because of his gender but also his honest love for Kiss, Cheap Trick's *Heaven Tonight,* and the Knack's *Get the Knack,* all of which were based on Beatlesque melodic pop melodies, not in-your-face screaming (even the "heavy" Kiss essentially wrote pop songs with massive hooks). Kurt was accomplished, a natural guitarist who was forced to pretend he was less gifted.

The lone pop song in Nirvana's repertoire, "About a Girl," composed after listening to *Meet the Beatles* for hours on end, was nearly hip-pocketed in favor of goofy but Olympia-approved Melvins' sound-alikes like "Hairspray Queen" and "Big Cheese." When it came time to record "About a Girl" for Nirvana's Sub Pop debut *Bleach,* in-house producer Jack Endino observed just how self-conscious Cobain was over the catchy song. "He felt like he had to make an excuse for it," Endino has said. "I hope the Sub Pop guys like it," Cobain said, shrugging, resorting to what would soon be the institutionalized standby mode of his generation: irony.

Cobain's famous envy of the Pixies ("Smells Like Teen Spirit" admittedly copped their patented loud-quiet-loud format) was not just musical. The Boston-based quartet had no such issues when it came to airing out their inner pop fan. The Pixies glided from the gothy and cred-correct UK label 4AD to the major Elektra with an almost blithe sense of entitlement, and therefore received no shit from their own college-town rock scene. When leader Black Francis placed a similarly unabashed pop song, "Here Comes Your Man," on their major-label debut, 1989's *Doolittle*, and released it as a single, it was a sign of their diversity and depth and not an act of an Indie apostate. The Pixies' 1987 debut EP, *Come on Pilgrim*, contained a song, "I've Been Tired," that satirizes collegiate self-righteousness viciously. "She's a real left winger 'cause she's been down south and held peasants in her arms," Francis sings in a high-pitched, intentionally mocking voice.

Cobain, a high school dropout full of divorce-kid rage, couldn't have shelved "About a Girl" if he'd wanted to. He knew this was just the beginning of a shift in his songwriting approach, and even as he played and partied in Olympia, he prepared himself for the inevitable: that he would be the Judas to make it all safe for the knuckleheads. His psyche was painfully split. Part of him was Kurt, who had a McCartney gift for melody and a Morrissey-like desire to throw fame and success in the faces of all those who had written him off. Another part was Kurdt, as he sometimes spelled his name: self-mocking and self-limiting.

Cobain's behavior in his twenties seemed to be a cross between that of an arrested child acting out and a determined and ambitious music-business player.

"He appears to be an introvert and he appears to kind of not give a fuck—but he [also] puts in effort and energy to be in this incredible, top-notch, groundbreaking band. He signs to a label that has the resources to make him famous. He gets a super powerful management company," says Moon. Nirvana had indeed signed with Gold Mountain, which also managed Indie darlings Sonic Youth. "He becomes a superstar, and then he puts his torment out there as his thing. He put it out there in the music and in interviews. Sure, the torment was real, but it was also a production. Axl Rose has his shtick, and Kurt Cobain has his shtick, and his shtick was his torment, and I'm not saying his torment wasn't real, but that's what he chose to have as his public persona." Nirvana's last single for Sub Pop, "Sliver," "tells the traumas of a child away from his parents for the first time," according to Cobain. "Mom and Dad go off somewhere and leave the kid with his grandparents and he gets confused."

When the band recorded the follow-up to *Bleach* with uber-producer Butch Vig at Smart Studios in Madison, Wisconsin, the tracks that came together had sturdy melodies that were instantly memorable, like children's songs: big choruses and melodic verses that Vig double-tracked to maximize the Beatlesque quality. "Everything I do is an overly conscious and neurotic attempt at trying to prove to others that I'm at least more intelligent and cool than they think," Cobain said. "Smells Like Teen Spirit," named, as legend has it, after a quip by Riot Grrrl hero Kathleen Hanna concerning a deodorant aimed at the young-girl dollar, was yet another form of hedging on

Cobain's part; a sort of secret language aimed at the K Records crowd telegraphing, "I know this is commercial." Roll eyes. Irony.

Cobain's Twee bona fides come in part down to his physical appearance. He was never less than angelic. Those parfait-colored Elizabeth Peyton portraits of him, which make him look like a character in a children's book, are not wide of the mark. He was portrayed in multiple magazine profiles as rock and roll's own Little Prince figure, a regal man-child with yellow bed head and a sensitive, searching perspective on the bustle of the music business. He would greet reporters in pajamas. *Rolling Stone*'s Michael Azerrad observed, "Cobain lies flat on his back in striped pajamas, a red-painted big toenail peeking out the other end of the blanket and a couple of teddy bears lying beside him for company." Yet another scribe compares Kurt and his entourage to Christopher Robin and Pooh. *Melody Maker*'s cantankerous and outrageous Everett True, an early supporter, described him as a "cherub faced misfit." There's a scene toward the end of *The Little Prince* that reminds me of both Cobain's appeal and the heartbreak that did him in. The boy spies commuters at a busy train station and questions the rush. "No one is ever satisfied with where he is . . . Only the children know what they are looking for."

Cobain's demons wouldn't permit him to linger in such a state of childlike grace for very long. If you have to try to be childlike, you are doomed to fail anyway. As with Morrissey, the divorce of Cobain's parents served notice that all was not bright and sweet in life, and he carried that around with him for the rest of his days. The suspicion and pain drew him out of Aberdeen, but by the time he found himself among worthy peers, he couldn't shake it. "I think he was ashamed," his mother told *Rolling Stone* at the height of her son's fame. "And he became very inward—he just held everything. He became real shy. It just devastated him. I think he's still suffering."

Other profiles feature him tending his pets, smelly turtles and rabbits, or fondling his transparent Visible Man and Visible Woman models (which would later figure into Nirvana album art). Kurt was even still in touch with his childhood imaginary friend, Baba. Add to this a juvenile fascination with organs, sex, fluids (how many Nirvana lyrics mention them?); that he may have briefly once lived, like a Dungeons & Dragons troll, under a bridge; and that in "Something in the Way," the string-driven ballad that closes *Nevermind*, you have a lost boy with animals as friends? Twee!

Once the Butch Vig tapes, featuring the monster drumming of new member Dave Grohl, got around, Cobain's defection from Indie was a fait accompli, and soon the apologies started. In a published letter to Edinburgh pop-Punk group the Vaselines, one of his favorites and clear members of the deliberate-amateur society, he apologizes for his "business-like" tone in parts. Cobain was seeking permission to release recordings of what are now famous Nirvana cover versions of Vaselines songs like the joyful "Molly's Lips" and "Son of a Gun." Sonic Youth, the venerated New York noise-rock band, and to a lesser extent the Pixies, provided some cover as they set a precedent, but Cobain was too handsome and talented to remain an outsider. "Sonic Youth took us under their wing," bassist Krist Novoselic told me in 2011, but Nirvana would not remain there long. With *Nevermind* recorded and ready for release, Nirvana supported Sonic Youth on a tour of Europe that was documented by filmmaker Dave Markey and later released as *1991: The Year Punk Broke*. "That was the last of Nirvana just being this obscure band. The calm before the storm. The end of our innocence. Mere months later we were the biggest band in the world and we had to deal with that," Novoselic said.

The next time Nirvana played in Europe they would be headlining massive venues, including the annual Reading and Leeds festivals. "I was traveling around Europe by myself for the first half of 1992," says the writer Sarah Vowell. "Every time I'd get to a new city, there would be posters for Nirvana's *Nevermind* tour plastered all around the train station. For the first time in my life I got to be culturally chauvinistic! They were huge! I bought a copy of *Rolling Stone* at the Utrecht train station and there was an article about Seattle and Scott McCaughey from the Young Fresh Fellows was quoted in it. A guy I had seen play at the Cat's Paw, a crummy bar in Bozeman, Montana, was quoted in a magazine! By summer, I was marching to Nirvana's sold-out Dublin show singing 'Smells Like Teen Spirit' along with seemingly every kid in Ireland."

As he became famous, Cobain was also reckoning with marriage, fatherhood, and drug addiction, as if any one of those wasn't enough to shake his already fragile system. While Courtney Love is demonized by many, if anything more of her should have rubbed off on him. One listen to the vicious takedown of the K Records scene's pomposity that is "Rock Star," the closing track on Hole's sophomore release *Live Through This,* and it's clear that she possessed the better weaponry of the two. "We look the same, we talk the same. We even fuck the same," Love sang, mocking the cult of Calvin Johnson with a send-up worthy of Dorothy Parker.

Maybe it was the heroin—a drug that pumps up, for a time anyway, a sense of "why can't we all get along . . . life is beautiful . . ."— that left him soft. For all the larynx-scraping vocals, Cobain was an old softy. "Seasons in the Sun," Terry Jacks's sappy, mellow 1974 hit, made him cry. The tragedy of Cobain's drug use is that it compromised his rage. Nirvana had great rage. Their name was an assault on the boomer generation's hubris and easy idealism, which the boomers had thrown under the bus en masse once they hit their thirties and started wanting bigger decks and longer vacations. The *Nevermind* buzz saw "Territorial Pissings" opens with Novoselic intoning the old Youngbloods lyrics: "Come on people now / Smile on your brother / Everybody get together / Try to love one another righttttttt nowwwwwww . . ."

Heroin was not a hippie drug, which is part of why it found such favor as the boomers ceded their culture power to the Xers. Nirvana smashing up their equipment was, at its core, another healthy and cathartic outlet for the good rage. Once it became shtick and everyone and their brother was watching, Cobain grew self-conscious and sedentary. Robbed of this release, he did more and more dope.

His marriage and parenthood was a fuck-you to the boomers as well. When he hooked up with Love, they almost immediately began nesting. Love's own parents were boomer nightmares, her father a Grateful Dead flunkie.

"I wouldn't wear a tie-dyed T-shirt unless it was dyed with the urine of Phil Collins and the blood of Jerry Garcia," Cobain once quipped. Only there didn't seem to be any glee in that statement, and during the course of the interview, Love calls him out for having planned that line.

Cobain never once seemed to take a moment to be proud or to enjoy his success. He doesn't even look like he's enjoying wearing a giant yellow prom dress on MTV's *Headbangers Ball*. It seems like some kind of duty, yet another token mea culpa for Olympia. "I think he was a constant ball of stress and pressure from the get-go once his band hit the super mainstream," says director Dave Markey. "In my film you see him smiling and having a good time on that tour in the summer of 1991. He was just a member of Nirvana. He wasn't the tortured artist and the media figure that he became, MTV's spokesman of a generation."

Kurt Cobain cherished Beat Happening's *Jamboree*. He even had the K Records shield tattooed on the top of his left forearm. When asked why, he told a reporter it was to "remind [him] to stay a child." What makes the rise of Nirvana both Twee culture's greatest triumph and biggest tragedy is Cobain's inability to accept that he was really never meant to remain Indie. He was simply too ambitious, too talented, and, with his humble origins in the tiny harborside city of Aberdeen, over a hundred miles from Seattle, too much of an outsider to ever remain very comfortable once he found his way in. Whether the suspicion that his actions came to be regarded with was actual or a by-product of his deep insecurity and drug-induced paranoia doesn't matter; he lacked the defenses to process it all, and it did him in. Part of him must have hated Olympia. Part of him would have taken them all with him if he could. There were no half measures with Calvin Johnson and his scene. While the K Records founder personally liked Cobain, and acknowledged that his band wrote great songs once they left Sub Pop for Geffen Records, they were part of the problem. "If a band that is operating on an independent level becomes really popular, there's really no difference between them and Janet Jackson and Justin Timberlake. They're just another band on a major label. It doesn't affect the underground. The underground is always going to be doing its own weird thing," Johnson says. It's kind of like the scene in *Goodfellas* where Paulie, the boss, hands the beleaguered Henry Hill a bankroll and says, "Now I'm gonna have to turn my back on you." It's not that Nirvana was no longer respected as musicians. It's the fact that they were slagged by Olympia after they became the biggest band in the world that so troubled Cobain; it's that they no longer *counted* to the people who mattered most to him.

Billy Corgan, of Smashing Pumpkins, arguably as talented a songwriter as Cobain and, fortunately for him, coated with an extra layer of Teflon, issued a sort of preemptive strike against the Indie scene with "Cherub Rock," the scene-scathing lead track off the Chicago quartet's major-label debut, *Siamese Dream*. So when Pixies and Nirvana producer Steve Albini dismissed them as careerists (actually, "pandering sluts" was the phrase he used in a letter to the *Chicago Reader,* printed in January of '94), it was actually only a rebuttal.

When people turned to him to actually hear what this generational spokesperson had to say, more often than not Cobain deflected attention to other, less popular bands. Nirvana didn't tour with their label mates once they started playing major venues, but took Japanese cutecore band Shonen Knife out instead. They did a split single with the Jesus Lizard. Cobain name-checked the Vaselines in the press, calling Eugene Kelly and Frances McKee "the Lennon and McCartney of the underworld." They covered three Meat Puppets songs at their *MTV Unplugged* taping and brought the Meat Puppets out to play them. Even Daniel Johnston, the mentally ill singer-songwriter from Austin, Texas, was offered a major-label deal with Elektra (the Pixies' label) thanks in part to Cobain wearing a promotional T-shirt for his *Hi, How Are You* album in press photos. Alas, Johnston ultimately declined the offer, as he feared that Elektra act Metallica was in cahoots with Satan and was going to kill him. (He would sign with Atlantic instead.)

"Kurt felt he had to compensate by saying, 'No, I'm into the Raincoats,' whenever he was asked. He existed in a realm very far outside the small music scene we started, so it became more important to assert the things he asserted," says Nils Bernstein, a friend and one-time publicist for Sub Pop. "You don't have to assert that you like the Raincoats when you're sitting around my house listening to the Raincoats. But when you're talking to a bunch of asshole frat guys that are fighting in your audience in an arena, then it becomes really important to talk about the Raincoats."

Cobain's self-consciousness converted, in the face of his knuckle-head audience, to an equally joyless sense of duty, and at the end of a long day of campaigning for the causes he believed in—gay rights, women's rights—who wouldn't want to unwind with a bag of dope? "At this point I have a request for our fans," Cobain wrote in the scathing liner notes to the post-*Nevermind* compilation *Incestsicide*. "If any of you in any way hate homosexuals, people of different color, or women, please do this one favor for us—leave us the fuck alone!"

Cobain, though physiologically more attuned to remain a little prince, was duty bound to become instead a real-life catcher in the rye, keeping the kids from going over the cliff as they ran with a kind of freedom he aspired to but could never quite keep.

When Nirvana played "Smells Like Teen Spirit" on the UK's *Top of the Pops,* eight years after the Smiths' historic debut, Cobain, clad in shades, sang the song as a dour, histrionic crooning, supposedly in tribute to Morrissey. As with Mozzer, the Nirvana leader enjoyed a good cardigan (he is wearing one in the *MTV Unplugged in New York* session) and a requited love affair with the British press—which might have also resulted in his undoing. It seemed nobody, not even the most hardened British journos, wanted to take him to task. Too much was riding on his benevolence. Now, in the years before the brothers Gallagher and Damon Albarn, the British music press finally had a new figure, the first since Morrissey, who sold papers every single time he was on the cover. "My body wouldn't allow me to take drugs if I wanted to, because I'm so weak all the time," Cobain insisted. And yet he was telegraphing his addiction left and right, recording an album with William Burroughs and showing up for interviews pin-eyed only to be described as "shockingly thin."

In today's ultra-scrutinizing, 24/7 media cycle, Cobain would be hazed straight into rehab and no dealer with a sense of self-preservation would go within fifty paces of him. But at the time, he was wink-winked into what became a deep and ultimately fatal addiction. I'm not saying *N.M.E.* killed him. I have been on tour with bands and watched them ingest drugs, then submitted features in which none of that behavior appears and is only alluded to. Nobody wants to be the narc at the party, especially after *Vanity Fair*'s Lynn Hirschberg drew so much ire for her profile of Love. Cobain might have benefited from a few more finks. At the behest of Courtney Love, he turned to R.E.M.'s Michael Stipe for some kind of answer. Stipe, the godfather to Cobain's daughter, Frances Bean, even planned to lure him to Athens to record a collaboration in an effort to get him to clean up. Nirvana hired Pixies producer Steve Albini as some kind of reclamation of their identity, recording the decidedly skronky *In Utero* as a sort of course correction back to the land of the Indie kids, where one could take "comfort" in feeling sad, as he sang on "Frances

Farmer Will Have Her Revenge upon Seattle." Cobain's own revenge was not satisfying enough to keep him from harm. He didn't trust himself as a husband or a father. He didn't even really know who or what he was anymore. "This whole [Indie] thing is based on a lack of commerciality," says Bernstein. "If it's the biggest band in the world, is it Indie anymore?" Perhaps it never really was.

"[With] most of the music that's underground, there's a temptation to say, 'Oh, I was into them before anybody,'" says Calvin Johnson, "but most of the music that we were into at KAOS and Sub Pop was never even going to be popular. It's not like, 'I was into Devo and their first single on an independent label.' It's, 'I was into this weird band on an independent label and they're still on an independent label—and they're never going to be anything else because they're too weird.'"

Today, that question—"Is it Indie?"—is almost never asked. In the years since his suicide in April of 1994, Nirvana's power over the young, like the Smiths', has not waned even as the reasons for his death seem more and more senseless. Cred is no longer an issue anymore; the great conflicts that the Clash and Rage Against the Machine wrestled with as major-label artists are moot. There are teens who love Nirvana and have absolutely no idea that at one point their leader fretted, Hamlet-like, about the band's fate.

The line between major and Indie labels is all but erased when a band on Merge can sell hundreds of thousands of copies and debut at number one on the *Billboard* charts. It's as if Cobain died from a disease called "cred" that we now have a vaccine for. "We're in a post-cred world," says local singer/songwriter Sean Nelson. "Culturally there's no such thing anymore. If you're under thirty, the idea of selling out simply does not exist. Who gives a shit?"

If great bands have unspoken contracts with their audiences, they are almost obliged to break them if they are going to grow. Bob Dylan going "electric" at Newport in '65 was a breaking of a contract with the folk community. John Lennon marrying Yoko Ono broke another. And would either have been the figure they were today if they hadn't? Nirvana remaining in Olympia, pretending to be the less-gifted Tad or even Mudhoney, would have been the true act of dishonesty and betrayal.

"When big Indie bands started going to major labels, it was very divisive. It does seem quaint now—our favorite bands playing bars instead of all-ages clubs and charging ten dollars instead of five. There were major cries of 'sellout,'" says Slim Moon. "There are people in their mid-forties who've forgotten that they were once mad at Sonic Youth for signing to Geffen."

Like Joy Division, the Modern Lovers, the Clash, and the Smiths, Nirvana can never disappoint. They can never break their contract, never issue a shitty album or do a silly concert film. They are perfect in death. When asked about Cobain, Morrissey told a journalist, "I admire people who self-destruct. They're refusing to continue with unhappiness, which shows tremendous self-will. It must be very frightening to sit down and look at your watch and think, in thirty minutes I would not be here." Or maybe it's that K Records tattoo, after all, that endears, and will forever. The struggle to stay pure when all around you there are temptations and pressures is something teens of any generation can relate to. "Nirvana has become the symbol for a lot of kids who are experiencing angst for the first time," Tavi Gevinson told me in 2011, the year that *Nevermind* turned twenty and Kurt Cobain would have turned forty-four. "They want to make themselves over the way that teenagers constantly feel they have to."

"Kurt amplified the Indie-Twee sensibility in an American sense. He created the American version of the great revolutionary figures like Ian Curtis and Morrissey," adds the journalist Paul Morley. "These people managed to pull off being icons without being sentimental icons. They did it by evolving elements of a female side and an intellectual side as well as their musical side. Brooklynization gained much more momentum because of Kurt."

Chapter 10

Do Something Pretty While You Can

In which Glasgow rises again: an improbably superstar group combines the fetishes of 1960s pop with '80s Indie, and, in the midst of Cool Britannia and coke-and-lad culture, the diffident and often reluctant Belle and Sebastian become the first true pop cult in a decade. Meanwhile the Internet (slowly) replaces the diary as the mode of expression for bedroom-bound Twees.

I'm not as sad as Dostoyevsky. I'm not as clever as Mark Twain. I'll only buy a book for the way it looks. And then I'll stick it on the shelf again." So went a memorable line from "This Is Just a Modern Rock Song," an early standout by Belle and Sebastian.

Kurt Cobain never lived to see Belle and Sebastian, who formed in 1996, two years after his suicide, but he almost surely would have had a chuckle at those lyrics from their wry, somewhat tongue-in-cheek bit of self-mythology. Cobain, after all, was the one who shoved his guitar into Super 8 filmmaker/Nirvana tour documentarian Dave Markey's camera during a solo and said, "This is a blues scale in E." When he was asked who his favorite authors were, Cobain said, "Burroughs, Beckett, Bukowski . . . you know, the B's."

Cobain didn't live to see the Internet take much of a hold of the greater imagination, either. But both for those who remembered Nirvana and those who discovered them after the fact, Belle and Sebastian were *the* band. They are the superstars of Twee, especially for the kids of the Internet age—really, the ultimate band for the kids who knew, more and more, what they should know and read and watch and listen to. Remember, Twee was and remains the hardest movement to credibly join. Applicants have to be on their toes, and here was the first band since Nirvana to seriously popularize not only themselves but also their tastes. Belle and Sebastian not only wore their pop-cultural tastes on their sleeves, they also *placed* them on their record sleeves. They wrote songs about them as well. Ordinarily such fandom among bands, whose motive is usually to get fans for themselves, can seem like a gimmick or a kind of faux deference. But one gets the feeling Belle and Sebastian were forced into existence by the fervor of listening to records and reading books alone, or perhaps sneaking off to the cinema for a revival. Would-be record-company head Stefano D'Andrea and his longtime friend and eventual partner Mark Jones were forced to do some pushing as well.

D'Andrea and Jones cofounded Jeepster Records with little money, a one-room office in the Camelot Center in West London with a few dozen eager scouts looking to make some money to go out and bring back the next cool thing. Jeepster, named for a T. Rex hit, had a roster of exactly: zero.

Friends since their teens, Jones and D'Andrea knew what they liked:

Reed, Bowie, and Ian Curtis. What they would get from these scouts was one Blur and Oasis sound-alike after another. These were the heady, coked-up, Union Jack–bedraped Britpop days when even a band like Pulp, who'd been skimming the surface for nearly fifteen years, could now headline a massive festival. Sometimes they'd find one band and get excited, only to learn that their one good song was . . . their one good song. They cast their net far outside of London as well, to Wales, the north of England, and Scotland, which yielded one four-song demo by a band that was at the time answering to the odd, American name Rhode Island. Can't you see it on a marquee?

"We thought all four songs were as good as each other," D'Andrea says today. "We hadn't heard anything in trolling around the country that was like this. It reminded us of other things but we couldn't put our fingers on it."

To listen to early Belle and Sebastian for the first time is to be perplexed and beguiled as you are almost challenged to spot the reference, whether it's a horn riff reminiscent of Love, a lyrical shout-out to the Left Banke, preglitter T. Rex, predisco Bee Gees, Lee Hazlewood and Nancy Sinatra's trippy duets, Burt Bacharach's elegant bachelor-pad pop, Donovan, Nick Drake, Bowie, Roxy Music, or 1980s Indie greats like Orange Juice and the Smiths. To make it swing without feeling like a pastiche was a good trick, and Belle and Sebastian were able to do it not only with minimal effort but also with a lack of concern for whether or not anybody else would respond. Or if it was even worth it to investigate. It wasn't DIY, it was DIYY—Do It Yourself . . . Yawn.

"We heard it once and then we went up to Glasgow and we found that Rhode Island wasn't even a band. They didn't have enough people in it to be a band. They weren't even called Rhode Island anymore,"

D'Andrea says. "They'd changed their name to Belle and Sebastian but were just an assemblage of musicians and café denizens who sometimes gathered to play at the Stow College music room. We found ourselves in the position to try to encourage the whole thing into formation. It was much earlier in the process than we thought—but the songs were fully formed."

While physically little more than a tape and a name, spiritually Belle and Sebastian the band were already beginning to create a complex myth around themselves, and a powerful sensibility built for endurance well beyond the bedroom fantasy realm. Murdoch populated this dream universe with fictional characters that seemed at once alive and familiar as they entered his songs. He gave them all proper names, as Lou Reed had done with Candy or Ray Davies had done with Lola. Murdoch himself could have been one of his characters, had he not created them with his pen. He was pale and handsome in a way that made him seem simultaneously athletic and sickly. He had a front man's charisma but the shy, even mischievous behind-the-scenes manner of a young Brian Wilson. Time he had spent housebound after a serous bout of chronic fatigue syndrome had forced him to be prolific and populate his room with friends both imaginary and real. While recovering, Murdoch would walk the city or ride buses and observe people passing by, living their lives, and record them in his notebooks, giving them stories, dreams, secrets, and shame.

"Riding on city buses for a hobby is sad," he admits in the lyrics to "The State I Am In," which would later be the first song on the first Belle album, *Tigermilk*.

Here was an outsider, naturally so, fascinated by those who were plugged into the rhythm of the city. These Glaswegians didn't know or care that Murdoch was studying them, and that they would be incorporated into pop songs. They largely ignored the odd, skinny young man with his furiously moving pen.

Murdoch set these lyrics to organic, handmade sounds, dark and folky. The songs became open and dreaming enough to host a wide variety of styles. The talent pool among the musicians, and especially Murdoch, was huge. It simply required a kind of superconfidence that needed a little coaxing to the forefront and, eventually, to the stage.

"He looked like a real star to us," says D'Andrea, "just physically—kind of brooding and a bit moody." But he had a tough streak, stubborn and suspicious like many of the Glaswegians we profiled a bit earlier when faced with eager record-industry (albeit Indie) folks up from London. "He didn't suffer fools gladly. I think he was prepared to have a fight with anyone who wanted to put his records out because he had such a fully formed idea of how he wanted them to look—how he wanted them to sound—the way he wanted to do things and the things he didn't want to do."

When Jones and D'Andrea encountered Belle's other star, the winsome Isobel Campbell, with her girly barrettes in her straight blond hair, they knew they had something in her as well. Campbell would soon help perpetuate that Twee fashion archetype, indebted to the Nouvelle Vague heroines and still mimicked by a few thousand young women every year to this day: a well-read, cultured, and liberated woman who could turn on a dime and be girlish without pushing aside her integrity as a musician or her feminine strength. Still, video footage of her proudly holding C. S. Lewis's *The Chronicles of Narnia* is akin to Twee porn.

"She was really important," D'Andrea says of Isobel. "People assumed she was just a muse to Stuart, but she had a lot more to her than that, and she quickly became a bit of an Indie goddess to the young record-buying public." Usually when Indie rock produced a woman this crush worthy, she was almost obliged to be a tomboy in the Kim Deal mode, a hellion like Courtney Love and PJ Harvey, or an intellectual like Liz Phair. Campbell was unique to the 1990s, equal parts swingin' '60s muse, Sarah Records–style cutie pie, and femme fatale.

While the early "This Is Just a Modern Rock Song" is an origin story, Belle and Sebastian seemed, to the Londoners, content to merely exist in a fantasy realm, a band on diary paper or sketch-pad page. "They made no effort," says D'Andrea. "They felt, 'If it's good enough, people will contact us. If you have to go and ram it down someone's throat and tell them how good something is, then it's probably not that good.' That was Stuart's way of looking at it."

Ironically, while not planning their career, they kept about meticulously designing it. Murdoch already had the sleeve concept for what would come to be their debut, *Tigermilk:* it shows a woman nursing a stuffed tiger toy, a bit literal but evocative of the Smiths sleeves and hard to ignore. The liner notes, printed up by the band, elaborated on the origin story of Stuart (Sebastian) meeting Campbell (Belle, an actual nickname of hers, and kismet once Murdoch found out). It was largely based on their actual encounter.

"He had placed an advert in the local supermarket," Murdoch writes, cannily investing fans in the band by offering them a backstory rendered with the same level of wit, wistfulness, and preciousness as the lyrics. "He was looking for musicians. Belle saw him do it." In reality the pair met on New Year's Eve, 1995 into 1996, at a DJ set by Orange Juice's Edwyn Collins, then a decade into his solo career.

They were dancing in a transvestite bar called Gillespie's and quickly began courting each other. Murdoch, shaky still from his convalescence, was smitten, and later exchanged letters with Campbell and soon began playing her the songs he'd written in his bedroom or on those bus rides around town. Campbell didn't need to learn anything. She was a record collector as well, wrote her own songs, and played the cello.

"It was strange. Sebastian had just decided to become a one-man band. It is always when you least expect it that something happens. Sebastian had befriended a fox because he didn't expect to have any new friends for a while."

The extremely patient Jeepster would not be able to issue *Tigermilk* until 1999, even though it was ready to go and clearly a world beater of a debut. Belle and Sebastian had refused, instead allowing Glasgow's Stow College label Electric Honey to issue one thousand vinyl copies. As a bone, they promised Jeepster "the next record," with the hapless label heads never hearing any music and having no way of knowing that that album, also almost completely written, would become an all-time British Indie classic, on par with *The Queen Is Dead* by the Smiths and the self-titled debuts by the Stone Roses and the La's.

But first let's travel back for a moment, to those innocent days when one couldn't simply steal something musical with a click. The sheer scarcity of *Tigermilk* thickened out the already carefully constructed Belle and Sebastian myth for the increasingly intrigued public. The band doesn't appear on the cover. Who were Belle and Sebastian? A folk duo? Who was making this gorgeous, erudite, gentle but wry music? It was impossible to hear "The State I Am In," "She's Losing

It," "We Rule the School" (embedded with a sort of early ethos or statement of band-purpose: "Do something pretty while you can"), and the hilarious, heartbreaking "I Don't Love Anyone" ("No, not even Christmas . . . maybe my sister") without putting down your pint or your book and asking, "What is this?"

"We helped them distribute it and send it to people," D'Andrea says of *Tigermilk*. Of the thousand copies printed, Stow College kept two hundred, and two hundred were sent to tastemakers. "Influential people we could think of in Britain and America," he clarifies. Recipients included Seymour Stein, the legendary Sire Records founder. "We thought we'd get a licensing deal in America," D'Andrea says. "That this music would go down well." A copy went to Morrissey. Others were sent to reputable Indie shops in London like Rough Trade. An original copy of *Tigermilk* today will likely cost you more than a Vespa scooter, but at the time, many of these offerings went straight into the bin, ignored.

"Most people looked at this thing and said, 'Why don't you send me a tape? Why'd you send me an LP?' We thought they'd be charmed by that," D'Andrea says. One who certainly was charmed was Mark Radcliffe, an influential DJ at BBC's Radio One, who played the album once and instantly received more late-night calls than he'd ever had before.

If you happened to live in Brooklyn in 1996 instead of London, Belle and Sebastian's debut was just as explosive as Oasis's *Definitely Maybe*. If you lived just about anywhere else, you probably never heard of Belle and Sebastian unless you were a cool college kid with a good dial-up connection. And if you owned an original copy, you owned it on vinyl and knew you were one of just one thousand to be able to touch it. Most people only had a bootlegged tape. Still, in the twilight of the pre-Internet era there were parties designed specifically for the communal listening of *Tigermilk,* which seemed in itself to be a part of Murdoch's master plan. A new cult was born around the band, and the fact that nobody could see them and they refused to tour only fed the fervor. "It was like back in the Sex Pistols days," says D'Andrea. "You couldn't see them live, so you wondered."

Inspired and excited by the buzz, Jeepster tried to plead one final time to the band, "'You could license it to us and we can put out a decent amount of records!'" D'Andrea recalls. "'Oh, no,'" came the reply. "'We've already gone on to the next one.'"

The second album, which was briefly going to be called *Cock Fun,* was built on what was already a key Belle and Sebastian formula. Murdoch's voice, clean, sad, a little acid, is at the top of the mix, speaking directly into your ear like a good friend. "It's about capturing somebody's attention and keeping it," he has said of the mix. At times these were pop songs. Others featured only a piano backing, as on "Fox in the Snow." Whereas Oasis's third album, *Be Here Now,* filled every empty space in the sound mix with a wailing guitar solo or helicopter special effects, feedback, and drums, this was just the opposite. *Be Here Now* was an inflated, coked-out monster and has been credited with killing Cool Britannia in one bite, a cyanide capsule of unrealized potential. Belle and Sebastian, Britpop's gentle antithesis act, wouldn't even release a single from their second album, now titled *If You're Feeling Sinister,* and remained faceless, almost invisible. *Sinister* did land them a deal for American distribution with Matador Records, but this didn't alter the band's approach to engaging with the media, whose curiosity was now fevered.

"Shops phoned us directly try to find out something about the band," D'Andrea recalled. "They kept reordering *Sinister*, which was now selling a couple thousand copies a month—not doing any promotion, just by being out there and people talking about it." Murdoch had been proven right. If you are good enough, they will come to you.

For every fan who ached over piano ballads like "Fox in the Snow" or spine-stiffening anthems such as "Dylan in the Movies" and sad relationship status reports such as "Seeing Other People," Belle and Sebastian's unapologetic preciousness inspired the kind of hate and backlash that the Smiths faced the decade before and that Coldplay would reckon with at the beginning of the new decade. Recall this exchange from the Stephen Frears and John Cusack adaptation of Nick Hornby's *High Fidelity:*

Barry: Holy Shiite. What the fuck is that?
Dick: It's the new Belle and Sebastian.
Rob: It's a record we've been listening to and enjoying, Barry.
Barry: Well, that's unfortunate, because it sucks *ass*.

Zeitgeist-wise, Belle had favor, though: there was an electric renaissance in full swing by the end of the 1990s, a disparate scattering of rock snobs, geeks, and losers now aligned via the still primitive, mostly dial-up Internet. Once online, they would rally (or spar over) the likes of Belle and Sebastian or other stubborn, precocious artists like Beck or Radiohead, who had wisely ditched Britpop much in the way that Bowie ditched glam twenty years earlier in favor of future music. *OK Computer* made jaws drop. *If You're Feeling Sinister* made hearts flutter. Still trapped in their bedrooms, often slaves to their parents' phone kibitzing, the geeks were inheriting a whole new virtual world. Slowly these small and rather dinky networks of music obsessives grew more and more sophisticated.

Spearheading this movement toward a kind of digital music-geek salon was a working-class kid living with his parents beyond the Minneapolis city limits, working and sometimes loitering in record stores and listening to Meat Beat Manifesto through his headphones. His name was Ryan Schreiber, and he was perhaps the modern age's first fan-as-prodigy. His talent was his ardor.

"Music at that point was already my whole world and my whole life," Schreiber says, "before I was able to speak. My earliest memories were sitting at a record player and listening to the records my family would bring me. I did have some friends, but my fonder memories were watching MTV and listening to Top 40 countdowns. My parents really worried there was something wrong with me. I'd be in my bedroom and they wouldn't see me all day."

Schreiber had just graduated from high school and spent his time buried in music magazines, fanzines, and any info about bands from alt-weeklies that he could pick up in his local coffee shop or record store, his favorite being Cheapo Records, where he'd sometimes try to dub new releases in their listening booths with a smuggled cassette but was usually busted by the management. Still, he spent so much of his allowance at the store that the owners couldn't afford to ban him: more often than not he left with the newest issue of whatever music publications came in that week.

"I always obsessively consumed them," he says. "And I noticed that a lot of these zines had interviews with some of the artists that I was really into." Schreiber was also lucky enough to have a local radio station (KJ 105) that played British Indie, like My Bloody Valentine and the Jesus and Mary Chain: "I was educating myself on this music." At the time, you could still be considered a bit of a freak for liking this stuff. "I wasn't the most popular kid in high school. I was sort of a loner. The music is so readily available now that it's hard to imagine a time where if you listened to Elvis Costello it was a liability."

Schreiber owned a big Mac computer with dial-up and determined that rather than paste and staple his thoughts on pop, it would be faster, cheaper, and more immediate if he placed them on the Web. "I just didn't have any faith in my ability to print and distribute material," he admits.

He learned the ins and outs of the nascent Web while working in Down in the Valley, another local record store, and was soon proficient enough to build a site. "At the time, there was nothing at all on the Web dedicated to Indie music. [There were] some fan pages for artists but none of them were trying to be publications," he says. "I really wanted to make the site into an actual zine. I started writing record reviews of records I would buy." The only other sites going at the time, Sonicnet and Billboard, were in New York City, with strong ties to the industry. Nobody was sending Schreiber, out in the Midwest, anything at all.

The site, originally called Turntable, launched in earnest in the fall of '95 and almost immediately ran out of music to review.

"I actually went in to the Minneapolis Public Library and asked the very nice librarian to look up telephone numbers for me for record labels in New York City. They were very sweet about it." Schreiber would cold-call these companies and explain his situation, and ask for access to their artists as well as new music. Sometimes they would send out promotional CDs; mostly they'd blow him off. "I was realistic about who I would be able to get time with—being an Internet publication was like a novelty to people. Labels didn't even have e-mail addresses yet."

Some forward-thinking Indie bands (Low, Jawbreaker) happily agreed to talk to the enthusiastic and autodidactic nineteen-year-old. "Other people were like, 'You're on the what?' 'I'm on the Internet.' What is that?' Nobody was reading it anyway, so we could do whatever we wanted to do and say whatever we wanted to say with no fear of repercussion."

Only Schreiber's parents suffered, as in order to post on his site their son would often have to engage the phone line for hours on end. "They were so mad. The line I was calling was long distance too." But slowly, instinctively, the kid was building a brand and gaining followers. This became evident when he received a cease-and-desist letter from a company already registered as Turntable. He chose his new name, *Pitchfork*, as a sort of homage to one of his favorite zines, *Puncture*, and the suggestion of an "angry-mob mentality" of people chasing Frankenstein through the streets with "sharp weaponry." He'd see a lot of pitchforks sticking out of hay bales as he drove from the suburbs into the city to see shows. "What solidified it as a sign was watching *Scarface* for the eighth time—in the opening scene they are interrogating him and he has a pitchfork tattoo and they know it means he's an assassin—and so I was like, 'This is so cool.'"

Slowly Schreiber acquired a staff, starting with like-minded soul Jason Josephs and expanding to a skeleton crew of mostly writers with backgrounds at alt-weeklies and decent dial-up connections. "I didn't have any money to pay them. I'd give him free CDs. That ended up being the arrangement with everyone for a while."

Pitchfork was updated monthly, then daily, and by the time Schreiber started receiving comments from people just as obsessed with music, books, and film as he was, he knew, "This is what I want to do with my life." And soon the notorious decimal point, the most Twee and precious of record-rating systems, was born.

While every music-media outlet had its established rating system— the *Village Voice's* Robert Christgau, the self-described "dean" of rock writers, had his letter grades; *Rolling Stone* had its stars; and *Spin*, for a time, its red-to-green color-coding—*Pitchfork* went one step farther, pioneering the decimal system. 6.8? Why not 7? Shit!

"We were looking at all those other rating systems and thinking, how do we make something a little different to distinguish and separate ourselves? We had a ten-point scale and we opted to break it down into decimals so it would be that much more accurate. It's kind of a scientific thing, sort of a gut thing. Reviewing so many records, as we did, we wanted to separate a flat 7 from an 8."

The site went from five hundred readers a day to thirty thousand a year later. "I thought, Well, we can't really get much bigger than this. Yo La Tengo and Built to Spill, these are artists who only sell thirty thousand copies of their records. This is the whole world. Today it's like five million visitors a month." It's also become shorthand for a kind of Brooklandian obsession with new music and obscure cult bands. There's an annual festival, feature-length documentaries, and as of the summer of 2013, a sister site, the Dissolve, devoted to film geeks. It's even been parodied on the Indie-Twee-skewering sketch show *Portlandia*, the ultimate honorific. The site is precious and essential as responsible as Napster and file sharing for putting down the big, bloated print magazines one after another, leaving only *Rolling Stone* and *N.M.E.* standing.

As the Web became more accessible, it turned into a sort of global bedroom for the burgeoning Twee Tribe. Now lonely people obsessed with bands, books, films, and art could find each other and pair off in a blink. Even analog forms were reaching out beyond the metropolises: public radio stations like Chicago's WBEZ produced *This American Life*, which began national syndication in 1996. This weekly story-driven show applied the same outsider-observing-life approach that became a kind of "What a Wonderful World" for Indie kids that wasn't saccharine or repellently chilly. There was sadness in the voice of host Ira Glass that was probably reflexive, but that made him seem invested—not only in the subject but in the weirdness of the "American life" too. Glass seemed big brotherly and became a friend to millions as the decade wore on; someone they would never meet like Morrissey or Stuart Murdoch but someone who knew them, and whom they felt they knew as well. Its thematic shows soon bred its own roster of Twee Tribe heroes, personal essayists like David Sedaris and Sarah Vowell, herself a former college Indie-rock radio DJ.

"Music was important in that subculture, but it wasn't all-important. Elvis Costello was God, but so was Kurt Vonnegut," says Vowell of this new world in which technology seemed to be surging by the minute, taking away the very notion of obscurity and cultishness with every inch it gained.

Chapter 11

Sic Transit Gloria

1996–2001

In which moviegoers are given an alternative to the established Indie-film tropes of gunfire and pop-referencing quips of the Tarantino variety, and another great 1990s auteur emerges as the quintessential Twee director and, stylistically, the constructor of his own self-contained cinematic universe, one that addresses, again and again, the coming storm of adulthood and the passing of time.

Another wave, as influential as the Nouvelle Vague, came in the 1990s with regard to cinema and produced a half dozen or so highly influential auteurs and one bona fide superstar to rival Quentin Tarantino, who, let's be frank, led his own one-man wave that was as anti-Twee as possible (save, to be fair, a bin-digging series of soundtracks).

From slight, bespectacled Todd Solondz's *Welcome to the Doll-house* in 1995 through Wes Anderson's *Bottle Rocket,* Whit Stillman's trilogy-closing *The Last Days of Disco,* and Sofia Coppola's *The Virgin Suicides,* from the polarizing (the cutesy-poo French farce *Amélie* and the often powerful, sometimes cringingly precious Miranda July debut *Me and You and Everyone We Know*) to the near unanimously acclaimed (*The Squid and the Whale*), these films defined a certain collective shriek that would resonate for a decade and find favor with directors from both the super-low-budget mumblecore school, profiled a bit later, and the Hollywood-studio-approved Judd Apatow conglomerate of actors and filmmakers. The noise was a reaction, primal but still somehow polite, to the simple passing of time as well as the question: What does one do when the body ages and yearns and grows and becomes less beautiful, and the world does the same? Simply, how do you, in the words of Belle and Sebastian, "do something pretty while you can," when you are acutely aware that the hourglass has been turned over?

"We'll be forty in five years. Forty is basically fifty, and then after that, the rest is just loose change," spacey, kinky-haired Hamish Linklater frets in Miranda July's 2011 film, *The Future*.

"What the fuck is going on?" Ben Stiller rages at his aging body and coming irrelevance in writer-director Noah Baumbach's *Greenberg*, released the previous year.

Even rugged matinee idol George Clooney's titular Mr. Fox in Anderson's stop-motion animated adaptation of Roald Dahl's *The Fantastic Mr. Fox* (2009) doesn't want to stop his youthful practice of stealing chickens even though it's become a threat to his safety. "In the end, we all die, unless you change," his wife, voiced by Meryl Streep, warns him.

"*Sic transit gloria,*" as Max Fischer says in *Rushmore*, which we will get to in a little bit: a Latin term for "Thus passes the glory (of the world)." Fischer saves Rushmore Academy's Latin program, but nobody is spared from Father Time: he's the shark or the giant gorilla or the vampire in these "monster movies." And his victims aren't always human. Ways of life, modes of behavior, and in the case of Anderson's latest film, 2014's *The Grand Budapest Hotel*, once elegant Old World palaces, are prone to falling into "shabby decay."

They are all, in their own ways, as angry and defiant as Peter Fonda and Dennis Hopper in *Easy Rider* or Joe Buck in *Midnight Cowboy*. They simply don't know what to do with that anger. "Bottle up and explode," as Elliott Smith sang. That was one option. It was like every film became an Indie-rock version of Laurence Kasdan's *The Big Chill* overnight, and instead of Motown, we got Smith and his sulky brethren to score them.

In the main, the mid-'90s saw an ongoing cultural debate about violence in cinema, peaking with the 1994 summer release of *Natural Born Killers,* Oliver Stone's Quentin Tarantino–penned, kaleidoscopic take on Terrence Malick's *Badlands.* But as with the years after Punk, and artists like Elvis Costello, the most potent form of violence is the roiling, internal kind. It's a quieter mayhem, and it informs just about every Twee hero of this era. Call it "talky violence"—the cinema of Hartley and Stillman, Baumbach and Solondz and Jonze, everyone but Coppola, whose characters don't seem to speak much at all, or Anderson, whose characters are sometimes struck dumb by the enormity of it all. Still, these are characters in states of severe unrest, and instead of shooting, they shoot their mouths off or shut them for prolonged spells to make their points.

"In the nineties, everybody was just nutty about super-violent films," says Whit Stillman, whose debut, the agitated comedy of manners *Metropolitan,* and its follow-up, *Barcelona,* both arrived during the rise of gunfire artists such as Abel Ferrara, Quentin Tarantino, and Robert Rodriguez. Tarantino alone transformed the nature of

"Indie" from the contemplative, deliberately paced, sometimes even spaced-out fare that Jim Jarmusch, Steven Soderbergh, and early Richard Linklater offered to the shoot-a-guy-then-quip thrill rides that were really no different from big-budget action franchises like the Die Hard and Terminator movies—just more clever and helmed by someone with a better record collection. Stillman, a Harvard grad with a background in advertising, was, in his own words, "totally on the outs."

Well, not totally. *Metropolitan,* which concerns the social lives of upper-Manhattan debutantes and the formally dressed escorts who love and use them, met with rave reviews and garnered an Oscar nomination for Best Original Screenplay in 1990. Still, the film seemed out of place somehow, a throwback to the gentler age of Bill Forsyth's early-'80s fare, before bombast was a requirement. The actual Manhattan of the late 1980s and early '90s was at its druggiest and most crime infested under Mayor David Dinkins. In life, New York felt more like *Midnight Cowboy, Mean Streets, The Panic in Needle Park,* and *Cruising* and less like a Rankin/Bass snowy Christmas spectacular— but in Stillman's world, as in Woody Allen's before him, the streets were safe. It was the psyche that was in danger, not the body.

His camera lingers lovingly on "old New York" touchstones like Scribner books, Henri Bendel, the Doubleday building, the Plaza Hotel, and, of course, the tree at Rockefeller Center. Stillman's characters, rosy cheeked and clad in Brooks Brothers and J.Press when not in tuxes, don't talk like WASPs with sticks up their asses. They rant and whine just like Woody Allen heroes. This endeared them to a loyal but small audience, and set up one of the crucial tropes in Twee cinema: relatability. It also, unsurprisingly, left others at a loss. They are films that require the patience of a novel-reader.

There's a pivotal scene in *Metropolitan* in which Chris Eigeman's Nick Smith walks with a pal down a city street at night, dressed in the full formal wear he and his young compatriots have grown comfortable in: top hat, tails, the works. This being a Stillman snow globe, there's no chance of being mugged. Nick looks both elegant and ridiculous, not quite a man despite his attire, and not quite an overgrown boy dressing up, either, but rather stuck in between. As he goes, he and his pal happen upon a box left out on the sidewalk for sanitation pickup. Nick stoops to inspect the contents and is mortified to discover that what he considers treasure has been deemed refuse: Steiff stuffed animals, an Aurora model car set, and a pristine Derringer pop gun.

"Do you remember the Derringer craze?" he asks his pal. "It's incredible the things some people throw away! The childhood of our generation is represented here and they're just throwing it out!"

Twenty years later, the same emotions are visited in the Oscar-nominated blockbuster *Toy Story 3,* only this time from the point of view of the discarded toys themselves. "We're all just trash waiting to be thrown away, that's all a toy is," says Lots-o'-Huggin' Bear.

The passing of time, without religion (and if these characters have a religion, it's pop culture itself, which prizes, as we know, all things young), can make people wise, but it can also make them mean. The marginal popularity of these films, beyond certain critics, comes down to the fact that their auteurs are unafraid to create a character who is, quite simply, a dick—from Eigeman in *Metropolitan* to Ben Stiller in Baumbach's *Greenberg* nearly twenty years later.

"When I read [the script], I always thought of that character as just the kind of guy who threatened me in high school," says Eigeman. "The unbreakable resilience of his arrogance. The dominance of his personality. In a way, Nick is a bully. This is a guy where you kind of want to be in his orbit, but you're also kind of scared to be in his orbit, because he could turn on you just as quickly."

Hence, the way these characters express themselves—in Stillman's films and later in many of Baumbach and Anderson's—can be construed as snappish. "Generally, they're kind of arch," says producer Joel Kastelberg, who worked on Baumbach's first two films, *Kicking and Screaming* (1995) and *Mr. Jealousy* (1997). "It can be off-putting to people who want a little more sugar in their experience. There's a wry, knowing quality to those guys in person and in their work, and it might be offensive to some people." These are characters in serious pain, well aware that an actual time-machine-style return to their childhood is no cure. Grade school, junior high, and high school were cruel too.

If there was an antidote to the perils-of-adulthood subgenre, it came from an unlikely place in the mid-'90s. *Fast Times at Ridgemont High* director Amy Heckerling wrote and directed a smash in the form of the aforementioned *Clueless* in the summer of 1995. It depicted a new kind of enlightened, post-*Heathers*, post-Nirvana popular kid: Cher Horowitz, played by Alicia Silverstone, and her best friend Dionne (Stacey Dash). Both characters were named for "great '60s singers who now do infomercials," as Cher says in her voice-over narration. Cher has her hormones in check and her shit together despite a dead mother and an emotionally absent father. "Hymenally challenged," she is saving her virginity for Luke Perry and is more motivated by the state of her soul than the churning in her teenage body. *Clueless* is not without commentary and certainly not without charm. The high school hallways are full of girls with bandaged noses, dozens of them, but Cher, egged on by her complaint-rock-listening stepbrother, Josh (played by Paul Rudd), is determined to leave the superficial behind and devote herself to performing good deeds: sharing her fancy coffee with her teacher, buying takeout for her hard-boiled father. Her greatest challenge: making over the "adorably clueless" Tai Frasier, a fashion-challenged transfer student played by the late Brittany Murphy. Still, the world of *Clueless* is a fantasy; loosely based on the Jane Austen novel *Emma*, it's a pretty fable when compared to that same year's primal scream, *Welcome to the Dollhouse*, a junior high exposé that feels more like *The Road Warrior*.

Directed by Todd Solondz, who is consistently the darkest, bravest, and funniest of the '90s Twee Tribe filmmakers, *Dollhouse*, like *The Breakfast Club* before it, asks the logical "Why?" in the face of student-on-student brutality, but it offers no easy, hopeful answers. When his chubby, bespectacled, hopeless-case heroine Dawn Wiener (Heather Matarazzo) gets in trouble for beating up a school bully, she justifies it to her horrid mother by claiming that she was only fighting back. "Whoever told you to fight back?" her mother retorts. A boomer, Dawn's mother is absolutely astounded that anyone would ever think to resist the nerd-jock order that marked American high schools and junior highs for decades. Her hair pulled back too tight, her sweater unfashionable, a permanently befuddled expression on her chubby face, Dawn needs a few dozen more allies; and alas, she has none, not even her computer-geek brother. When she endeavors to draft like-minded peers into the "Special People's Club," she's informed that "special people equals retarded. Your club is for retards." Solondz wasn't buying into the Hughes lightness, and had no fear to go pitch-dark.

"I think in parts it was probably a reaction against what I saw on *The Wonder Years*," he says today. "When you make a movie, particularly when you're young, you try to put something fresh out there—something you felt you haven't seen captured before." *Dollhouse* and, more so, the two films that followed it—*Happiness* and *Storytelling*—were raw, fearless, sweet, and subversive tales about what happens when the system releases these schoolyard victims into the real world. *Dollhouse* was a surprise hit, and Dawn Wiener became a sort of Norma Rae figure for nerds. "I think I was moved by her plight," Solondz says of his greatest creation and possible alter ego. "Her flaws and her failures. It endeared me to her. And the reaction [from the public] was unexpected. Even Cindy Crawford said at one point, 'Dawn Wiener, that was me.' It struck some sort of chord."

Belle and Sebastian saw a kindred spirit in Solondz and would later record a soundtrack for *Storytelling,* which turns its eye to the social structure of the American liberal-arts college. "All nine of them came out to Hoboken!" Solondz remembers of Belle and Sebastian, to work on the music.

"I think people saw Dawn as a hero," Solondz says. Especially when contrasted with Cher Horowitz, Dawn Wiener seems so much more tangible. "They started using expressions like 'geek chic,'" Solondz recalls. "Like there was something hip about her and the attitude towards her. But I think certainly 'geek chic' is something that's embraced by people who haven't had that epithet hurled at them." Solondz clearly had, and wasn't buying into it. Still, even though he kills off Dawn (her death is mentioned in his later film *Palindromes*), he hasn't ruled out resurrecting her. He's done so with characters in the past. He's even cast different actors in signature parts, which he may have to do again, as Matarazzo seems to have permanently distanced herself from Dawn. "It's possible the character may reappear at another point," Solondz says. "I did want to bring Heather back, but she emphatically never wanted to play this character ever again. She didn't want the role to define her."

In a way, killing off Dawn was an act of mercy. Many of Solondz's characters simply cannot navigate adulthood. Their misadventures and miseries behind closed doors validate every fear expressed by modern cinema teens. When you grow up, your heart not only dies, it slowly rots first. *Dark Horse,* Solondz's 2011 film, concerns a charmless, bloated man-child (Jordan Gelber) who lives at home, in middle age, with his elderly parents, played by Christopher Walken and Mia Farrow—the latest in a series of major stars who've clamored to work with Solondz since *Dollhouse*—in a room surrounded by vintage toys. "It's a kind of death in life," the director says. "It's also a very class-oriented issue. [Not growing up] is a problem of the privileged in a world that's kind of become a consumerist paradise."

There are those who might look at Twee cinema as the absolute moment that the "strong, silent type," so admired by Tony Soprano was lost forever. John Wayne in *The Man Who Shot Liberty Valance*. Gary Cooper in *High Noon*. The Stillman characters and their offspring in Baumbach and Anderson's films are never silent and never very strong, despite being mostly beautiful on the outside. There's trimness and rosiness to all Twee characters, and usually a hollow, or at least dysfunctional, core.

Baumbach was barely out of college when he returned to the world of academia for *Kicking and Screaming* in 1995, released in the midst of the popularity of 1994's *Reality Bites,* Gen X's first assertion in

Hollywood. That movie featured much bigger stars than Baumbach's, like Winona Ryder and Ethan Hawke, but trod the exact same period of young-adult life.

In order for *Kicking and Screaming* to get financed as a shoestring affair, another movie star, Eric Stoltz (a veteran of Hughes's *Some Kind of Wonderful* and Tarantino's *Pulp Fiction*), had to agree, via a fax sent from Scotland, where he was filming *Rob Roy,* to appear in a small part. That part hadn't even been written. Baumbach would have to pencil in for him the role of Chet, the all-knowing bartender at the local college-town tavern.

"I got the script from Mary-Louise Parker while we were shooting *Naked in New York,*" Stoltz remembers. "She said it was really good—but there were no roles for either of us. So I gave it a read, it's always nice to read something good. Joel Kastelberg was producing, so he arranged a meeting with Noah Baumbach. I thought he seemed a fine fellow, and we agreed I was to play the video clerk. Then I went off to Scotland to shoot *Rob Roy,* and during that summer I got a fax from Noah saying that the original lead of the film had dropped out, and that Trimark—the company financing the film—needed a "name" within a week or they'd pull the money. I wrote back that there was really no lead role that I was appropriate for, and Noah wrote that we could make one up. He came up with Chet, the older guy at the college who never graduates and works as a bartender. I agreed, even though my agents were a little thrown."

The quality of the writing seemed to put the producers at ease despite Baumbach's inexperience. "Noah hadn't been on a film set. He'd never even directed a play. But he had a presence that was inspiring," says Stoltz.

In a way, Baumbach is the poster child for the bedroom scholar who, like Morrissey and Stuart Murdoch, formulated a stance strictly by absorbing and filtering other artists' work. Baumbach's mother, Georgia Brown, and his father, Jonathan Baumbach, were both writers and cinephiles. "Noah was instantly in his element as a director," Stoltz recalls.

"It was a fun set to be on, as everyone was there because they loved the script," Stoltz says. "That's one of the great things about small independent films—since no one is really making any money, the cast and crew tend to be there for the right reasons, and the work often reflects that."

The film's plot concerns a group of recent graduates of a Vassar-like university (Vassar was Baumbach's alma mater) who are reluctant to head out into the world and conquer it. *Kicking and Screaming*'s heroes create a de facto bunker in a cramped, off-campus hut and attack each other like Pinter heroes until, one by one, they break down. Nothing has happened to them to warrant such sadness or hopelessness. They are simply the new, soft men, the first generation who did not have to—and did not know how to—fight.

"I'm nostalgic for conversations I had yesterday," Chris Eigeman's Max complains. "I've begun reminiscing events before they even occur. I'm reminiscing this right now. I can't go to the bar because I've already looked back on it in my memory and I didn't have a good time."

Max is the prototype for the coming generation of tech-propelled young people who want their glories accelerated without the burden of paying any dues. "There's this sort of world-weary pose coupled with being incredibly naïve at the same time," says Eigeman of the character. In another scene, pacing and smoking, he announces, "I wish we were just going off to war."

"I think he's really sincere," Eigeman says of the sentiment. "Those kids really wished the big events of their lives were behind them and not in front of them. It's a pose that's easily adoptable."

As the postgraduates wait, Vladimir-and-Estragon-like, for the love and glory and life that they don't fully believe in to happen to them, they grow listless. Instead of sweeping up a pile of broken glass, Max simply places a hand-drawn sign on it, reading: BROKEN GLASS.

They test each other on useless trivia too, naming the Friday the 13th films in order. "The obsession with trivia is a way of avoiding the bigger questions in life," says Hamilton, who plays the closest thing the film has to a romantic lead. Grover, like Max, is inert, but whereas Max shrugs and muses at his fate, Grover keeps convincing himself that he's all right. The shortcuts he aspires to are not just macro; they are micro too. He is the kind of guy who reads enough of a book to be conversant. Hamilton is such a winning screen presence that Grover is less punchable than he should be when dismissing his girlfriend Jane's sincere desire to explore the newly tourist-friendly, somewhat cliché, Prague. "Oh, I've *been* to Prague," he tells her. When she points out that in actuality, he hasn't left the campus in years, much less visited Prague, he snaps back, "Well, I haven't *been-to-Prague* been to Prague, but I know that thing, I know that 'stop shaving your armpits, read *The Unbearable Lightness of Being*, fall in love with a sculptor, now I realize how bad American coffee is' thing."

The film was only a modest success, although it is now prized as a cult classic.

"There is a whole new wave of people who've found it," says Hamilton, "so obviously whatever it touches upon is not changed. If anything, it's even a bleaker situation, graduating from college now."

As with any artistic trend, Twee doesn't become a movement until it gets its own household name. He arrived in the corduroy-draped, beanpole shape of Wes Anderson.

"I don't know how Wes Anderson does it," says Whit Stillman.

For one thing, he isn't a New Yorker. Anderson was born and raised in Texas. He skirts Hollywood, even though he is a studio filmmaker. As with his musical contemporaries like Belle and Sebastian, he's found a way to make films that are at once indebted to older masters, whether it's Satyajit Ray, Louis Buñuel, Hal Ashby, John Cassavetes, George Lucas, or even the 1980s teen-angst school of John Hughes, *Risky Business,* and *Heathers,* but he has created a cinematic language all his own. He has a signature tempo and rhythm, instantly identifiable like Altman's or Quentin Tarantino's. From all of this, Anderson builds a universe as detailed and signature as that of Orson Welles's early films or George Lucas's *Star Wars.* Everything seems to fit, every detail has a thought behind it; nothing is simply hung or placed in a Wes Anderson movie.

The distinctness of Anderson isn't only down to the way actors speak or what they say: it is also what they don't say. Tarantino fills every frame with noise. Anderson's hushed, haunted, too-smart-to-smile debut *Bottle Rocket* has heroes often staring into the distance, lost in thought and in life. Visually, Anderson is a frame saturator. His films are cluttered and compulsively designed, and as his now classic American Express commercial implies, there's not a detail that hasn't been puzzled through, from a swatch of wallpaper to the right hat. Anderson's father worked in advertising in his native Houston and it's the selling of a vision, almost ad-campaign-like, with a kind of requisite certainty and conviction that has rubbed off. This is why, like Charles and Ray Eames before him, Anderson has always been a sought-after commercial director.

Anderson could not have gotten there without the likes of Stillman, but his alpha stance has afforded him a gift that only Tarantino had previously enjoyed: a seemingly blank check. Tarantino and Anderson are, in this way, the Francis Ford Coppolas of their generation, wildly respected by their peers, with money and power contributing to a kind of gifted-child indulgence that could ruin either of them if they ever missed. But both are fairly crack shots.

Anderson wasn't always a visual maximalist. His beginnings were as DIY and stark as Indie film gets. In its first incarnation, *Bottle Rocket*, a twelve-minute short cowritten with his University of Texas classmate Owen Wilson and shot in 16 mm, was a low-budget black-and-white caper. The soundtrack was cool jazz—Artie Shaw, Chet Baker, and selections from Vince Guaraldi's score from *A Charlie Brown Christmas*—and the film was set in Austin, already a key Twee Tribe hub like New York, L.A., Chicago, Portland, and Seattle. But from the start, Anderson's output swings with a sense of inspiration that lifts what is essentially a heist story.

Owen Wilson's Dignan and his emotionally troubled friend Anthony (played by Wilson's real-life younger brother, Luke) steal a coin collection from Anthony's mom. But the attitude and the humor of the movie are as much at play as the unchecked love for filmmaking itself. The *Bottle Rocket* short caught the eye of Oscar-winning writer, director, and producer James L. Brooks via Polly Platt, ex-wife of Peter Bogdanovich. Brooks was known for Oscar-winning films such as *Terms of Endearment* and groundbreaking television like *Taxi*. Platt sensed that here were filmmakers who shared the spirit of the new-Hollywood insurgency she'd been a part of in the 1970s. These were the Beattys and Redfords of their generation: clean-cut, all-American, but troubled and sometimes dangerous.

Reshot as a feature under Brooks's guidance, *Bottle Rocket* added a love story and a few more local, if improbable, heists (including a strip-mall bookstore), as well as James Caan. Stillman and Baumbach were independent filmmakers from the East Coast in the old tradition. Brooks and Caan signaled something else entirely. Anderson and Wilson were the new Hollywood. *Bottle Rocket* was not a hit, though Anderson's current poise tends to overshadow his early false starts. In the mid-'90s, audiences did not want their criminals this inept, running around like little kids in jumpsuits, spewing code words into walkie-talkies. But rather than correct his course, Anderson doubled down and set about creating, with Owen Wilson again, an even more Twee universe, without a trace of self-consciousness.

Rushmore, Anderson and Wilson's next script, opens with a sort of mission statement in the form of Max Fischer (Jason Schwartzman) daydreaming about solving an unsolvable math problem. Here is the can-do spirit of the young and contrary Gen Twee member, personified. Nothing is impossible. Max is haunted by the death of his mother and ashamed of his father, a simple but loving barber. Max is almost compulsive, an overachiever, founding clubs and societies, participating in lacrosse, debate, astronomy, trap and skeet, beekeeping—as well as the Max Fischer Players. This Twee theater troupe turns to Anderson's beloved 1970s films like Lumet's *Serpico* and

Coppola's *Apocalypse Now* for inspiration. The film itself might have been just a string of set pieces had it not been emotionally grounded by Schwartzman, who won the part after an extensive search. Olivia Williams's Mrs. Cross, a comely widow—her dead husband haunting the academy—and Bill Murray as Herman Blume, the world-weary titan, also add relatable emotion.

Blume, Vietnam vet, unhappily married, with spoiled numbskull kids and a sense that life's rewards are nothing more than a big swindle, is returned to his youth via Max's spirit. Through Max, Blume experiences, albeit briefly, all the raw emotions of his past—joy, hope, amusement, lust, and rage. He is literally given a jolt of life by Max, whereas before he is flirting with drowning himself in his backyard swimming pool. With its 1960s pop soundtrack full of Donovan, the Kinks, and the Who, *Rushmore* is operatic but never bombastic. It's a quiet film in its own way, talky but more concentrated than *Bottle Rocket*. Audiences left the theater in 1999 feeling restored and willing to pay for whatever the team of Anderson, Murray, and Schwartzman offered next.

Was Anderson the most talented of these new-school filmmakers or just the one with the most certainty of vision?

"I saw *Rushmore*, and I thought, He's comfortable making his own genre," Noah Baumbach said. Following *Kicking and Screaming*, Baumbach, the would-be wunderkind, hit a skid. His follow-up, *Mr. Jealousy*, released only a few months before Anderson's *Rushmore*, cast Eric Stoltz as Lester Grimm, a New Yorker with trust issues bordering on the pathological. Annabella Sciorra was cast as his girlfriend, Ramona Ray, the source of much of his agony. Chris Eigeman plays Dashiell

Frank, a famous novelist and one of Lester's foes, whom he spies on in a group-therapy session, hoping that details of an affair will be revealed.

Critics who had praised *Kicking and Screaming* as a smart, new voice were now tepid. A Janet Maslin review in the *New York Times*, in particular, destroyed the momentum. "I'm not sure [why critics didn't like it]," says Stoltz. "Perhaps they could sense that it was a bit more formulaic, perhaps they didn't like Noah doing his own narration. Who can say? Perhaps the leads should have been a bit older—I've found that older men, say, in their forties, tend to have serious issues with jealousy much more than twenty-somethings, who tend to be less threatened by experience. I think it's a very good film."

"Baumbach has described his second film, *Mr. Jealousy* . . . with reference to the directorial pantheon," Maslin wrote, "invoking film-makers from Billy Wilder to Francois Truffaut to Ernst Lubitsch as inspirations for his own comic style. Without knowing that, it would be easier to cite the two most imitated contemporary influences on independent comedies, Woody Allen and *Seinfeld* (in that order)." She went on to describe Stoltz, Sciorra, and Eigeman as "strikingly mis-cast," although she did concede that the film was "better written than staged."

"The distributors became reticent about it," the film's producer, Kastelberg, now says. "There wasn't a clamor to get this movie out, despite the critical success of *Kicking and Screaming*. They just pulled the plug. It was very hard for Noah to get a film made after that."

Baumbach earned a deal with ABC and wrote several pilots for the network. He made good money doing so, but it wasn't until he was imbued with the defiance of *Rushmore* that he had the nerve to shrug off his critics and continue pursuing his cinematic vision. "He was frustrated that he wasn't making movies. Then Wes Anderson came along, and it was amazing for him. It enabled him to get going again," Kastelberg says.

Anderson and Baumbach had met while their first films were traveling the country on the festival circuit. Baumbach now decided to up his game and take more risks. He began writing a story about his own Max Fischer, a boy—perhaps his alter ego—and the way he reacts to the divorce of his Brooklyn-intellectual parents in the 1980s.

"I read the script for *The Squid and the Whale* years before it was made," says Dean Wareham, former front man for the band Luna, who contributed a song to the soundtrack of *Mr. Jealousy*. Wareham created the now-iconic score for *The Squid and the Whale*, finally released in 2005. "It was a long journey to get that film made."

Meanwhile, Anderson had carte blanche. His production company, American Empirical, already stood for a certain level of quality. Following the success of *Rushmore*, an even more eager array of major movie stars like Gene Hackman, Danny Glover, Anjelica Huston, Ben Stiller, and Gwyneth Paltrow wanted to join Murray and the Wilsons in the next Wes Anderson film.

If *Rushmore* is informed by *The Catcher in the Rye*, then *The Royal Tenenbaums*, Anderson's first true masterpiece, is saturated with Salinger's Glass family from *Franny and Zooey* and *Nine Stories*. Even as it pushes all the Twee Tribe pleasure buttons (1960s soundtrack, smart humor, studious detail, children's-book-drawn palette) it confirms their greatest fears: *sic transit gloria*.

The Tenenbaum siblings, former acclaimed playwright Margot (Paltrow), financier Chas (Stiller), and tennis pro Richie (Wilson) are all gifted children—geniuses even—turned pathetic adult messes.

They are all dysfunctional to the point that they have become self-destructive and hurtful to those around them. They're all bound for terrible things until their estranged father, the scoundrel patriarch Royal (Hackman), falls down on his luck and tries to reconnect with his wife, Etheline (Huston), as a last resort.

The now-iconic Futura-font credits bearing his "An American Empirical Picture" production-house credit, and the whimsical ice cream colors, animal-print wallpaper, Dalmatian mice, and butterscotch sundaes cannot erase the fact that this movie is a dark affair about trust and secrets, lies and how family both saves and ruins our souls. Royal falsely claims to have cancer, though Glover's Henry Sherman, whose wife *did* die of stomach cancer, soon discovers the lie. Richie is secretly in love with Margot and is driven to a suicide attempt (set to Elliott Smith's brutal junkie ballad "Needle in the Hay"). Margot is cheating on her husband (Bill Murray) with an overpraised and drug-addled would-be Cormac McCarthy (Owen Wilson's Eli Cash). The marriage of pain and *Peanuts* freed a lot of filmmakers and gave Hollywood a new context, and the confidence that audiences everywhere now wanted complexity, singular vision, better detail, and a soundtrack that would send them to the newly ubiquitous search engine Google. More young auteurs were required.

Almost as improbable as the rise of Wes Anderson from outside Hollywood's establishment was that of Sofia Coppola from inside. Coppola was as connected to the 1970s Indie revolution as someone of her generation can get, having grown up the daughter of Francis Ford Coppola. Until the new millennium, however, she was known only for ruining *The Godfather: Part III*. Coppola was cast as Michael Corleone's daughter, Mary, after Winona Ryder pulled out, instantly inspiring cries of nepotism. Were there no qualified, "serious" actresses available? Coppola's only real film experience to that point had been observing the old man and cowriting his contribution to the anthology film *New York Stories*, "Life Without Zoe." The short film features Zoe, a sort of Eloise figure who lives virtually alone in the opulent Sherry-Netherland Hotel. She's the privileged daughter of a world-famous but absent flautist and a vapid shopaholic mother. Zoe is obnoxious. Her rich friends are even more obnoxious. "I've talked to Morgan Fairchild on the telephone for an hour in my room," the wealthiest one, a boy named Abu, brags. Zoe's servants (Don Novello, also known as Father Guido Sarducci, among them) smile through gritted teeth. Homeless people in boxes wearily accept her gifts of Hershey's Kisses when they'd rather have a sandwich. It's as tone-deaf as can be, and only worsened by the sharpness of the other two contributors, Woody Allen's "Oedipus Wrecks" and Martin Scorsese's "Life Lessons," one of the director's most satisfying "deep cuts." Scripted by the great Richard Price, the latter captures the art and social scene of New York of the mid- to late 1980s as it really was.

Nobody finds other people's offspring half as charming as their own. Most show-business veterans were aware that nobody tells Francis Ford Coppola what to do, but since the early 1970s there's been an even stronger axiom: you don't fuck with *The Godfather*.

The Godfather: Part III was probably the most anticipated film of all time. Only the late-'90s Star Wars prequels had more buzz. When *Part III* was released over the Christmas 1990 holiday, critics were mixed on the film, but nearly all of them (with the exception of the *New Yorker*'s Pauline Kael and *Entertainment Weekly*'s Owen Gleiberman) agreed that Sofia Coppola's "Am I getting my lines right?" performance, especially her death scene, was disastrous. When the hit man, dressed up like a priest, puts a bullet in the center of her chest, she doesn't look particularly pained, just sort of confused—but overall it's no worse a piece of overacting than Andy Garcia's or Joe Mantegna's. She took the hit for the film because she was the director's daughter and she wasn't Winona Ryder.

The controversy was so great that Sofia appeared on the cover of *EW* under the headline THE GODDAUGHTER and spent much of her twenties as a punch line. Even the inherently sweet *Gilmore Girls* made mean-girl jokes about the death scene. Twee cinema's bête noire is always the slickie: the handsome, privileged foe. In *Metropolitan,* Eigeman is riled by Rick Von Sloneker, a womanizer with silky hair and a tan. In *The Squid and the Whale,* Jeff Daniels's estranged wife (Laura Linney) takes up with a younger, impossibly handsome tennis pro (Billy Baldwin).

To many, Coppola, a hip model, Hollywood party thrower, and muse to fashion designer Marc Jacobs, was the slickie of her day, someone who was fun to hate on and as far from an underdog as possible. So when her adaptation of Jeffrey Eugenides's *The Virgin Suicides* was released in 1999, nobody was expecting much, but even if the bar had been set high, the film would have cleared it. It's among the first to establish a poetic and empathetic but almost anthropologically distant window on the gold-lit, twisted private world of girlhood. The doomed Lisbon sisters—Cecilia, Bonnie, Mary, and especially Kirsten Dunst's lovely but mostly mute Lux—are locked away by their God-fearing mother (Kathleen Turner) and hapless father (James Woods). Dunst, like future Coppola hero Scarlett Johansson, acts intensely with her eyes, conveying lust, boredom, contempt, regret, terror, elation. Coppola's scripts must be about thirty pages each. Only recently with her teen caper, an adaptation of writer Nancy Jo Sales's *The Bling Ring* (2013), do her characters get coked up and verbose.

Outside the pink bedrooms of the Lisbon girls, with their scented makeup and teddy bears, there's sin. Within, they are safe. Local boys circle the house like wolves. You can almost see hormones on the screen. Josh Hartnett's Trip Fontaine, with his 1970s wig and polyester trousers, locks eyes with Dunst, and what might be John Waters– or Todd Haynes–like is treated with a deep and abiding understanding by Coppola.

As with Anderson and Baumbach's films, Coppola routinely fills her soundtracks with retro music, but it's not as obviously cool. The songs she chose for *The Virgin Suicides* soundtrack were more kitsch: "The Air That I Breathe" by the Hollies and "Magic Man" by Heart. The mid- and late '90s was the time when the generation that grew up on *The ABC Afterschool Special, Schoolhouse Rock, The Midnight Special, Sha Na Na,* and *The Muppet Show* began choosing the songs to punctuate the emotional templates of their films, so music from the 1960s and '70s reigned. Even *The Ice Storm*, directed by future Oscar-winning director Ang Lee and adapted from the Rick Moody novel (and a critical hit but a box-office bomb at the time of its 1997 release) uses a kind of knowing array of '70s kitsch to lift certain key scenes. That film's teens are, in typical Twee fashion, wiser than their parents. Fourteen-year-old Wendy, played by a young Christina Ricci, is following the Watergate scandal and the abduction of Patty Hearst by the SLA while her superficial parents sneak around, having affairs and kvetching about golf handicaps. Ricci calls her dad (played by

Kevin Kline) fascist, and he calls her kiddo. The kids court each other with gifts of chewing gum and Devil Dogs or shout-outs to Dostoyevsky. Today the film is a Criterion-approved classic, with plenty of resonance among the Twee Tribe.

Wes Anderson is likely a factor in the second life of Sofia Coppola, as he reinvented Bill Murray as the go-to daddy figure in Indie film. Sofia Coppola chased Murray, who famously has no agent, only a telephone number and an answering machine. She vowed she wouldn't make her next film, a self-penned romance set in Japan, if Murray didn't play the part of Bob Harris, a faded movie star flown out to Japan to shoot a quick payday commercial.

Lost in Translation, the independent film hit of 2003, uses actual weariness as a metaphor for world-weariness. America had been on terror alert for two years since the attacks of 9/11. A second war was launched that year in Iraq, and increasingly intelligent mainstream movie audiences wanted their sweetness with a little nod to just how fucked up everything seemed, a sort of enlightened escapism. Scarlett Johansson was as blond and comely as the girlish Kirsten Dunst, but she had a huskier voice and an older-than-her-years quality (already demonstrated alongside Thora Birch and Steve Buscemi in *Ghost World*) that was squarely in the zeitgeist. Her "Is this it?" frown is the same as Murray's in *Rushmore*. They are united in displeasure before they even share a frame of screen time.

Her Charlotte, newly married, stranded in a lonely hotel room while her vapid husband (Giovanni Ribisi) is off photographing a band, evokes the same sense of frightened, postcollege stasis that Baumbach's men of *Kicking and Screaming* are plagued by. She makes up for it by being snippy. "Why do you have to point out how stupid everybody is all the time?" Ribisi asks. He begs her not to smoke. She smokes. He leaves her alone in her hotel room, and when her self-help tapes don't placate, she decides to have an affair—one of the mind and not necessarily the body. Bob Harris, Murray's former movie star now riding on nostalgia and kitsch, is spirit-revived by a younger foil.

"I'm staging a prison break," he confides to her over his cocktail. She's in. Together they "make a run for it" into the blinking, chaotic neon of Tokyo by night, where grown men dress and act like children and strippers gyrate to bad dance music. It's a series of sensory overload and comedown, arcades and house parties, hospitals and hotel rooms.

"I'm stuck. Does it get easier?"

Coppola, like Anderson and Baumbach, is a child of divorce. In 1986, when she was just fifteen, her brother was killed in a boating accident. She was briefly married to Spike Jonze, but by 2003 the marriage was ending. He is clearly referenced in *Lost in Translation* in the form of Ribisi, a skinny hipster earning a living filming bands. This film made Johansson a movie star. Like Baumbach, Coppola succeeded after a serious professional setback by facing the darkness and using it, rather than attempting to outrun and escape it.

Audiences and critics instinctively sensed the bravery in *Lost in Translation*, and, like Baumbach, Coppola was nominated for an Oscar (as was Murray). Baumbach and Murray lost. Coppola won.

When new-Hollywood directors like Bogdanovich, Hopper, De-Palma, Friedkin, Scorsese, Spielberg, Lucas, and Coppola Senior became the establishment, they blew a lot of studio money—sometimes on ambitious flops, but occasionally to create an award-winning gem. On a smaller scale, the *new* new Hollywood, dubbed the millennials by some—or "the American Eccentrics," by Armond White—followed a similar path as their careers carried on through the decade.

With Owen Wilson now a full-fledged movie star, Baumbach and Anderson became writing collaborators. Though both visually striking, neither Anderson's *The Life Aquatic with Steve Zissou* nor *The Darjeeling Limited* carried the shock of the new that was *Bottle Rocket* and *Rushmore*. Meanwhile Coppola's *Marie Antoinette* was opulent and ambitious but oddly empty at the same time. Critics seemed to seize on the film's emptiness even while taking it its sumptuous art direction and costuming.

The millennials didn't have Roger Corman, the exploitation film impresario who nurtured the '70s Easy Riders like Coppola, Bogdanovich, and Scorsese, to teach them how to make films. But they did have skate videos, which were distributed hands-on like zines in the '70s and '80s. And they had MTV. A sort of companion school of soon-to-be-respected directors emerged out of music video production in the '90s and early '00s and created a half dozen films that stood proudly alongside the new, young post–Easy Rider auteurs, but stood out as well. The works of Spike Jonze, Coppola's ex-husband, were not too far removed from a film like *Marie Antoinette*. Here were the boys dressing up and playing with record-company and later film-studio money (what is Jonze's most famous music video, the Beastie Boys's "Sabotage," if not a case of dress up and frolic?). Coppola appears as a gymnast in the Chemical Brothers' 1997 "Elektrobank" video, directed by Jonze, to whom she was still married at the time.

The films of Jonze, Frenchman Michel Gondry, and others by-passed the '70s as influences and were instead throwbacks to the candy-colored, trippy '60s and early '70s (films of their childhood, ostensibly: *Logan's Run, Day of the Dolphin, The Omega Man, Soylent Green,* and *Planet of the Apes*). Other times they were impossibly sweet but bizarre, and called to mind *Bedazzled, Head,* and other drug-culture informed, deceptively dark comedies. The best of them, Gondry's *Eternal Sunshine of the Spotless Mind* or Jonze's recent *Her,* feature characters who want the same thing as Max Fischer or Scarlett Johansson's Charlotte: they want to belong, to be loved, to figure out this big, scary world. They're haunted characters existing in a world where the whimsy is not as neatly boxed as it is in Anderson's creations. It feels homemade, like the costumes in Gondry's *Be Kind, Rewind,* and just on the verge of falling apart, à la the hazy end of Jonze's *Adaptation.* MTV before "Sabotage" and other Jonze videos like Bjork's "It's Oh So Quiet" and Weezer's "Buddy Holly" lacked a certain playfulness (Gondry's clips like Cibo Matto's "Sugar Water" and especially his later videos for the White Stripes would keep this quality alive). The clips seemed harder, less art pieces and more products designed to move other products; more teen friendly with a real need for Twee spirit. Even Nirvana's videos were moody and murky (with the exception of "In Bloom"). Only the young Beck seemed to get the joke of rock stardom and its attendant promotion and pressure—and the fun one can have with it. When these Twee video directors leaped over to feature films they brought this sense of dark whimsy and visual experimentalism with them, and like-minded artists like Beck (a little too arty, aloof, and on-his-own-planet-unique to pass as pure Twee) and Bjork (same) followed, loaning credibility and occasionally a song or two to a soundtrack. Childhood is never far; it haunts these heroes—take Jim Carrey bathing in the sink or slyly jerking off in *Eternal Sunshine of the Spotless Mind*. It even haunts the chimp trapped in the apartment of Cameron Diaz's and John Cusack's characters (practitioners of a very Twee and outré art form, puppeteering) in *Being John Malkovich*. When faced with a real man's man, like Nicolas Cage's Charlie Kaufman in *Adaptation*, these directors' boy-men shrink in confusion.

With *Being John Malkovich* and *Adaptation*, Spike Jonze, who'd made his name with street-smart skater videos before virtually taking over MTV in the mid-'90s with one innovative video after another and then as a cocreator of the *Jackass* franchise, became respected as a serious—not just a "kid"—filmmaker. But once he was given a chance to have a carte-blanche career, what he chose to do was a murky adaptation of *Where the Wild Things Are*, which had none of the zest and humor of his previous films.

The film is shot in dusky light, with strange pacing. It's full of pregnant pauses. The *Wild Things* monsters, the great showpieces of the film, are just as brooding and neurotic and damaged by life as Max, who turns to them for diversion. In a 2013 profile of Jonze for *Time*, Joel Stein succinctly described the film as "a kids' movie so true to what it feels like to be a kid that kids didn't see it . . ." Once they had hits and power, the millennials seemed determined to tell even more personal and polarizing stories that drew them farther and farther away from the box office and deeper into their childhood traumas.

Similarly, Baumbach's *Margot at the Wedding* squandered much of the goodwill the director had banked with *Squid*. "Nicole Kidman's figure is polarizing, and a lot of people did not respond to it," says musician Dean Wareham, a friend and collaborator of Baumbach's. "I kind of think people will accept the behavior of the Jeff Daniels character, the father, that way, but they won't accept it in the mother—they'll accept a man being a selfish prick." No longer having to keep their Twee in check, it ran rampant in tandem with the out-of-control war effort and created a sort of backlash that was usually reserved for winking foreign films full of big-eyed scamps, like Audrey Tatou in the polarizing *Amélie* and anything starring Roberto Benigni.

"I hate the idea of 'Oh, this is the new trend we have to kill,'" says Whit Stillman of the Twee cinema backlash, started in the mid-2000s, that even affected financing for his comeback film, 2011's *Damsels in Distress*. "You get so much hostility it's amazing. It's a very perverse thing going on. I think if the world is upside down, we should be watching delightful 1930s escapism—and charming comedies. In 1935 our imaginations were at their apex and the world was in the worst spot it was going to be in. Ten years of absolute horror, and yet they made these gorgeous, wonderful films." Similarly, as the world skirted another depression and a pair of seemingly endless wars, Twee films began to become more fantastical . . . and profitable.

Next came the stop-motion-animation retelling of Roald Dahl's *The Fantastic Mr. Fox* (with no less than Meryl Streep alongside Clooney) and the magnificent *Moonrise Kingdom*, a love story set in the fading summer of 1965 between Suzy and Sam, troubled young runaways who share a brief but idyllic campsite on the shore of a remote island in New England. In this film, Anderson's best and most commercially successful so far, there's a literal storm coming to threaten the blissful, pure childhood of its two heroes. Anderson doesn't even bother with masking his metaphors any longer.

When that film was released in 2012, it seemed only the crabs were vocal. The film charmed just about everyone else. The author and screenwriter Bret Easton Ellis, newly emerged as Twitter's greatest and most lethal culture critic, tweeted, "The 'Moonrise Kingdom' review in NYTimes is the whitest review I have ever read about the whitest movie ever made," while newly minted Generation Twee heroine Lena Dunham gushed, "Moonrise Kingdom couldn't be more pleasurable."

At least Donald Fagen, the Steely Dan cofounder who took Anderson to task during the *Life Aquatic/Darjeeling Limited* period for repeating his tropes, came around. In his 2013 memoir, *Eminent Hipsters,* he expressed cynicism-free affection for *Moonrise*. "I think one of the reasons we're intrigued by Anderson is that he seems to be fixated on the sort of geekish, early-sixties adolescent experience that he's too young to have had but that Walter [Becker] and I actually lived through. And yet he nails the mood precisely, using comedic exaggeration and fantasy to do the job. Although it was no picnic, it's too bad everyone's coming-of-age can't take place in the early sixties."

Sometimes even Anderson veterans took shots at the maestro. Hosting an October 2013 episode of *Saturday Night Live, Moonrise Kingdom*'s scout-troop leader Edward Norton appears in the horror spoof *The Midnite Coterie of Sinister Intruders*. The short is narrated in the fashion of *Tenenbaums* by Alec Baldwin ("From the twisted mind . . . of Wes Anderson"), and Norton, doing a spot-on Owen Wilson, observes a gaggle of maniacs in his front yard through a set of vintage binoculars.

"Wow, look at him! He's got the meat cleaver. And a record player!"

Anderson, who at the time of this writing was deep into the

production of his latest film, *The Grand Budapest Hotel*, was likely oblivious to it all. I went to see the film on its opening day in March 2014 and realized just how far he stood above the haters. He seemed to straddle them, his head far too high in the clouds to even hear or acknowledge them. The film's main action (there are flashbacks and flash-forwards) takes place in a lavish hotel in the fictional Republic of Zubrowka during the weeks and months leading up to a "tricky" war, as concierge M. Gustave (Ralph Fiennes) describes it. It's obviously World War II, but specifics are not mentioned and plot (an art heist) as intrigue is not really important. It's a Wes Anderson film about Wes Anderson's latest vision. "[The film] is about the spiritual heritage and the political force of those long-vanished styles," Richard Brody writes in his *New Yorker* review "about the substance of style, not just the style of his Old World characters but also, crucially, Anderson's own." I also realized in the lobby that the openings of Anderson's films are akin to a new action film starring a bevy of Marvel comics heroes; they are events, full of triggers (cameos by beloved Anderson collaborators like Owen Wilson, Bob Balaban, and of course Bill Murray) and signals to his devoted ("Rudeness is merely the expression of fear," one character declares). It's the real world, with only a "glimmer of civilization in the barbaric slaughterhouse we know as humanity," as another character complains, that's got the problem, not Anderson, the filmmaker as pastry chef; the one-man preservation society. With every great, old palace, like the Grand Budapest, that falls into "shabby decay," Anderson, another catcher in the rye figure like Cobain, seems determined to be there to point out the shame.

Chapter 12

Extremely Loud and Conveniently Local

2001–2009

In which catastrophe and war separate the real men from the man-children in the worlds of literature and activism, and the fate of the modern age hangs in the balance. Would it be the end or the beginning of something better, kinder, and more hands-on?

The world was going to end. The giant rabbit with the gnarled teeth predicted it. *Donnie Darko*, the cult film directed by Richard Kelly is a long, occasionally funny bad omen. Donnie (Jake Gyllenhaal) is an insomniac, overmedicated, and over-psychoanalyzed troubled teen in the fall of 1988. He may also be dead. In another bit of horrible coincidence, a part of a jet airplane has fallen on his house. He exists now in a sort of netherworld, a Holden Caulfield figure in purgatory, obeying the call and parsing out the cryptic utterings of a giant, Harvey-like bunny. *Donnie Darko* is a great Twee film because it's suffused with dread, darkness, and humor à la Anderson's oeuvre, and because it reduces its adult characters to either helpless or deluded. In terms of production and setting, *Darko* takes Anderson's ardor for the unremembered 1960s and places it in the 1980s; it's set on the evening of a George Bush–Michael Dukakis presidential debate. In 2001, teens rallied around *Darko,* making it an almost instant cult hit, largely because it was spearheaded by a credible film rebel in Donnie—but also because by this point, thanks to technology, the unremembered '80s could be virtually experienced. Echo and the Bunnymen's "The Killing Moon," Duran Duran's "Notorious," the Church's "Under the Milky Way," and especially Tears for Fears's "Head over Heels" and the haunting cover of "Mad World" by Michael Andrews and Gary Jules made going back in time seem preferable to the actual madness that had descended like falling debris.

Few other works of 9/11-informed art ring as true as *Darko,* probably because it was filmed before the attacks and has prescience on its side. Even pop saint Bruce Springsteen's *The Rising* feels somewhat exploitative, having been recorded after the attacks. Artists had the means to respond to catastrophe faster in the twenty-first century, and perhaps this was not such a good thing. There was a good decade's worth of simmer between J. D. Salinger conceiving of Holden Caulfield, taking him to war, processing what he saw in Hürtgen Forest and at Dachau, and ultimately writing *The Catcher in the Rye.*

After the 9/11 attacks, there was also the prevailing sense that the adults needed to be in charge, not an increasingly infantilized and hybrid generation of teens. The Bush-Cheney leadership treated Americans like children, instructing us to do some shopping if we felt like helping, carrying on as if nothing happened at all. But as with

World War II, the world had changed forever, and answers were not coming clear or fast enough to satisfy, well, anyone.

September 11, 2001, brought with it, more than anything else, a sense of confusion and disorientation. Were we going to get hit again? Who was hitting us, anyway? They didn't wear uniforms. Why do they hate us? It was left to our elected officials and public servants to produce concrete answers and to our artists to address the abstract. Some looked forward. Others looked backward for precedent, and a few, perhaps unwisely, looked at the still-smoldering and tension-electrified present.

"Our good fortune allowed us to feel a sadness that our parents didn't have time for," Ewan McGregor says in voice-over in Mike Mills's bittersweet love story *Beginners*. Now the sadness was ours. We had our own World War II, our own Vietnam, and few of us had the sure-handedness or the ego of the Boss. What would we do with it? Would we handle it well, or would we clam up or blow it with self-absorption? It behooved our young artists to figure it out, even as the pit was being cleared of smoldering metal and ash and the air smelled deadly. Clarity was key.

"I don't think 9/11 had much bearing on me writing about history," says Sarah Vowell. "In fact, I was finished with a book of historical essays and had to scramble to write another, what came to be the title essay of *Partly Cloudy Patriot*, which was a tip of the hat to Thomas Paine. I will say it had a drastic impact on my music consumption. I used to have music playing around the house all waking hours, and I switched to news overnight and never really went back. It sounds silly now, but I slept with my radio tuned to my NPR affiliate for at least six weeks because I wanted to know the second they took bin Laden into custody. I did not anticipate that would take ten years. Though the first thing I did when I heard was put on Joan Baez singing 'The Battle Hymn of the Republic.'"

Brooklyn writer Jonathan Safran Foer, today a divisive literary figure, should at least get credit for his attempt to write his literary equivalent of *The Rising.* Foer's Oskar Schell, the nine-year-old hero of the novel *Extremely Loud and Incredibly Close,* is a precocious waif in a ski hat and backpack who has the run of the city until tragedy strikes. When he loses his father in the attacks on the World Trade Center, New York is no longer his playground but a haunted house. Oskar, like Holden Caulfield obsessing over his ducks, spends much of the book and subsequent film adaptation searching for the lock to a key the old man left behind. Here is a somewhat broadly drawn boy genius, but also one who has every right to whine and brood. There were many orphans made that terrible day.

And yet at the time of the book's publication, four full years after the attacks, there were readers who cried again and again, "Too soon," or "Not concrete enough." More than a decade on, that seems unfair. An artist's themes and topics cannot be dictated by the public, no matter how disturbed. But bin Laden was still at large. Support for the wars in both Afghanistan and later Iraq had yet to fizzle out and turn many against the president. There was no new Freedom Tower rising at Ground Zero. There was no balm at all, really. A good writer tends to ask more questions than provide answers, and this is useless in a panic.

Foer's previous novel, 2002's *Everything Is Illuminated,* was a best seller and announced the arrival of a major new voice. *Extremely Loud* stopped that momentum cold.

When asked whether he had second thoughts taking on 9/11, Foer responded, "I think it's a greater risk not to write about it. If you're in my position—a New Yorker who felt the event very deeply and a writer who wants to write about things he feels deeply about—I think it's risky to avoid what's right in front to you. None of the ways people were talking about 9/11 felt right to me."

That this new, murky conflict was a religious war forced the literary thinkers of all generations, especially the new, young heroes who had all the media attention (even those who were, at their core, utterly secular), to reflect on questions of spirituality. There was a pressure to select a faith and use it as a survival tool; a sort of zealot envy pervaded. The enemy, if there was an actual enemy, certainly had a fanatical investment in faith.

"I want to talk about God in a literary way," Foer said. "But I think I would have a very hard time praying to God." Despite the bravery and the sincerity with which he wrestled with these serious themes, Foer's Twee visage is what really did him in. Nobody questioned his talent. They took issue with his glasses; people confused him with Oskar. He looked like a boy, a spelling-bee champion. When an actual actor replaced Foer in the popular imagination and gave us an alternate face of Oskar, however, things just seemed to get even worse.

Images of a falling man—at the back of the book, in a kind of child's flip book design—showed a real-life victim who committed suicide by jumping from the tower, rather than dying from heat, fire, smoke inhalation, instead floating back up into the smoky window. To some this was seen as not poetic but exploitative. After 9/11 people asked if irony was dead. They might have inquired about whimsy as well.

The film version of *Extremely Loud* was Oscar bait that salted the wound. Worse, it was a falling Tom Hanks. The actor *is* America, representative of everything we trust and are proud of, the Jimmy

Stewart of his age. And here was this adaptation nobody wanted, killing him and making us relive that dreadful Tuesday all over again.

Especially in New York City, the knives came out. Manohla Dargis of the *New York Times* wrote: "It's about the impulse to drain that day of its specificity and turn it into yet another wellspring of generic emotions: sadness, loneliness, happiness. This is how kitsch works. It exploits familiar images, be they puppies or babies—or, as in the case of this movie, the twin towers—and tries to make us feel good, even virtuous, simply about feeling. And, yes, you may cry, but when tears are milked as they are here, the truer response should be rage." Lou Lumenick of the *New York Post* compared the film to one of "those framed 3-D photos of the Twin Towers emblazoned with 'Never Forget' that are still for sale in Times Square a decade after 9/11."

Even Art Spiegelman, who took on the Holocaust and was so careful not to profit from his *Maus* series, lest he be criticized as exploitative, was compelled to address—carefully—the events of 9/11. In 2004 the artist issued *In the Shadow of No Towers*; an oversize meditation on the day, which seemed, especially when compared to his previous epics, somewhat tame. "I never liked those arrogant boxes," he writes of the towers, "but now I miss those rascals, icons of a more innocent age." He compares the air in the days after the attacks on New York, acrid and toxic, to his father's description of the air at Auschwitz, but that's as far as he'll go. Foer, younger and perhaps braver, was willing to risk his reputation to really go there, through the eyes and heart of a scarred but plucky child, and in some ways his career has never recovered.

If there's an invention of the 9/11 era of letters that's critic-proof, or rather critic-oblivious, it's McSweeney's, which today feels more and more like both an empire and an important literary school on par with the existentialists and the beats. At a recent symposium at Laemmlein & Leah Buttenweiser Hall at the 92nd Street Y in Manhattan, a few hundred young men and women—slouching in their black vintage dresses, clunky shoes, nerd glasses, ski hats, and beards—filed in to hear some of the magazine's key contributors over the years discuss the origins of the quarterly turned website turned publisher, once raggedy and prided on printing pieces that were rejected by other publications. This is where the movers and shakers of popular culture come to lecture, whether it's Dr. Oz or Suze Orman, and in its own way, McSweeney's has similarly imprinted its design for living on millions.

Founder Dave Eggers was himself a refugee from the standard publishing world, which was clearly too staid and catty for him. One can imagine him recoiling and devising ways to chuck all the rules. He was a student of the post-Punk British Indie scene of the early and mid-'80s, so the example was already there when it came to eliminating the middleman, staying true to an ideal, and operating with a social conscience. He was also a student of the heroic and rebellious Maurice Sendak, having read *Where the Wild Things Are* at age five. "I just reacted with pure terror. But then I used to hide under the couch during *The Wizard of Oz*. I think what frightened me the most was that I couldn't work out if the Wild Things were nice or nasty. There was a moral ambiguity to them which really disturbed me," he has said.

Eggers, then a new father himself, wrote the script to the Spike Jonze adaptation of Sendak's classic, as well as a full-length novelization. "I wrote it between our two children being born," he said. "I wanted to write something that might have the same sort of effect on a kid as the books I read when I was young had on me. I can remember exactly where I sat when my teacher first read Roald Dahl's *James and the Giant Peach.* It's like the cement is still wet when you're that age; every little mark can become permanent."

Following the success of his 2000 memoir *A Heartbreaking Work of Staggering Genius,* which deals with him raising his younger brother, Christopher (Toph), following the back-to-back losses of both parents to cancer, Eggers could have benefited from the established publishing-business structure and committed himself no further than the delivery of a highly lucrative follow-up. Instead he invested in McSweeney's and printed the next book, now hugely anticipated, himself.

McSweeney's Quarterly Concern, christened with Eggers's mother's maiden name, was founded in 1998 as a literary quarterly, a sort of new, modern version of *Granta* or *Paris Review.* By the release of 2002's Eggers novel *You Shall Know Our Velocity,* it was regarded by Great Britain's *Telegraph* as "the most influential literary magazine in the United States." This was down to the talent, of course (contributors included Jonathan Lethem, Michael Chabon, and Ann Beattie, among others), but also the presentation. *McSweeney's* the publication felt like a fetish object, like an old piece of vinyl. David Foster Wallace famously wrote a short story on the spine of one issue. Some were packaged in boxes, others in letters. They were gilded and giftlike, and to read them was to carve out a small bit of identity for yourself as a *McSweeney's* adherent.

Eggers, who seemed to know what to do with his new power, later founded the tutoring center 826 Valencia in San Francisco (and would establish outposts in cities across the country, as well as London and Dublin), applying his pragmatism to his social work by encouraging the creative writing and artistic skills of children ages six to eighteen. The programs were established with expediency and a kind of middleman cutting that called to mind the models established by Calvin Johnson at K Records or Ian MacKaye at Dischord. In a climate where people were growing further and further removed from each other thanks to the advent of social networking—and where even in art it was becoming increasingly common to muse, fantasize, or self-infantalize rather than tackle small problems incrementally with an eye toward a better world—Eggers, the literary child-rebel, did his networking on a person-to-person level.

"The tight-knit community we had is the foundation for what became 826," says Sarah Vowell. "The only thing I know about the influence of McSweeney's is that if you value your free time, do not take Dave Eggers's calls. He's a real roper-inner."

"McSweeney's as a publishing company is built on a business model that only works when we sell physical books. So we try to put a lot of effort into the design and production of the book-as-object," Eggers has said. He found a printer in the Detroit area, Thomson-Shore, and took pride in the Made-in-the-USA-ness of it all. "The fact that they're in Michigan makes it easier to communicate," he has said, "to reprint, and to correct problems . . . I don't mean to beat a made-in-America drum, but I would be lying if I said it doesn't feel somehow right to be printing books in the U.S."

Only Jack White rivals Eggers as a twenty-first-century Indie maverick, creator, and operator of his own idealistic microcosm. The former White Stripes leader founded Third Man Records in 2001, the year that the duo broke through with its third album, *White Blood Cells*. Today he owns and operates a self-contained record store, performance space, and record-company office in the same Nashville compound. It's a throwback to the days of Sun Records in Memphis, Chess in Chicago, and even Motown in White's own Detroit. There's even a darkroom for developing promotional photos. Like Eggers, White hired an old-school factory crew (United Pressing) to locally press the vinyl that's cut at the nearby studio. "We have a great relationship with them," White told me in 2009. "We had a meeting with them before I even bought the building. I said, 'Listen, I want to turn around records really fast. If I bring you a record, how fast can you do it? They can get us a hundred and fifty copies in twenty-four hours."

The juxtaposition of sometimes-chauvinistic traditions of blues-rock lyrics and White's more childlike and unaggressive tendencies was a bit trickier. As the White Stripes got bigger, they had to reckon with the Nirvana problem of drawing knuckleheads to the pit. I once saw White stop a concert midsong to lecture an overzealous fan with "This is a Marlene Dietrich song!" as if to imply that moshing to an old Weimar cabaret number was absurd.

By the time the White Stripes were winding down, White had relocated to Nashville and, like Calvin Johnson, divided up his talents and attention among several different recording and touring concerns, among them the Raconteurs and the Dead Weather. It was there that he became, like Dave Eggers, a modern, real-life Willy Wonka, with an analog-is-better aesthetic and everything made in America.

The culture's tendency toward crafting begins in the post-9/11 era. Movie stars can be seen with knitting needles in their Birkin bags. Anything tangible, perennial, "old school," and pure—a book, an LP record—is akin to a kind of cultural comfort food. And while the Net sped this up, even the most marvelous of modern marvels would take a turn inward toward the personal, with blogs and message boards exponentially growing and vying with more corporate retail sites for space and attention.

"I never had WiFi at home," Eggers has said. "I'm too easily distracted, and YouTube is too tempting . . . I've never read a page on an e-reader." McSweeney's saved paper the same way Wes Anderson's Max Fischer saved Latin in *Rushmore* and Jack White saved the American vinyl presses. "I would like to set the computers on fire," White told me in 2009. "We are in an age that is the antithesis of what I am trying to do artistically. It's a constant battle." The success of McSweeney's and Jack White, both wildly popular, can be seen as a triumph of the older, slower, but truer way over modernity, speed, and economy. It was fueled almost entirely by a sort of cars-with-fins-were-better sense of romance, quickly becoming not only a subculture in the twenty-first century but a new kind of cause. "I'm the poster boy for gas-lamp technology," White joked.

"I totally admire what he did," Jonathan Ames, a *McSweeney's* contributor, says of Eggers. "He was so exuberant. Like his generation's George Plimpton [founder of the *Paris Review*]."

There is a website—*McSweeney's Internet Tendency*—as well as an online store, but you won't find the founder on it. "I can say that with regard to the Web, Dave was utterly befuddled," says John Hodgman, another early *McSweeney's* contributor. "He found the idea that there was going to be a website somewhat confusing, and indeed the Web *McSweeney's* became a different animal. Dave's passion is to create these beautiful, innovative books. *McSweeney's* as a journal is about tremendous writing, but it's also about the art of making printed materials. And at the same time that Dave was creating these beautiful artifacts, sewn with golden thread, on the other side the website was pointing to a different kind of future. One where people would put up short material to be read all over the world." Faced with loss (Eggers's sister was, for a time, publicly unhappy with her portrayal in *Staggering Genius* and committed suicide in 2001) and the start of his own family,

Eggers might have remained solipsistic and precious, and indeed there are elements of that in his work. *McSweeney's*, along with the worst of the Foer book (and film), is dismissed by some as too cute, given the times; a sort of catchall buzz word for everything clever and Twee in publishing. With *The Believer*, a monthly magazine; *Lucky Peach*, a culinary-focused volume; and the *Wholphin* anthology DVDs, it's certainly a large enough multimedia concern to take fire.

"People hate whimsy," Hodgman says. "I think people are suspicious of it—because it seems un-serious in some way. Whimsy, in my mind, is defined as a kind of playfulness and a pleasure in playfulness—wordplay or cultural references or inside jokes. It is controversial not merely because it's disconnected from the hard social realities around us, but also because it doesn't care and it is not going to feel guilty about it. And a lot of people have trouble with that. I don't know that you could ever accuse Dave himself as a writer as being unconcerned with the world."

Eggers's subsequent books have taken on a sort of open-eyed global consciousness that will again hopefully find him leading by example. *What Is the What*, his 2006 novel, examines the crisis in Darfur, and *Zeitoun* is a 2009 nonfiction account of the displaced, post-Katrina residents of New Orleans. McSweeney's still exists in a kind of grace state because of this balance of whimsy and taking on the big issues of the world. "Part of his life is profoundly concerned with the world around him," says Hodgman, "but one of the reasons people still get mad is that he'll create the drop-in tutoring center but he'll also put a pirate-supply store in front of it. Or a superhero-supply store in front of it. It'll be playful and it won't apologize for being playful, and why should it?"

Chapter 13

Welcome to the Mumble

2003–2011

In which a trilogy of psychic salves—reality TV, YouTube, and social networking—alleviate the stress of a post-9/11 world and make stars of people without talent, connections, or even ambition. Simultaneously, a school of young artists with talent and ambition and sometimes an affinity for the oversharing that blights the new techno-driven world begin to connect. Soon they find themselves in the Hollywood game, having their purity challenged.

A would-be artist used to have to leave the bedroom in order to make an impact on the world around him. By 2003, all that had changed. All you needed was a laptop with an iCamera application, or a cell phone with high-definition video, and you could conduct a new kind of diary keeping—no pressed flowers between pages here—and you could become rich and famous doing so. You didn't even have to be enrolled in art, fashion, or film school. And if you really had something to say, you became influential. Here was a generation that grew up with computers as pets, rather than daunting and frequently malfunctioning machinery. They were aggressively encouraged to "Think Different" with their candy-colored iMacs, which seemed like the hardware manifestation of Steve Jobs's spiritual utopianism. Here were powerful but not cynical machines that could, it seemed, function as friends and creative partners. Jobs, a college dropout and adopted child who grew up poor, did not pass judgment but rather wanted the world, especially its children, to achieve spiritual, creative, and financial excellence with the help of his innnovations. He literally made it easier for someone like Ryan Schreiber and millions of other bedroom-bound, antisocial, obsessive, and passionate weirdos to excel and eventually prosper. In the new millennium, Twee Tribers could not only see themselves represented on film like never before and feel less alone, they could represent themselves without going broke and maxing out credit cards like Robert Townshend and Robert Rodriguez famously did in the 1980s and '90s, respectively.

The rapid gains in visual technology—cameras on phones, digital cameras, easy-to-use film-editing software such as iMovie—marked the postmillennial school of cinema, which reduced the base budget of filmmaking to zero. Plot suddenly seemed unnecessary. The only thing required was to never, ever stop talking, and a message would eventually be hewn. Silence was deadly in the '00s as the culture moved toward constant, twenty-four-hour self-documentation.

"It became an editors' medium," says Sean Nelson of the movement that became known as mumblecore by 2005. Nelson starred in director Lynn Shelton's quasi-mumblecore offering, the charming country mouse–city mouse buddy flick *My Effortless Brilliance*. "Editors make those movies," Nelson continues. "Basically what they capture on the set is a lot of rambling shit from actors who are not generally directed. Certainly not given language—they talk and talk and talk and talk and the editor finds the one minute of what they just said that's useful. In a way you could make the case that it's pure cinema. In another way you can make the case there is no intentional language in these films [and] that it's a fake naturalism."

Mumblecore was polarizing from the start. Its godfather is commonly considered Andrew Bujalski. Bujalski was at Harvard in the late 1990s, majoring in Visual and Environmental Studies. He looked the part of a modern, intellectual wallflower, with shaggy hair, big glasses, and inherent shyness. Bujalski was a fan of big Hollywood movies, but found that whenever he left the multiplex and the spectacle was over, he felt empty.

"I've always objected to the idea that if it's a movie like *The Avengers,* you have to see it on a big screen, but if it's a movie about people talking you have to see it on a small screen," Bujalski says. "I think it's the opposite. The big giant movies will kind of do what they're doing in any format, whereas something that is quieter really benefits from having your attention in that dark room."

Why couldn't the types of films that felt more intimate and real play on the giant screens? Didn't a good conversation with another person who really got you give you a more sustainable sense of satisfaction? Bujalski also grew weary of the classical modes of storytelling, where characters telegraph their desire and everyone has to have a conflict to overcome. Why couldn't people just hang out and be sweet to each other, help each other through this screwed-up existence? He didn't want to surround himself with schemers. Schemes were tired.

"I certainly know a lot of polite people, and I find that there is a lot of drama in those interactions," Bujalski says. "It's obviously less broad and less explosive. But I think the struggle to be nice when conditions don't seem to support it—when you don't know how to do it, or when your being nice rubs somebody the wrong way—there's a lot of story there."

"He knew he wanted to make movies," says Justin Rice, a fellow Harvard student who would work on Bujalski's early films. "But he didn't want to move to Hollywood."

Bujalski began seeing his friends as characters, specifically a spacey, young brunette woman named Kate Dollenmayer. He'd observe her, write down things she'd say that inspired him, and find himself fashioning a story around her personality, much in the way *Annie Hall* was an amalgam of Diane Keaton's mannerisms, family history, and relationship with Woody Allen. "I wrote [*Funny Ha Ha*] with Kate in mind to do it," Bujalski says. "I had the idea of putting her in a movie before I wrote a word of script."

Funny Ha Ha, shot with no budget in the Boston area, is the story of Dollenmayer's character Marnie, a kind of postslacker beauty who is a bit lost after college. Marnie is Lena Dunham's Hannah Horvath, ungentrified. There's also a bit of Keaton's doomed Theresa Dunn from *Looking for Mr. Goodbar*. Every man Marnie meets is smitten with her, and she has absolutely no idea what she wants. Even Bujalski himself, cast as a sweaty, stammering potential suitor, tells her, "You know, ninety percent of the guys you know are head over heels in love with you."

Marnie is both amused and a little horrified by the courtship rituals. "What's my deal?" she replies to a date. "I'm sorry that's such a terrible question."

Bujalski's world of boys and girls is full of fumbling and kissing, followed by prolonged apology. If there's a sharpness and rigidity to this meandering, it's in the execution. Here, the director's laissez-faire approach is discarded in favor of dogma. Bujalski shot the film shortly after 9/11 in black and white, with a 16 mm camera. None of the angles were fancy. He clashed with his ad hoc sound and lighting crew when it was suggested that they try some effects. "Part of the nature of making a film is the conflict between the director wanting the performance and the DP wanting things to look right," says Justin Rice, who did sound on *Funny Ha Ha* and would later star in Bujalski's follow-up, *Mutual Appreciation*.

"The DP wants to put up lights and the director just wants to shoot. But for Andrew, it was definitely clear to all of us that he didn't give a fuck [about lights]. He was just thinking it had to stay off the cuff. Always rolling. Ready to shoot at a given moment, and the more time you spend staging things, the less of that shambling vitality you get."

Like Wes Anderson, Bujalski invented a cinematic language, only nobody could quite make it out. A few years later, his sound director Eric Masunaga, in an affectionate bit of mockery, named it "mumblecore." The sound, already compromised, was further muted by the marble-mouthed, untrained actors that Bujalski insisted make up his world. There's a comfort to *Funny Ha Ha* that would be impossible if it was cast with professional, trained, capital-A Actors. It was as if Bujalski had to know them and observe a certain inner quality before he would cast them. "A politeness," Rice says. "He picked people who had politeness to their essential nature. Polite people portraying polite characters. I remember something he said to me: 'It's about people looking for a chance to be kind to each other.'" It was as far from Hollywood and business as it could possibly be, but *Funny Ha Ha* was about to imprint the movie industry in a major way.

The film was completed at a time when word of mouth was faster and more powerful than ever before. Specialized sites, once the province of gamers, chat-room haunters, and the antisocial, were now common places for fans of bands, films, and authors to connect and for once in their lives enjoy a sense of popularity (in the years before it was measured by "likes" and "followers").

Over the next three years, as Bujalski cut and screened the film and attempted to get a distribution deal, the legend of *Funny Ha Ha* grew. Here was a film that didn't talk down to its young audience but presented a raw, funny reflection of that audience that was both comforting and flattering. There was no hard sell necessary, no weekend window in which to make back all the money for a film like this. It was the first film of its kind to meander into profitability at its own pace, and was so ahead of the curve that it had the luxury of aggregating a myth before finally hitting proper theaters in 2005. "We were really lucky in that it had this weird, uncanny lifespan. That's something unrepeatable, to have a movie that has a three-year word-of-mouth build," Bujalski says.

By the time the film was playing in major cities and Bujalski was being heralded as an exciting, new voice, he was already shooting his next film in Brooklyn. *Mutual Appreciation* is again the story of a somewhat bewildered Twee hero, navigating a world where cynics have agendas. As with Dollenmayer, Bujalski had an actor in mind when he wrote the script, this time envisioning Rice as the lead. "He asked me to do it based on the relationship that we had, and not necessarily any aspirations that I had to act," Rice now says. A fan of the director's vision, Rice agreed. *Mutual Appreciation* was an even bigger success than Bujalski's debut (success in this new world being applause at festivals and, if you were lucky, some bookings in art houses and a distribution deal to screen on cable channels like IFC, which launched in the mid-1990s but a decade in began to stop rerunning classic independent film in favor of newer, younger voices).

Rice, with his bed head, skinny tie, and blazer, looked like he could have been the sixth member of the Strokes, and became the first heartthrob of the nascent genre—or at least the closest thing to one. In real life, Rice's rock band, Bishop Allen, was gaining a following too. That said, the real star of *Mutual Appreciation* is the new Brooklyn.

"I lived for a while on the sixth stop of the L train, the Morgan stop. In one month, thirty people got mugged on my block, and one time we found a finger in the snow. There were cars burned up on the street. You could see the smoking husk of the car. Now, right around the corner from where that was, is Roberta's Pizza, this beautiful, amazingly cool restaurant. They grow their own food. Bake their own bread. Have their own radio station. There were a lot of like-minded people coming to Brooklyn. The process was under way when we were shooting *Mutual Appreciation*," Rice says. Nearly a decade before HBO's Brooklyn-set *Girls*, this was the first time the new, young, Indie Brooklyn was captured on film for those outside of the five boroughs to witness. And they liked what they saw.

Mumblecore took on a life of its own after *Mutual Appreciation*. It was a phrase, like "the Brat Pack," that the media could seize on and studios could place in context. Suddenly there were big opportunities for Dollenmayer and Rice. "I thought of it as a *Lord of the Rings* scenario," says Bujalski, "where Kate held the ring, which was the power of being a tremendous natural actor, wildly charismatic and watchable onscreen—and she just didn't want it. She threw the ring into whatever that mountain is with the fire that destroys it. People asked her to be in their films and she politely demurred. Which is funny to me since she's always broke. I thought, 'You should sell out just a little. Make some money.' I believe the casting director of *Talladega Nights* sent her the script. Kate read it and said, 'This is kind of dumb.' And that was the end of that. That was her Hollywood career."

Bujalski remained Indie despite the cachet that two underground critical hits afforded him. "I came to understand that selling out is as much if not more work than just doing what you care about and love—given that choice, I always defaulted back to doing what I love." Bujalski's third film, 2009's *Beeswax*, was an even more meandering and casual account of polite people coping with an impolite world.

Beeswax, unlike *Funny Ha Ha* and *Mutual Appreciation*, was shot on digital video. In the years since Bujalski's first two films, cameras became smaller, lighter, and more high-tech than they had ever been before. Most phones were embedded with video cameras that could produce sound and video of a quality not too far removed from that of many low-budget films.

"There's no way I could have done the movie if those cameras were not on the market," says Alex Karpovsky, the star of *Beeswax*, who would begin making his own low-budget films like the documentary *The Hole Story* (2005) and the thriller *Red Flag* (2009) around this time. Karpovsky would later find wider fame as poor Ray, the struggling, bitter, Andy Kaufman–obsessed café worker on *Girls*. Says Karpovsky, "There's no way there'd be this explosion in independent film that we've seen in the last six or seven years if it wasn't for the digital paradigm shift, making cameras that allow for an aesthetically presentable format on a financially acceptable level."

The technology included new computer software like iMovie that enabled aspiring young filmmakers to edit on their personal computers rather than rent an expensive Avid system. These advances, combined with the critical context of mumblecore as a viable subgenre, led to the support of major film festivals, which were now thriving as both a business pool and a sort of social circle. "The festival circuit is where I met most of the people that I ended up collaborating with," says Karpovsky.

Joe Swanberg was one of the aspiring filmmakers fascinated by the improbable rise of Bujalski. A film student at Southern Illinois University, he had an amused, mischievous squint and preferred more radical fare. "*Funny Ha Ha* was heavily influential to me," he says. "In a sense it provided a chart of all the things I didn't want to do with my first movie." A firebrand and button pusher more than a basic entertainer, Swanberg felt that, if anything, Bujalski's "kind" world was a bit too quaint. He'd worked in a video store as a teen in suburban Illinois where he could mail-order independent films. By the time he was graduating, he felt he'd already consumed the classics of the 1980s and '90s: the independent films of Jim Jarmusch, Hal Hartley, Spike Lee, Todd Solondz, and Quentin Tarantino as well as New Wave directors like Eric Rohmer. "There's a nostalgic quality [to Bujalski] that I didn't relate to at all. Shooting on sixteen-millimeter, it was a throwback to a certain kind of independent film that I didn't have a need for in my life. I was ready to make movies about where the culture was that second. I didn't want it to look old. I wanted it to look oppressively current. I really embraced that video look, that kind of handheld reality-TV look." If Swanberg afforded Bujalski any respect at all, it was for the barriers the older director had knocked down. "He was a big inspiration because here was this guy who made this really small movie with his friends, and I'd gone and bought a ticket and seen it in a movie theater."

The first film Swanberg made after graduating from film school was called *Kissing on the Mouth*. Shot on digital video, it covers similar ground as *Funny Ha Ha,* but its depiction of postcollege relationships, infidelity, and insecurity is much more in-your-face. Swanberg cuts the soapy travails of his leads Ellen (Swanberg's then-girlfriend, Kate Winterich) and Patrick (Swanberg himself) with documentary-style interviews with real-life new college grads. "With that first movie I just wanted to make something really important to me. I'd been out of film school for like seven months and I hadn't done anything. Everything about *Kissing on the Mouth* was about practicality. My girlfriend, who is my wife now, and two of our friends did everything on the movie, acted in it and wrote it."

Swanberg, like Bujalski, features in his own work, but only out of necessity. "I wanted to put this really explicit sexual stuff in there, and I know that I'm comfortable doing it so I know there's one less person I have to talk to about this." Specifically, there's a scene where Patrick masturbates to ejaculation in the shower. It's shot very matter-of-factly, as if it's the most boring, routine thing in the world, creating an uneasy sensation in the viewer. The rawness of this new movement in film seems to be a kiss-off to the sort of neo-Reagan values that surged back under the Bush-Cheney administration. "Early on I was really angry that I wasn't seeing this stuff in movies. It just made no sense to me that as adults there seems to be a fear of putting this stuff on the screen—coming out of film school, I was really annoyed by the lack of courage I was seeing in Indie films," Swanberg says. "We were living in a weird, new Puritan age."

The fearless sexuality and attitude of Swanberg's early films made an impact at Austin's South by Southwest festival, where, for basically the cost of application dues, a young filmmaker could carve out a name for his low- or no-budget feature. "It wasn't until I got to Austin that I realized that the main advantage of the film festival was to meet people and see new work. That week at SXSW in 2005 was completely life-changing for me. In the span of seven days I met more people who are still important to me than I ever will again."

Aaron Katz, the most sophisticated visual stylist of the new movement, was also there that year with his debut, *Dance Party, USA*. Essentially a day in the life of attendees of a suburban keg party, it's teens with cheap cups of beer talking about life, squinty-eyed, stoned, and unintentionally hilarious. "You know what shit fucks me up? The clit," one says. The verisimilitude is astounding, and the digital color scheme feels deep, like old Super 8 home movies.

Also at SXSW, Mark and Jay Duplass, two brothers from New Orleans, were premiering *The Puffy Chair*. The film concerns a young man who enlists his brother to travel to pick up the titular piece of furniture, won in an eBay auction, to present to their father on his birthday. It's a road-trip movie, à la Alexander Payne's *Sideways*, with higher production values and a greater sense of "someone took time to actually write a script here" than most mumblecore offerings to date. The Duplasses are also the least meandering of the early mumblecore directors. Swanberg was representing with his next film, *LOL*, which had become one of several dozen acronyms, in this case for "laugh out loud," instantly known and constantly employed by the new, fast, social-media generation. The film is a quickly made hodgepodge of donated footage bound together by the theme of technology as something that brings people closer in an illusory way; it consists almost entirely of phone messages left for people.

"I was desperate to get back," Swanberg says. "I came home from the last SXSW and immediately started working on [2006's] *LOL* because I knew I wanted to be back at that festival the next year. I never wanted to not be part of that conversation and part of that community."

"There were all these great regional film festivals that bring filmmakers together [in the 2000s]," says the writer-director-editor Lynn Shelton. "I think a lot of new filmmakers emerged, and especially those making really small films with their buddies and figuring it out on their own. It's like we were in the trenches alone and we'd completely bond when we'd meet each other at these fests because our families and friends didn't have any idea what we were doing. They couldn't really relate to the blood, sweat, and tears and then the massive effort it takes to make a movie."

"They were critical," Duplass says of the mid-'00s festivals. "Jay and I often credit Sundance with the reason we have a career in the first place. But it was also a place where we met our peers and made some of our longest-lasting friends. Also, there was a new breed of young filmmakers working with the new technology in the early mid-2000's, and we all just sort of gelled."

Previously, a director or producer would show up at a festival sweating over whether their relatively expensive production (sometimes the product of a maxed-out credit card) would sell and allow them to eat. Now the pressure was more like, "Will my peers like it and encourage me to continue?" These films were so cheap, the professional stakes were in the basement, and art was everything.

LOL is also noteworthy as the film debut of Greta Gerwig. If *Funny Ha Ha*'s Kate Dollenmayer was presented with the option of being mumblecore's breakout female movie star and rejected it, Gerwig, a student at Barnard College, was happy to have the job. Swanberg met Gerwig through a mutual friend, Chris Wells. Wells and the director became acquainted at the Telluride Film Festival, and Swanberg sent him a copy of *Kissing on the Mouth*. "He'd shown it to Greta and some of his other friends at Columbia. She was just his girlfriend at the time and kind of interested in acting."

At the time, Swanberg was shooting a Web series for IFC called *Young American Bodies*. The newly launched channel was all over mumblecore, as it was inexpensive and intriguing. Gerwig inspired the director to begin writing for her.

"I had a good time shooting a scene with her, and started putting together *Hannah Takes the Stairs*," Swanberg says. "She confessed to me later that she knew I was going to do another movie and that she was purposefully around." Gerwig wasn't simply opportunistic. She was also a writer, studying English and philosophy. She brought ideas and did not shy away from the subject matter. "Shooting a movie without a script required actors to generate a lot of their own material, and at the time scenes were pretty sexually explicit, or at least sexually realistic, and she was somebody who didn't seem to be fazed by all that—I was impressed by that aspect of her—and I also thought that her presence was really magnetic."

The statuesque, blond Gerwig was, relative to the mousy mumblecore actresses, a kind of Gena Rowlands among two dozen Peter Falks; a conventional beauty with a good complexion. She had a quirky, sometimes goofy demeanor that seemed authentic, despite her Hollywood-ready looks. "She almost seemed to me like somebody who was already a movie star," Swanberg now says. "I just sort of knew she was up for the challenge and I also knew she was excited about doing a film, which was a major criterion for me."

"I think Greta is just a star," Duplass (who stars alongside her in *Hannah Takes the Stairs*) says. "She's odd, likable, funny, cute, raw. I love working with her and hope to do so again—she also has that wonderful extra skill of being a talented writer, so her improvisation is particularly astute."

The production values of *Hannah Takes the Stairs* are not that different from those of *LOL,* but Gerwig makes *Hannah* explode on-screen. Like Dollenmayer, she is a postgrad who's unsure of what she wants. She works at a website (where Bujalski, in a cameo, is also employed) and dates around. But here was a mumblecore star who actually wanted to be famous, and the whole scene just took off. "It was instantly a way bigger movie than we expected," says Swanberg.

Features in *Rolling Stone*'s annual "Hot" issue, *Filmmaker,* and the *New York Times* followed. "Artists who mine life's minutiae are by no means new, but mumblecore bespeaks a true 21st-century sensibility, reflective of MySpace-like social networks and the voyeurism and intimacy of YouTube. It also signals a paradigm shift in how movies are made and how they find an audience," Dennis Lim wrote in the *Times.* The IFC Center, a newly opened movie house on Sixth Avenue where the old Waverly Theater used to be, launched a ten-film mumblecore series that summer.

"At first, we all laughed at the word *mumblecore*," Duplass says. "It seemed a bit pejorative, but in the end if the *New York Times* was going to write about our tiny little movies, we figured they could call them whatever the hell they wanted."

With the heightened attention, of course, came the inevitable backlash. "For a lot of people, those movies sucked," says Swanberg. "I didn't really absorb that hurt until much later—I think it was shocking. We'd been in a little bubble of the cinephile world, but basically for a week owned the New York film scene. It felt like a big deal to all of us, and then within a couple of days it felt like everyone hated it and we all had targets on our chests."

"I do think the term is a bit limiting now," Duplass says, "and maybe doesn't apply to the disparate styles we all have. It's almost come to be synonymous with 'microbudget,' which is just too broad to be useful. Most importantly, I think the term sounds downright artsy-fartsy. And I'd hate for any viewer to stay away from one of my movies because they think to themselves, 'Mumblecore? Dumb word. Sounds pretentious. I'll skip that one.'"

Some audiences avoided mumblecore or anything that smacked of it as a nuisance at best, a rip-off at worst. "It's amazing to me the currency that word has had," says Bujalski. "I remember the moment in 2005 when I repeated it to a journalist. Then it kind of lay dormant for a couple of years. When Swanberg was getting the most hype around *Hannah Takes the Stairs*, it just exploded. The last thing I ever thought that my movies would be was provocative—it shocked me that they could drive people to anger."

Others, of course, embraced the movement as a kind of salvation, seeing characters just like themselves on screen for the first time. The films were short and easily screened on laptops. They were funny, sexy, and bore the fingerprints of their creators. These fans ran to mumblecore openings at top speed. "I thought it was sort of an umbrella term that was used by programmers and publicists and film-festival programmers to promote these movies," says Karpovsky. "And that's great. It got them more attention than they would otherwise, and I think that's wonderful."

Mumblecore was proving adaptable. The Duplass brothers transposed the subgenre's smart, talky, low-budget qualities onto genre films: in 2008 they made *Baghead*, a kind of *Blair Witch Project* for smart people. It takes place in a cabin in the woods, where a bunch of Indie filmmakers "hole up to write a feature film that stars us." It's both a satire and a viable product that expands what a mumblecore film can be. Gerwig costars as one of the would-be victims of the titular Baghead. Was it a joke? Baghead literally wears a bag over his head. And if it was a joke, who was it on?

"Jay and I are plot whores," Duplass says of the difference between a Swanberg free-form experimental film and a Duplass production, which feels more conventional and "movie-like." "We love to keep our movies moving forward inside of a genre with plot pumping along, rather than a more navel-gazing, dialogue-driven structure."

Similarly, Lynn Shelton delineated herself by having excellent sound, a tight sense of plot, and wry scenarios that would fit nicely with any smart Hollywood comedy. Simply put, the once-amateurish school was becoming more sophisticated.

Swanberg, an outsider to the end—though friends with both the Duplasses and Shelton—worried that Gerwig was getting stars in her eyes.

"Greta picked up a lot of bad habits from other actors on that movie [*Baghead*]," says Swanberg, who reunited with Gerwig to film *Nights and Weekends,* which would be released in 2008. This would be a full collaboration, with Gerwig cowriting and directing the story of a breakup, but the divergent ambition of Swanberg, who wanted to stay Indie, and Gerwig, who was hearing the call of mainstream Hollywood, was palpable. It was a fraught production with multiple stops and starts even as the two filmmakers continued to tour *Hannah Takes the Stairs* around the country to adoring film-festival crowds.

Humpday, Shelton's follow-up to her debut *My Effortless Brilliance* (starring Harvey Danger front man Sean Nelson as a pretentious author), appeared in 2009 and concerned Ben (Mark Duplass) and Andrew (Josh Leonard, a veteran of the actual *Blair Witch Project*), another pair of estranged old buddies who entertain the notion of filming a gay porno movie as an art project. Ben is living in middle-class comfort. Andrew is freewheeling and calls his friend out on his lifestyle. For an uncomfortable moment, Ben takes the bait for the sake of the creative breakthrough. "Google 'porn.' It's all been done. There's not a lot of dude-on-dude who are not gay," says Andrew, goading his friend.

Shelton's commentary on bored and restless privilege was much needed at the time, as if to say, "Just because it's cheap to make a film these days doesn't mean we have to film everything, people." "Something just hit me," Ben admits before the deed is recorded and uploaded. "I think we might be morons." Critics adored the absurdity and the fresh sense of existential confusion that hadn't been seen since the days of *The Graduate.* Similarly, *Breaking Upwards,* by Zoe Lister Jones and Daryl Wein, finds a New York couple, also privileged and also bored. As an experiment, they decide to take a consensual break from each other and date other people. The film was shot for only $15,000 but features name actors—Olivia Thirlby, who would later star in *Juno* and *Bored to Death,* as well as acclaimed Broadway actress Julie White—and a relative lack of improvisation. As it went with Michael Stipe after a few R.E.M. albums, the mumblers were beginning to enunciate.

"In terms of the postmumblecore universe, yes, our attention to production value, scriptwriting, and trained actors was a definite choice," says Lister Jones. "I think we felt frustrated that DIY filmmaking had come to mean a lack of all of those things, and we set out to prove that a microbudget could still account for narrative arcs, dynamic actors, artful lighting, and muscular dialogue. *Breaking Upwards* was also a response to the way in which our generation was overwhelmingly portrayed on film as meandering, lost, and mopey. We didn't feel represented, and so we wanted to shine light on a world of driven, neurotic, emotionally articulate twenty-somethings instead."

Meanwhile, Swanberg and Gerwig were quite literally meandering, lost and mopey, trying to complete *Nights and Weekends* under the pressure of following up their hit *Hannah Takes the Stairs.* "We were not on good terms," Swanberg says. "It was a terrible experience. Through the process of making *Hannah Takes the Stairs,* I became completely infatuated with Greta. She felt the same about me as a director. It made my relationship uncomfortable and her relationship uncomfortable. It's the thing about these kind of movies. Because there's no script, it's self-generated. The shooting atmosphere and the way the movie is put together is always really intimate. And it definitely bleeds into real life." Sexually explicit and raw, it's hard to watch *Nights and Weekends* and not feel a little creepy, like you are witnessing an actual rift. "At the time I was very gung ho about having this very freewheeling artist life. I was happy to have the movie and real life mixed up. That's the power of the movie. It's what I was going for."

Gerwig, by contrast, was becoming more and more removed from the process and more and more professional. When they'd get together to film, Swanberg noticed her becoming increasingly mannered. "It was really different. She had all these tics and new things she was doing. I was excited about her in *Hannah*. She was totally unformed and un-actory. We got into a lot of arguments."

"There isn't a normal dynamic between us," Gerwig admitted in 2008. "Our entire relationship is based on work, and because of that, it's sort of like we don't know how to be any other way than completely intense and absorbed with one another. It's never really been like, 'Oh yeah, let's just go grab coffee for an afternoon.' It always ends up with, like, screaming accusations." Perversely, the film itself depicts the two actors in near-pornographic sexual congress.

Ironically, it would be through Swanberg that Gerwig would meet the director who would give her a breakthrough "movie star" role opposite a proven box-office king. "I'd gone and seen *Margot at the Wedding*, which I thought was awesome," said Swanberg, perhaps unsurprisingly, of Noah Baumbach's most polarizing film. He sent Baumbach a fan letter and discovered that the older director had been a fan of *Hannah Takes the Stairs*. Baumbach had made something of a proto-mumblecore film in the late '90s following the production of his second film, *Mr. Jealousy*. *Highball*, shot on a low budget with a bunch of friends and regular actors like Annabella Sciorra, Dean

Wareham, and Justine Bateman, had an improvised script, no context, and was never meant to be released. "It was just a ditty," says Joel Kastelberg, producer of Baumbach's first two, "proper" films. When it was released, the director had his name removed from the credits. Still, the freedom of creating a film on a borrowed set with nothing but a loose story line appealed to him. In the mid-'00s, he'd been observing the mumblecore movement from outside, an established director for over a decade, with major movie stars in his films. Swanberg and Baumbach would collaborate briefly on an off-the-cuff ensemble piece about a play production, *Alexander the Last*. "I remember at some point in the summer of 2008 we all hung out together," Swanberg says of how Baumbach came to cast Gerwig in his 2010 film *Greenberg*. "It was a period when everyone was interacting. I certainly didn't sit them down together and introduce them."

Baumbach, married to *Fast Times at Ridgemont High* actress Jennifer Jason Leigh at the time, may well have been fascinated by Gerwig, but more likely he was energized by the speed and honesty of mumblecore-style filmmaking. Baumbach's subsequent films, from *Greenberg* to *Frances Ha*, would both star Gerwig, by then his girlfriend and creative partner, and create a sort of genre offshoot that would marry mumblecore lightness and speed to classical screenwriting and filmmaking techniques.

Gerwig soon disappeared from Swanberg's orbit for good. "She did almost zero promotion for *Nights and Weekends*," he now says. "That was the last period of time that I really talked to her or hung out with her." Not exactly bitter, Swanberg isn't a fan of this postmumblecore hybrid either, the union of Hollywood and the digital Twee cinema.

Of course, it's hard to classify *Greenberg* in any way as a sellout. It's a difficult film, beautifully shot in sunny, smoggy L.A. and almost cruelly unsparing in its treatment of the *Kicking and Screaming* college kids reckoning with forty. They are no longer rehearsing or becoming *anything*. This is it. If they didn't make it (in Roger Greenberg's case, as a rock star), they aren't going to. Those who have kids are parents. Those who don't . . . won't. Greenberg (played by a subdued Ben Stiller), fresh out of a stay in a mental hospital after a nervous breakdown, is fine with that, as he is committed to "doing nothing." His plan is that he will drift through the rest of his days and wait around to die, swallowing pills to keep the demons away. Then he meets Florence (Gerwig). In lesser hands, she'd be a manic pixie dream girl, that well-established Hollywood cliché of the younger, plucky woman who lifts the spirits of the usually older, lost hero. But Florence is as screwed up as Roger is. When they fall in love, it's plausible. They fit. He's terrible, borderline abusive to her, but he also makes her mix CDs. "Hurt people hurt people," she tells him, and it's somehow illuminating. *Greenberg,* which also features Duplass in a small role, is both a commentary on postmumblecore preciousness and a beneficiary of its energy. "All the men out here dress like children and the children dress like superheroes," Greenberg observes.

At the film's climax, Stiller's sad hero, once a would-be rock star and now driven to the nuthouse with anxiety and regret, is wired on a line of coke and surrounded by twenty-somethings at a house party. They snicker as he compliments them on the quality of their drugs. "You're mean," he says. "The thing about you kids is you're all kind of insensitive. I'm glad I grew up when I did. Your parents were too perfect at parenting. All that baby Mozart and Dan Zanes songs. You're so *sincere* and *interested* in things . . . There's a confidence in you guys that's horrifying." If *Kicking and Screaming* is Twee's restless *Easy Rider, Greenberg* is its resigned *Lost in America.*

Critics were divided yet again. It was definitely a love-it-or-hate-it offering. "Greta's amazing in that movie, but I think it's not good at all," says Swanberg. "I don't feel this way anymore, but at the time, I thought, 'Why would you spend eight million dollars to make this? If you're going to try to shoot a little handheld movie in natural light, why cast movie stars and spend all this money? Ben Stiller looks like a guy that's had plastic surgery, not the kind of real person that these movies were sort of about. But Greta is amazing."

Gerwig found herself at a crossroads after *Greenberg.* She was hot, but it was a slippery slope. Following in the footsteps of Chloë Sevigny, she opted to work with established auteurs, filming a small part in Woody Allen's *To Rome with Love* and taking a lead in Whit Stillman's *Damsels in Distress.* She made a play for major movie stardom alongside Russell Brand in an unnecessary remake of the Dudley Moore classic *Arthur* (in the Liza Minnelli role) that cooled both stars' careers for a time.

When Lister Jones and Wein were given a relatively large budget to shoot the follow-up to *Breaking Upwards,* they cast Gerwig as Lola in the title role of *Lola Versus,* a sort of updated version of her searching, urban Hannah character, without the same freedom. "Well, we went from fifteen thousand dollars to five million, and we thought we had hit the jackpot," says Lister Jones. Debra Winger and Bill Pullman play Lola's parents. "We took a pretty brutal beating with critics and trolls alike," Lister Jones says. "I think there is always a backlash when Indie goes corporate, because people can sense the tension between the two in the work itself. And they feel betrayed by something being represented as Indie when it has a number of super-commercial elements. The wolf in sheep's clothing. There's no way to avoid it, especially in this technological age when everyone is a critic, and those critics who are established have to be cruel in order to get an audience. It's sad. But Woody Allen said something like, 'If you listen to them when they love you, you have to listen to them when they hate you.' So I guess the trick is to never listen to them at all."

Gerwig returned to Baumbach as his collaborator and muse in 2013 for *Frances Ha*, another young-woman-in-the-city film that fared much better with critics. Meanwhile the Duplasses, and to a lesser extent Lynn Shelton, joined Richard Linklater and Spike Lee in attempting to work within the studio system with major movie stars while not dispensing with their Indie ethic or compromising their vision completely. Mark Duplass seemed able to pivot from appearing in big-budget studio films like Kathryn Bigelow's *Zero Dark Thirty* and generating, with his brother Jay, charming, no-budget comedies like *The Do-Deca-Pentathlon* (which features two rival brothers and the childhood athletic competition they cannot let go of) with real aplomb.

"Jay and I always wanted to make money writing in the system, kind of like John Sayles," Mark Duplass says. "We thought we'd write for money, take that money, and make little films. We've found that we can exist a bit more peacefully inside the system as filmmakers as well. Also, my acting career has really brought in some great awareness and income to make the movies we want. But, yes, in the end we always hoped we could exist in the system enough to make a decent living, own a house, and have a family without starving."

Today, each of the Duplasses' new releases is a kind of event for film critics, and ironically, it may have been their example that convinced holdouts like Swanberg and Bujalski to dip their toes into the Hollywood pool. Swanberg's *Drinking Buddies,* released in the summer of 2013, featured Olivia Wilde, star of the mega-budget flop *Cowboys & Aliens,* as well as Anna Kendrick of *Twilight* and Jake Johnson of *New Girl.* "I've felt it's time to not just be a self-absorbed filmmaker," Swanberg told the *New York Times* upon the film's release. "It's about time that we grew up a bit." As with his other films, *Drinking Buddies* is improvised, and, discounting the explicit sex (now long gone), it's not that far removed from *Hannah Takes the Stairs.*

"It's still the same kind of movie I've always been making," Swanberg swears. "The actors are well known, but they still have to show up every day and make up the dialogue. What's gone forever is the need to have to be best friends with the people I'm making a movie with."

Bujalski's *Computer Chess* is only slightly more plot driven, but the white-saturated home-video style did not appeal to anyone beyond the art houses when it was released in the late summer of 2013. It remains firmly in the context of his older work: documentary-like, wry, talky, and sweet. That he worries it might be a bit more commercial somehow is part of Bujalski's considerable charm. Still, most of the mumblecore school of the new century, many of its practitioners now in their thirties or early forties with families to support, are inevitably headed into the mainstream. "I kind of can't put that off any longer," Bujalski told the *New York Times* when *Computer Chess* was released. Will they keep their Twee stubbornness, innocence, and "shoot till you can't shoot anymore and cut until you find the truth" methods intact? We will have to stream and see.

Chapter 14

It'll Change Your Life

2002–2008

In which Indie's three-decade-long, slow and steady rise toward commercial and cultural dominance is manifest, and Brooklyn emerges as its taste-making center, thanks in part to a film . . . about New Jersey.

Rock and roll at the start of the twenty-first century wasn't very sexy, and then it became sexy again, and then it became resolutely unsexy and stayed that way. As the 1990s ended, rock was the province of either thudding mooks who ripped off the Pixies' loud-quiet-loud motif, like Limp Bizkit, or sensitive singer-songwriters, new James Taylors and Dan Fogelbergs, like Chris Martin of Coldplay and John Mayer. Then, in the fall of 2001 and into the winter of 2002, bands like the Strokes, with their skinny jeans and Chuck Taylors, along with their "garage rock" contemporaries such as the White Stripes, Interpol, and Black Rebel Motorcycle Club, did what seemed impossible: they brought late-1970s Punk rock to yet another phase. This modern rock renovation was one informed by the digital "modern age," pop savvy in that plugged-in, fully-informed-fan way, but with a firm footing in the past and its gloriously rudimentary primitivism. Black leather jackets were the uniform again, now cropped and tight.

N.M.E. and *Melody Maker,* the only two big print music week-lies around, went batty for everything about this sound, and soon a generation of British bands, the Libertines the most talented among them, were adopting the druggy downtown style themselves. Punk was back, and then, within eighteen months, it was over again, brought down just as it had been before by hype, drugs, power strug-gles, and burnout. Just as had happened with Punk heroes in the late '70s, there were thousands of kids worldwide who liked the Strokes fine but could never dress like them and were intimidated by their seemingly effortless urban cool. The Strokes' white belts would soon join the safety pin in the museum, and a gentler, more sensitive strain of Twee Tribe–friendly rock would become even more commercially valuable, and a major cultural force. Many of these bands—the Shins, the Decemberists, Death Cab for Cutie and its offshoot the Postal Service, Rilo Kiley, Sufjan Stevens, and Beirut—predated the Strokes or were their contemporaries. The problem was that these bands were hopelessly unhip. Then, when uncool became cool and white belt hip-ster fatigue set in, as it inevitably would, they seized their chance. They were post-hip superstars. There was a book released in the UK in 1986 called *Like Punk Never Happened* that described the shift from Punk—lean, mean, three-chord rock and roll—to cuddly, marketable stars like Boy George and George Michael. By 2004 it seemed that the same thing was happening. It was as if the Strokes never existed.

After two stellar albums (*Room on Fire* and *Is This It*), this fab five decided, like their '90s heroes in Pearl Jam did, to retreat some, exhausted and over it. Some got married and had kids. Others went down drug holes and came out the other side, but they would never be the same band again. Meanwhile Jack White became more or less his own man, following his unshakable vision and the occasional band. Into the rock void came the Twee soundtrack and a series of bedroom-geek-approved, *Pitchfork*-endorsed bands that were, almost uniformly, more gentle, thoughtful, and cuddly. They wore no leather, but rather neat sweaters (Vampire Weekend). They played old-timey instruments like the French horn, the cornet, and the accordion (Beirut). Some were almost inevitably Canadian (Arcade Fire), but most came, or at least migrated to, Brooklyn, rehearsing in an old pencil factory by the river in Williamsburg and releasing music directly to the fans who prized them as their imaginary friends.

Almost none of these bands were inferior to the Strokes. Many of them, Vampire Weekend and Arcade Fire certainly, proved even more consistently great. It's just that if you ran into them in a dark alley, you would not feel a chill up your spine and reach into your pocket to protect your wallet. It was, frankly, disorienting for those who covered the scene, as I did at the time. One minute I was up all night, drinking Pabst Blue Ribbon with the Strokes, and the next I was in the basement of an old social club somewhere in Brooklyn, discussing stamp collecting and bird-watching with a clean-cut, dead-sober Sufjan Stevens. "I've got a *Peterson Guide* [for bird-watching] and all that stuff," Stevens told me excitedly. When I ventured into Brooklyn to find Zach Condon, who traveled Old Europe collecting sounds and instruments and then recorded his first albums in his New Mexico bedroom under the moniker Beirut, I could barely find his walk-up, in the middle of what was then a Hasidic Jewish enclave far off the Bedford Avenue strip. It felt like being in Poland or Prague. "It's a different city," Condon said of Brooklyn in 2006. "You can only see the rooftops of Manhattan, and that's about it. I actually get frustrated there. It's too much like Disneyland. I'm really affected by the space I'm around. I'm super sensitive to aesthetics." Brooklyn was proving a blank slate where musicians like Condon could build their own universe as they envisioned it, a kind of new "Old New York" that suited their romantic notions and didn't have the peer pressure and the coked-up pace of Manhattan. Much of the music shared the tempo.

"So much of it does not rock. Not in any sense," says Simon Reynolds. "One of its hallmarks is other instrumentation. The guitar does not function as the dominant instrument anymore. It's what depresses me slightly about it, that it's so tightly linked to class now. College-type people listen to it. The fact that it's covered by NPR basically seems to indicate that it's become a sort of class marker."

Danger was being phased out in stand-up comedy as well, in favor of a Twee boyishness—or, in the case of Kristen Schaal and Sarah Silverman, acid-tongued girlishness. Andy Kaufman and Steve Martin—no longer Lenny Bruce, Richard Pryor, John Belushi, George Carlin, or Sam Kinison (all druggy, edgy, and doomed to rides either short or extremely bumpy)—seemed to be the new heroes. Kaufman, an oddball from an upper-middle-class Long Island family, debuted in the autumn of '75 on the inaugural season of NBC's late-night sketch comedy *Saturday Night Live* and became yet another eventual Twee hero.

His breakthrough act, the one that made him nationally famous, was honed in the comedy clubs of New York and Hollywood. It found him standing nervously alongside a mounted turntable as it played the theme to *Mighty Mouse*. He'd twitch and wait for the chorus—"Here I come to save the day!"—lip-synching with an almost camp fervor for a few brief moments before falling back into his timid stance. And thus was introduced an "Is this real or a put-on?" sense of enjoyable paranoia to popular culture. Kaufman only enhanced this with powder-keg appearances on *The Tonight Show* and, most famously, *Late Night with David Letterman*. Kaufman, like Richman, could push and push, singing "Old MacDonald" ("With a moo, moo, here and a moo, moo, there . . .") until he broke the crowd and had them. "There are no punch lines to anything I do," he once said. Anyone waiting for the wink would wait forever.

In *Girls,* Ray (actor Alex Karpovsky) owns almost nothing of value but a signed cutout of the late comedian. Kaufman and very early Steve Martin made stand-up comedy safe for the young at heart. In order to be a popular stand-up during this period, once Woody Allen vacated the art form for film, you had to be raunchy and manly: Richard Pryor, George Carlin. The only other alternatives were the buttoned-down, classy observers with their bow ties and dry, radio-announcer deliveries. Kaufman and early Martin (iconic prop arrow through his head) were deeply in touch with their childhoods. Martin's "Happy Feet" routine was as much a whimsical notion as Kaufman's Mighty Mouse bit. He'd stop a serious monologue with the warning, "Uh-oh, I'm getting . . . happy feet," then break into a goofball soft-shoe, his hands flailing wildly, before returning to the staid banter. These were boys in men's suits doing humor that was not too far from the schoolyard, whereas someone like Richard Pryor was a grown man, courting and wrestling with darkness.

"If you showed one hundred people a clip of Andy Kaufman doing a character or doing the bit with the phonograph, the last thing that any person you showed it to would say was, 'That's a man!'" says veteran stand-up comedy manager Barry Katz today. "If you saw Steve Martin doing 'Happy Feet' in an era he was in, or bunny ears, if you showed a hundred people that clip, they would not say, 'That's a man!'" Kaufman and Martin would both adapt their popular stand-up acts to television and became even more famous as the masses somehow accepted their inherent strangeness and precociousness, their lack of the conventional setup-and-punch-line structure. They were dangerous and unpredictable, of a piece with Punk and post-Punk but with a boyish sweetness and cleverness they wore very much on their sleeves.

Kaufman seemed to pour all of his residual darkness into a character named Tony Clifton, a vulgar lounge singer in the Vegas-Sinatra mode. Clifton, who drank, smoked, whored, and burned bridges, seemed to exist so that the painfully awkward Andy Kaufman could remain and take his audience out for milk and cookies after a performance at New York's revered Carnegie Hall. Martin became a movie star, and in underrated films like *Pennies from Heaven* and *Dead Men Don't Wear Plaid* backed away from his stand-up persona. Even his goofball comedies would have small grace moments, as in *The Jerk,* which briefly suspends the broad comedy to find Martin strolling seaside, plucking a ukulele, and harmonizing on "Tonight You Belong to Me" with paramour Bernadette Peters. It's a serious and highly romantic moment, until Peters produces a cornet from nowhere and takes a solo.

Still, for all their shunning of reality, without both Twee comedy pioneers, there would be no Indie strain of the comedy sect today. Bill Hicks and Mitch Hedberg, perhaps the last of the progeny of Carlin and Pryor, ceded the stage to the likes of doughy, nonthreatening stars like Mike Birbiglia, who, in his oxford shirt, is more of a child of monologist Spalding Gray. Demetri Martin, Kristen Schaal, and even the relative veteran Sarah Silverman can be boyish or girlish and powerful in part because of the context we can now place them in. They will never fill arenas like Dane Cook or Kevin Hart, and may always play the best friend or the weird neighbor on TV shows (whereas Steve Martin and Andy Kaufman were leads), but they are free to be their occasionally and sometimes gleefully stunted selves and prosper.

TV too backed off the darkness of *Twin Peaks* in favor of a new gentleness that seemed to speak to the new generation directly, if not to the masses. MTV, after the alternative revolution, continued to phase out music videos in favor of event programming geared toward the new Internet-savvy audience. It picked up the soon-to-be-canceled *My So-Called Life* from ABC in 1995 and reran nineteen episodes, introducing the low-rated series to a wide audience. Angela Chase, played by a teenaged Clare Danes, is on the cusp of adulthood (as represented by her neurotic parents) and at a social crossroads at her high school. (Her goony-sweet next-door neighbor Brian Krakow is going nowhere socially but is dependable. The handsome-but-vacant Jordan Catalano is sexy but unaccountable.) She's not a popular kid, but not a loser either. It's a sophisticated portrayal of an identity crisis set to the new platinum Indie rock. She spends much of the groundbreaking show frowning furrows in her forehead, aghast at the enormity of it all. Will she ever get to college, or will the Buffalo Tom concert have to suffice? Here were the first teenagers ever portrayed in pop culture, to deliver the message: "We know this system is insane."

"I think it was the first TV show to deal with adolescence in a realistic and respectful way," says Devon Gummersall, who plays the hapless, kinky-haired Brian Krakow, a kind of teenage saint of unrequited love. "It's really difficult for writers who are in their thirties or forties to do justice to the teenage years—we all have a natural selective memory." MTV got it and played *My So-Called Life* constantly. "MTV established it in a lot of ways," says Gummersall. "They played it for five years. They overplayed those nineteen episodes incessantly. It was great; that was where we became a cult show—that's where it started to become a lasting thing in the public consciousness."

The animated *Daria,* which premiered in 1997, featured a protagonist like Clare Dane's Angela Chase, another questioning loser hero. Her sister, Quinn, is a golden girl. Her mother is a distracted businesswoman. Daria is mortified by them both: "I don't have low self-esteem," she says, "I have low esteem for everyone else." In 1999, *Freaks and Geeks* offered a portrait of high school in the early 1980s that sated the desire for all things Reagan-era with even more satisfying detail, as it was staffed by people who were actually in high school in the early 1980s: creator Paul Feig, executive producer Judd Apatow, and writers like Mike White. The story of Lindsay Weir, her little brother Sam, and their high school experience mines some of the terrain covered in *My So-Called Life*. Lindsay is a mathlete and a geek, but she's also a secret rebel, drawn to the freaks, who smoke pot and listen to Rush and Styx in the parking lot. Her parents are nuts (*SCTV*'s Joe Flaherty and Becky Ann Baker, who would go on to play Hannah Horvath's mother on *Girls*). Her teachers are worse.

The show combines elements of *My So-Called Life's* drama and sensitivity with a healthy sense of classic '70s and '80s stand-up humor. When both elements came together, as they did on the classic late-season episode "The Little Things"—when Seth Rogen's Ken learns that his new girlfriend, Amy, was born with both male and female reproductive organs and was made female by her doctors—it set a template for the kind of gross-out comedies with hearts of gold that would be the new Apatow blockbusters of the twenty-first century: *The 40-Year-Old Virgin, Knocked Up, Bridesmaids.*

Freaks and Geeks lasted only one season, and, like the earlier show, amassed a cult, quote-spewing following. It was an expensive show to produce, jam-packed with costly retro pop and New Wave (its theme is Joan Jett and the Blackhearts' "Bad Reputation"), and the authenticity that did it in was part of its appeal.

Stars Hollow, the fictional town in Connecticut that is the setting for *Gilmore Girls,* is a kind of snowy Narnia where there's no violent crime—another sweet universe, not unlike the burgeoning Kind Brooklyn. The only nuisances there are trolling troubadours like Grant Lee Phillips. Stars Hollow was a safe little corner of the world for Gen Twee.

Created by Amy Sherman-Palladino and first aired in 2000, *Gilmore Girls* is Twee fantasy. It asks, "What if my daughter really was my best friend?" The rift between parents and children, endemic to all youth-oriented popular entertainment, is finally erased. We know it's fantasy because mother Lorelai (Lauren Graham) and daughter Rory (Alexis Bleidel) consume nothing but pizza, hamburgers, and black coffee but remain perfectly trim. And yet the fantasy is almost never questioned because reality, increasingly harsh on the outside, has no place in Stars Hollow. When it does intrude, everyone learns from it.

Lorelai was pregnant at sixteen, "the scandal girl." Her life upended, to the chagrin of her wealthy and standing-conscious parents, she didn't go off to college and instead left home and pledged her life to raising the child (also named Lorelai but known to all as Rory) the right way. Lorelai has character. She's a flake, but her sacrifice gives her grace. Lorelai is also, crucially, raising her daughter idealistically. She is the parent all Brooklandians want to be. *Gilmore Girls* is all about references: Dawn Powell, Sid Vicious, Ruth Gordon, Judy Blume, Slint, Steely Dan, Artie Shaw, Black Sabbath—you have to be quick to process them all, and Sherman-Palladino doesn't wait for you.

"There's a preponderance of secret language," says Chris Eigeman, who played Lorelai's love interest, Digger Stiles. When the show was released on DVD, it came with a glossary. It's the first great show of the search-engine age.

And then there was Charlie, the hero of Steven Chbosky's *The Perks of Being a Wallflower*. Released in '99 on the MTV Books imprint, the novel would sell over a million copies. Charlie is a lonely kid whose best friend recently committed suicide. He's haunted by the death of his aunt Helen, and upon transferring to a new school isn't expecting more than the usual pain and tension. But he makes friends with a crew of like-minded misfits who are proud of their outsider status, even revel in it. It defines them, and suddenly he feels warm and "infinite." *Perks* is a leap forward, part of the next step beyond Nirvana's alterative revolution. "When you can buy flannel shirts at the Gap, they stop being the flannel shirts that we fell in love with in 1990," says Chbosky. "Style, substance, music, art, movies, and television never stand still. Invariably what happens is those kids that need to be iconoclast and need to be a step away, they're going to find the next thing because they're the trendsetters and they're the trailblazers and it's never been different."

Instead of moving forward into a new world of technology, many teens of this generation simply went backward, Jack White–like, and invested in things of permanence. The era of vinyl records being sold in Urban Outfitters begins here.

"An LP is not going to be updated," Chbosky says. "It's physically healthy. It feels grounded and trustworthy. You can't put it on a phone. You can't delete it. In a modern world where everything is portable, there's something lovely about having something that's grounded."

The notion of books and records as friends is treated reverently in 2004's *Garden State,* written and directed by Zach Braff. Braff was, at the time, the star of a fairly mainstream sitcom, *Scrubs.* The show had its own devoted following and a madcap sense of humor, but few could have predicted the notes Braff would hit with his debut film, or how it would alter the lives and careers of once comfortably small Indie rockers. Mainstream Hollywood came to them, as the East Coast advertising world and MTV had already done. It took a bit longer, but the conflicts were eternal.

Twee's biggest overground moment, however, was not concocted in MTV's Times Square conference rooms. It seemed to come out of nowhere, a long-circulated, potential vanity project from a TV actor. Braff had been slowly circulating a script set in his hometown of Orange, New Jersey, for years. The film was about a troubled young man who returns home for his mother's funeral. It was a charming enough script to attract major movie stars, like Natalie Portman, then appearing in the Star Wars prequel trilogy, as well as respected, young independent film actors like Peter Sarsgaard. Produced by Danny De-Vito, it was still an under-the-radar affair.

"We'd meet up at Thirty-third Street," says Armando Riesco, who appears in the film as Jessie, an improbable overnight millionaire thanks to his invention of "silent Velcro." "And a van would take us out to New Jersey. I got the sense that people believed in this film strongly. You don't get Natalie Portman and Peter Sarsgaard on board because they're your friends."

Like *The Graduate*, its most obvious predecessor, the film opens on an airplane and is driven from start to finish by its evocative soundtrack (also featuring Simon and Garfunkel). The film's most iconic scene takes place in a doctor's office. Andrew Largeman, played by Braff, is back in his New Jersey hometown from Los Angeles, where he's a struggling actor and waiter. His mother, who drowned in the bath, had been crippled in an accident that Largeman blames himself for. Complaining of headaches, he goes to a doctor recommended by his aloof shrink father, played by Ian Holm. Waiting in the office, he encounters Natalie Portman's Sam, in jeans and a sweater with big retro-style headphones encircling her head. They chat and he casually asks what she's listening to.

"You gotta hear this one song. It'll change your life, I swear," she promises.

It's "New Slang" by the Shins, a three-year-old track from their Sub Pop album *Oh, Inverted World*. The band's front man had been around for a decade, recording in Albuquerque under the name the Shins since the late 1990s. The song is gloomy and jangly, not unlike an old Kinks track, but there's a soothing quality to it that is instant. We can see its healing effect on the grieving, tormented Largeman.

"The music was written in," Riesco says. "He knew what song was going where before anything was shot. Zach basically handpicked these songs to be on the soundtrack to his movie."

Garden State's soundtrack album, released in the summer of 2004, sold almost a million and a half copies in North America, won a Grammy, and made major rock stars out of the Shins. It also established a cultural field upon which other Indie rock bands could follow suit, bands that had nothing to do with the film but shared a gentleness and a Brooklyn-ish quality, as well as a certain professionalism. Politics and revolt were not only unnecessary, they were a liability. "Music became Twee in that middle-class Brooklyn artisanal urbanite who went to college in the nineties. It's not that I have something against that stuff. It fits into society, and what you get is niceness and contentment," Riesco says. Somehow the rise of Nirvana and the Strokes felt like triumphs of the underdog, with a strong tether to eighties Indie, both British and American, while the rise of groups like the Shins, Modest Mouse, and the Decemberists to the top of the pop charts felt like a shrug, as if, unthreatening and uncontroversial, they always somehow belonged in a Starbucks. "It was music for people who didn't buy into the ethos of cool that goes around rock, the danger element," says Riesco.

The world of *Garden State*, like Stars Hollow, was a place these cool-shunners wanted to go back to again and again. To play "New Slang" was to return to that scene and feel something. "It was the beginning of the numbness everyone feels today," says Riesco. "People texting and walking at the same time, unable to really connect with people."

Braff's shell-shocked hero is a refugee from Prozac nation. "There's a lightning storm in my head," he moans. Largeman's so numb with guilt and chemicals that he doesn't even recognize love the first time he sees it, in the form of Sam. When he meets her, in fact, she asks him if he's retarded. The answer is, of course, yes, but only emotionally. Largeman, with his motorcycle and sidecar, is Marlon Brando's Johnny, the Wild One, for his generation. Portman's Sam is his deliverer to the world of authentic emotion. This is, of course, utter fantasy, just like Lorelai and Rory Gilmore's diet. Sam is a classic "Manic Pixie Dream Girl," the term coined by Nathan Rabin in his review of Kirsten Dunst's performance in Cameron Crowe's dud romantic comedy *Elizabethtown* the following year.

Sam keeps and buries a lot of hamsters. She still has a piece of her baby blanket (named Tickle) and sometimes reboots her brain by making funny noises. There's footage of her figure skating while dressed like an alligator straight out of Sendak. She's chaste but also, crucially, sexy, warning Largeman, "We're not gonna make out or anything" when he enters her bedroom. Sam doesn't exist anywhere in nature—only in the minds of writers—but there's a darkness that she initially conceals and Largeman is too self-absorbed to detect. It gives her depth and makes her more real. Sam is an epileptic. That's why she is at the doctor's office, blocking out the reality of the situation by blasting Indie rock into her brain. She's terrified, with her body betraying her at times.

"I look forward to a good cry," she tells Largeman. Largeman looks at her as though he no longer knows what that word even means, but by the film's end she not only has him primal-screaming into an open crevasse, washed clean in a rainstorm, but sexually heals him after all—in the very tub that his mother drowned in, of all places.

"This is good! This doesn't happen often!" Sam swears to Largeman as he is about to go back to Los Angeles to resume his dead and hopeless life, the familiar. We wonder if he will wise up or get on the plane. He wises up. He runs to her, literally, and they are saved, these two broken heroes for a broken and terrified world.

Braff and the box-office success of *Garden State* would be chiefly responsible for the homely but sweet new leading men, your Michael Ceras, Jonah Hills, Jesse Eisenbergs, and Seth Rogens. "There's Channing Tatum, and then there's those guys," says Josh Hamilton, star of *Kicking and Screaming.*

In a 2012 essay in *Esquire,* the writer Stephen Marche observed of the post–*Garden State* era, "All the rebels are fey in quirky America." But are they true rebels, or was the very notion quaint in a post-post-everything world, constantly on orange alert?

Ellen Page's Juno McGuff is the closest thing the era has to a true Punk. She abhors the then-current trope of the sexy nerd: "Jocks like him always want geeky girls who play the cello and read *McSweeney's* and want to be children's librarians when they grow up," she says of her crush object, Michael Cera's Paulie Bleeker. When she and Bleeker do consummate their mutual attraction, Juno is impregnated on the first try and must reckon with this "diddle that can't be undid, home skillet," as Rainn Wilson's drugstore clerk tells her.

Diablo Cody didn't go undercover in a high school like Cameron Crowe, and the dialogue of *Juno* has no "this is how they really speak now" verisimilitude. As with *Clueless,* Cody simply nailed the attitude of young and modern Twees, and inevitably they began speaking in the Cody-invented vernacular in tribute. Like all mainstream Twee fare, *Juno* is rich in the secret language of detail: Juno's hamburger phone, her pipe, Bleeker's orange Tic Tacs. These quirks used to be the domain of the "best friend" or "weird uncle" in movies. Now they are for the leads.

The soundtrack to *Juno* was an even greater success than the *Garden State* soundtrack, although, in a post–*Garden State* culture, perhaps not the same surprise. It topped the *Billboard* charts, and the film earned more than $100 million at the domestic box office. It was nominated for Best Picture, and Cody, who'd also written a clever memoir, *Candy Girl,* about her brief time as a stripper, won the Best Original Screenplay Oscar.

Juno has the wide-of-the-mark quality of a dozen after-school specials and *One to Grow On*–style PSAs on its side, most as tone-deaf as rapping Barney Rubble. Never has teenage pregnancy and abortion been taken on in a way that hasn't seemed self-righteous or, worse, condescending. It's broad, almost farcical, and achingly real. When Mr. McGuff says, "I thought you were the kind of girl who knew when to say when," Juno responds, "I don't really know what kind of girl I am."

Instantly all the Holden Caulfield–like tough-kid slang melts away and we, the audience, are faced with Juno's terrifying dilemma and the immense responsibility that goes with it. She is not even fully formed herself as her baby is forming inside her. "It has fingernails," an anti-abortion protester tells her. This is why Cody got the gold statue.

Jason Bateman's Mark Loring, once a promising musician, is as arrested as Juno in his own way. His 1990s heyday is long in the rear-view, but he cannot let go. His wife, Vanessa, played by Jennifer Garner, is tired of "waiting around for him to become Kurt Cobain." She wants to be a mother and can no longer reckon with being married to a man-child.

Mark is astounded by Juno's facility with retro Punk rock and splatter-film auteurs and falls in love with her for her taste and the youth that she reminds him of. Of course, it's the teenager who proves herself the mature one, not only surviving her outsider status but also placing the baby with Vanessa even after Mark leaves to pursue a happiness that's almost guaranteed to elude him. The film ends with a grace note: Juno, reunited with the baby's father, Paulie, being childlike again, playing guitar and singing the Moldy Peaches ditty "Anyone Else but You," an update of the Velvets' sweet duet "I'm Sticking with You."

Suddenly the Celine Dions of the pop world were the minority and the Elliott Smiths were everywhere. The Moldy Peaches performed the song on *The View*. Cera and Page became both romantic leads and action stars without having to spray anyone with machine-gun fire or make Stallonian quips. More TV shows with a sweetness at their core were green-lit, from CBS's *The Big Bang Theory*, costarring *Garden State*'s Jim Parsons as a socially awkward physics wiz, to HBO's *Bored to Death*, starring *Rushmore*'s grown-up Jason Schwartzman as a hapless novelist moonlighting as a private detective. "I wanted an ethos of kindness underneath everything," *Bored* creator Jonathan Ames says of his Brooklyn-set farce. "It came to that after I got exposed to other TV writers. I was supposed to have a staff. I saw in those people's scripts that I was sent—everybody was mean to each other. It sounds like a schoolyard thing to say. A lot of the humor came out of put-downs and mockery, whether it be mockery of characters the way they were written or the way they spoke to each other. I didn't want that kind of humor anymore."

Chapter 15

Dorks Incorporated

2005–2011

*In which the post-abovegrounding of Twee swells the battle be-
tween haters and the Twee Tribe. Lines are drawn over girlishness and womanhood and the question is raised whether one can
be a true feminist if one wishes everyone looked like a kitten. Also,
"Girl" becomes a megabrand, but is it really shorthand for "White
Girl"?*

What do you do with bullies? If you're Australian teen Casey Heynes, you snap. You pick them up and body-slam
them. If you're Fairuza Balk (a real-life actress whose
name seems to come from the works of Roald Dahl) in the make-
believe high school revenge saga, you use the powers of witchcraft
to attempt to exact bloody revenge on them (or like Rachel True's
character, at least make their pretty blond hair fall out in clumps in
the swimming pool). A decade after *The Craft*, the box-office hit *Mean
Girls* finds a premeltdown Lindsay Lohan confronted with the same
quandary. What do you do with bullies? Do you join them and rule

the school, or do you fight them back? *Mean Girls* reduces it to an anthropological question, and maybe that's what it is. Through the ages, the "life-ruining" plastics are always going to try to rip the sensitive kids to shreds. There will be freaks and there will be geeks. But what happens when the world, pop culturally speaking, begins to resemble high school, and technology and the anonymity of the Internet turns us all into mean girls? Do we go with or against the flow? It's an existential question best answered by modern-day philosophers like Taylor Swift: "Someday I'll be big enough that you can't hit me, and all you'll ever be is mean." If there's a flaw in this theory, it's that the bigger one seems to get, the more blows one takes from haters. We may be living in a postsnark age, when the bullies themselves get tagged with names like "troll," but it is also threatening to become a leaderless age, one without its innovators, Beatles, Stones, Godards, and Wes Andersons, because to put anything out into the world these days is to risk it being ripped apart by coyotes. It's getting harder and harder to keep the social pact that our stars have with their fans. Ever since the 1960s, when young audiences stopped looking to their often ephemeral pop stars for pure entertainment and began expecting them to lead, the contract between star and fan has been a tricky one with regard to levels of fame. As I've mentioned, there is a part of Morrissey that can never be unfaithful to the *idea* of Morrissey. There's a point where the ascent of beloved stars can seem like a personal victory for their fans, but if they pass that point, resentment begins to fester. As Morrissey himself sang, "We hate it when our friends become successful . . ."

This is, of course, a horrid liability for the artist. Part of making great art is to break the rules and defy expectations. And yet, with the advent of TMZ and similar sites and the rise of the Internet troll, a particularly cowardly, mostly anonymous strain of social commentator, came a heightened watchdogging. We police our stars now, via some kind of electronic caucus. In the spring of 2013, Zach Braff turned to the crowd-funding website Kickstarter to raise a budget for *Wish I Was Here,* his long-awaited directorial follow-up to *Garden State*. It had been nearly a decade since that film made a mark, and Braff's career had cooled some. It wasn't a given that a studio, even a large Indie, would hand him a blank check anymore. The teenagers who'd made the Shins famous had grown up. They didn't even go to the movies as much anymore, preferring to binge on Netflix and on-demand cable. Some viewed it as a bold DIY act. Others found it vulgar, as if to say, "We invested in him. We bought our tickets to see his film. We bought the soundtrack album. We even sat through a few episodes of *Scrubs*. It's in syndication now. He's gotta be rich. And I'm freelancing! Fuck that guy!"

What may truly be at issue is the question of whether Braff has anything left to say. Is he putting one over on us? Can he speak to our pain again and heal us as expertly as he managed to in '04? People are happy to pay for quality. It's why the green-market phenomenon, and, to a lesser extent, the rise of Whole Foods, has been so pronounced in the last decade. Everyone wants to be able to feel good about their produce. But you know what you're getting with the tomato. With Kickstarter, it's a gamble and a matter of trust in the artists. The consensus on Braff, by the way, seems to indicate that he was worthy of trust, as his film was fully funded.

And so, with the rise of the great electronic democratic voice and a more empowered, hands-on approach to all forms of consumption comes an age of suspicion and, frankly, distrust when dealing with artists—especially our once-favorite artists. Nobody gets our hate more than the ones who once got all our love. Take the case of Miranda July. Nobody came with more cred correctness than the young July. Here is someone who first found her voice as part of the original Riot Grrrl movement in Olympia. She was and remains friends with Carrie Brownstein of Indie-rock trio Sleater-Kinney and released spoken-word albums on the same label, Kill Rock Stars. Her short stories appeared in the *New Yorker*. Her performance pieces were reviewed by serious art critics. She was mentioned in the same breath as alternative-culture saints like Kathy Acker and Lydia Lunch. And then she got famous.

July's low-budget feature-film debut, 2005's *Me and You and Everyone We Know,* showcased for a larger audience what had previously been a niche matter of taste. Her wobbly voice, gawky beauty, and performance-artist mien was not for everyone. "I'm going to be free!" she promises at the start of the film, "I'm going to be brave." She is also going to be pilloried. The film itself is beautiful, with moments of grace (a quiet shot of a bird in a tree, a poignant and sad performance by the great John Hawkes), but it's also hater bait, with July dialoguing with a goldfish in a bag as it wobbles precariously on the roof of a moving car. "I didn't know you but I want you to die knowing you were loved . . ."

July *was* an acquired taste. But was she full of shit? Why the investment in girlishness at the onset of her thirties? July was thirty-one when the film came out. Why was her character sitting at home, waiting for a boy to call, like some lovelorn teenager? Was she renouncing her feminism? July made the cover of the *New York Times Magazine* in July of 2011. The headline read: MIRANDA JULY IS TOTALLY NOT KIDDING.

Is this scrutiny sexist in nature? Probably. *Thumbsucker*, the debut of July's husband, the designer turned director Mike Mills, is even more Twee than some of July's conceits, and nobody called for his head. Yes, the film that Miranda July was promoting in that *New York Times* cover story was partially narrated by an abandoned kitty, but who's to say she isn't 100 percent invested in that? "To her detractors ('haters' doesn't seem like too strong a word)," the *Times* observed, "July has come to personify everything infuriating about the Etsy-shopping, Wes Anderson–quoting, McSweeney's-reading, coastal-living category of upscale urban bohemia that flourished in the aughts."

"I always liked authenticity, but authenticity can be very complex and shaded," says Kill Rock Stars founder Slim Moon. "I never much liked irony, the whole sort of slacker thing. I always thought that was really just an expression of suburban entitlement or insecurity. I hate to pick on them, but to me Mudhoney was kind of an example: 'We're gonna really rock—but we're also going to only half commit, and you're always going to wonder if we mean it or if it's a big joke.' I see how Miranda befuddles people and they think it might be a big joke, but I think she's a complex artist who is very shaded. I don't think she's pulling our leg one bit."

Zooey Deschanel was, for almost a decade, a talented actress from a show-business family and on a path toward a solid, respectable career, vying for roles with the likes of Michelle Williams, Kirsten Dunst, and other "serious actresses" with a penchant for dark, complicated material.

In Adam Rapp's *Winter Passing*, for example, she's as sullen as the young Winona. Rapp's movies are a subgenre unto themselves, full of depressed people taking drugs and sometimes working in the sex industry. To appear in one of his films or plays is to send a signal: "I'm serious. I'm not afraid of the edge."

Over the course of the film, she snorts coke, has impassive sex, and mopes around, mostly looking for more coke. Her voice is flat, depressed, perhaps medicated. She's sickly, pale, sallow, and druggy. She is also morally compromised. Her father, played by Ed Harris, is a famous writer. When a publisher offers her a large sum of money to retrieve his letters, she heads home to confront him. There she finds he's in a relationship with a doting British woman close to her own age. The two clash, and in one exchange, Deschanel quips, "Why don't you go back to Narnia or wherever the fuck you're from?"

In the years since that film's 2005 release, many once-intrigued fans of Deschanel found themselves asking the same thing of her. Maybe there's always been a dichotomy to Deschanel. People are complex, after all. Maybe she was warning us with her choices of roles.

In the same year that she appeared in David Gordon Green's bleak *All the Real Girls,* a kind of Bruce Springsteen album track come to life on film in which she plays a greasy-haired blonde trapped in a dead-end town, she also made John Favreau's *Elf,* a sunny holiday classic in which she sings "Baby It's Cold Outside" with Will Ferrell's overgrown Santa's helper. She was Shelley Duvall in Kubrick's *The Shining* one minute, and Shelley Duvall in *Fairy Tale Theater* the next. Brooding. "Actressy." "The girl" to Will Ferrell's showboating. She also played "the girl" to Jim Carrey's showboating in *Yes Man.* Or perhaps it was just a question of receiving the kind of style makeover that public figures and artists receive all the time. They reinvent, they get better clothes and cooler hair, they start dropping the right names.

"She had no style and she was mousy-looking," says *Daily Beast* contributor Tricia Romano, who would post one of a trilogy of controversial essays in 2011, the year the new, retro-cool Deschanel went supernova, "and it was like she had gotten this sort of look and once she adopted this look, everything changed."

The change in appearance seemed timed to what would become Deschanel's signature role, the 2009 hit romantic comedy *(500) Days of Summer.* Zooey's character, Summer, with her bangs and sundresses and handiness with Smiths lyrics, is the ideal girl, a smart, funny, but gorgeous dreamboat. She also leaves poor Joseph Gordon-Levitt's Tom destroyed because she cannot be possessed. "You don't think a woman can be free and independent?" she asks his dimwitted friend. She drives Tom to tears, but she also wakes him up, moves him from his literal summer to his more world-wise autumn.

She is the free spirit who quotes Belle and Sebastian in her high school yearbook page ("Color my life with the chaos of trouble . . .") but also compares herself to Sid Vicious in her breakup speech to Tom. There's a clip of the two reenacting a scene from Alex Cox's cult classic *Sid and Nancy,* and Deschanel is sure enough the doomed junkie. She was even in talks to play Janis Joplin on film, and she does an authentically bluesy version of "I Put a Spell on You" with her Indie band She & Him. That duo (which also features singer-songwriter M. Ward) is one of the very few actor-led bands that isn't a punch line. They've put out three volumes of smart retro pop on big Indie Merge Records, and have respectably high *Pitchfork* reviews.

In Blakeian terms, she was a Tyger and she was also a Lamb, a complex and puzzling and captivating young star, and then, at some point, the Lamb ate the big cat and she became a Super Lamb. Then the knives came out. And heads were scratched: "Wait. Is she for real? And if so, what the fuck happened?"

I don't mean to be reductive, but I should probably point out that in 2010, the winter after (500) Days of Summer, Deschanel turned thirty. Leaving her twenties, her actual youth, prompted her to pick up a ukulele and never look back. The cynic might just observe that she fell into something marketable, which everyone in show business seeks to do: something to dispense with job insecurity, establish dominance in the cutthroat industry, and sell something.

"Now we only see this character of her—a quasi-version of herself," says Romano. "We don't know what she's actually like, but she's got to be a pretty shrewd businesswoman. But we don't even see her being a tough bitch. We just see cutesy girl, and the problem is everyone wants to be the cutesy archetype too." Deschanel quickly got blamed for leading a march backward, away from the perceived ground gained by the feminist movement. The character of "Zooey the Retro dork" was, to her credit, so appealing that many, especially the young and searching, happily followed her there, many of them unaware of her earlier, edgier work. It was as if the first Cure song you ever heard was "Friday I'm in Love" and you never bothered to explore anything that came before.

"Deschanel's artful kookiness has, as her star has ascended, threatened to engulf her entire persona—which would be an unfortunately toothless end game for an actress who displayed such edgy mettle in her early films," Salon observed.

Deschanel, like everyone in the Internet age, was aware of the criticism and managed it well for a time. When *Saturday Night Live* cast member Abby Elliott portrayed Deschanel in the recurring sketch *Bein' Quirky with Zooey Deschanel*, all the commentary about her was there, as were her now signature brown bangs. She stopped being the kind of actress who disappeared into roles and became a movie star whom people tailored the roles around—and who essentially played the same character every time. Deschanel got the joke. When she hosted *SNL* herself, she, of course, appeared on *Bein' Quirky* as Mary-Kate Olsen, looking waifish, complete with huge sunglasses and blond wig.

Still, the self-deprecation only went so far, and soon Deschanel, like Cobain before her, found herself as something of polarizer—both a Twee Tribe icon and an Indie apostate, as she seemed to not only advance her persona but also blatantly go for the cash with the website she cofounded, HelloGiggles. The site is a digital universe of everything girly and quirky on the surface ("Live Owl Cam Cuteness" ran one feature; "Adventures in Thrifting" is another). There are "Nails of the Day" photos and also serious, issue-based columnists. Visitors just have to dig past all the Tweeness to find anything serious.

HelloGiggles had the misfortune to launch in the same era as another pair of "girl-aimed" sites. Former *Sassy* editor Jane Pratt started *xoJane*, originally a collaboration with Tavi Gevinson, who had been blogging on her own *Style Rookie* site since her very early teens. Pratt's Indie bona fides were set in concrete thanks to her founding and editing of *Sassy*, which in 2011 was something of a legend; its features "Cute Band Alert" and "It Happened to Me" are now part of the Indie vernacular. Chloë Sevigny had been an intern there. *Sassy* had a glow that surely must have been catnip to a cool teen like Gevinson. Pratt herself in a *New York* magazine profile in 2012 placed her "emotional age" at fifteen. But somehow the supergroup never clicked. "Tavi and her dad couldn't come to terms, and backed out," *New York's* Carl Swanson revealed in his Pratt profile. "Now Tavi has her own site, Rookie. On its masthead, Pratt is listed as its 'fairy godmother.'" Romano attempted but failed to interview Gevinson for her *Daily Beast* piece on the puzzling and troubling "girliness" of the new wave of female-targeted websites. "I kind of feel like Tavi was like, 'Yeah sure!' and once she saw what *xoJane* was, she probably wised up and said, 'That's not at all what I want my brand to be.'"

Instead Gevinson launched her own website, really a Web magazine, *Rookie,* and despite her age quickly surpassed both *HelloGiggles* and *xoJane* as the only authentic voice for girls and young women; ironically, it seems like the cooler, Punk rock older sister site to those magazines, which are run by pop icons in their, respectively, thirties and fifties. A banner ad on *Rookie* recently featured Doc Marten boots, whereas *xoJane* was advertising a Rachel McAdams romantic comedy. Still, none of them offered much to the culture-hungry adult woman.

"I thought, I don't understand why all these websites have a girlish tone. Does everything have to end in an exclamation point and have a sort of valley girl tone to its language? There's *Jezebel,*" Romano says, singling out the serious political and feminist-culture site, "but it can get shouty and enraged. I want to read about political figures without exclamation points."

Then, at 3:02 P.M. on June 4, 2011, Deschanel tweeted to her millions of followers, "I wish everyone looked like a kitten." A simple, wistful, not entirely serious "wish." Suddenly it was as if Gloria Steinem, Joan Didion, and Courtney Love had favorited and retweeted it and the feminist movement was done.

Deschanel's carefully styled and marketed cult was, at the time, bigger than ever. She was no longer just an actress; she was an ideal. And now she was about to star as the lead in her first television series for Fox, *New Girl.* The buzz was already great. The show, created by Liz Meriwether, was talked about in the same breath as classics like *Seinfeld* and *Friends:* witty, urban, sexy. Others worried that it did little more than showcase a woman over thirty tacitly saying to her increasing fan base that in order to get ahead, you had to act like either a sexpot or a little girl.

In February of 2011, NBC's *30 Rock* had run a much-discussed episode entitled "*TGS* Hates Women." Shamed by feminist website *Joan of Snark* (clearly *Jezebel*), Liz Lemon hires a new staff writer, Abby Flynn. Before long, Flynn, who wears pigtails, gym socks, and short shorts and speaks in a gooey, giggly baby voice à la Zooey, vexes Lemon and beguiles the male staff with her "sexy baby" talk. Fed up, Liz asks her to meet outside the offices, by a statue of Eleanor Roosevelt, and tries to disabuse her of the idea that she has to play dumb and immature to get ahead in the male-run industry. "Look, I know it can be hard. Society puts a lot of pressure on us to act a certain way, but *TGS* is a safe place, so you can drop the sexy-baby act and lose the pigtails," Liz says, attempting to be big-sisterly.

"I don't have to explain myself to you. My life is none of your business," Abby counters. Lemon's retort: "Except it is, because you represent my show and you embarrass me."

Overnight, Deschanel seemed to become a similar enemy and, to some, a symbol for what was going wrong in the broader popular culture. If someone was marketing overpriced crocheted narwhals on the arts-and-crafts-marketplace website Etsy, it was Deschanel's fault.

As this resentment built, Fox's marketing campaign for *New Girl* was inescapable. Deschanel was on the side of city buses "bein' quirky" with the phrase SIMPLY ADORKABLE over her head. Writer Julie Klausner, who also hosts the weekly podcast *How Was Your Week?*, posted a piece to her personal blog entitled, "Don't Fear the Dowager." It quickly became viral after being picked up by *Jezebel*. "There's so much ukulele playing now, it's deafening," Klausner, a huge pop-culture enthusiast and keen observer, wrote. "So much cotton candy, so many bunny rabbits and whoopie pies and craft fairs and kitten ephemera, and grown women wearing converse sneakers with mini skirts. So many fucking birds." Klausner lamented the fact that women were not able to be mature, sophisticated feminists. "Women with master's degrees who are searching for life partners, list 'rainbows, Girl Scout cookies, and laughing a lot' under 'interests' on their Match.com profiles," Klausner jokes.

Klausner implied that companies were profiting off this by selling ridiculously girlie clothes to mature women. "When I shop now, I have to make sure that garments I think are dresses, are not actually rompers." And the women themselves, who were acting like sexy preteens instead of serious-minded, sophisticated adult women, were motivated by similarly less-than-selfless ends. "We all know these manic pixie Muppet Babies are really just in it for the peen."

"I wrote it knowing I would be heard in the sense that I edited it a bunch of times," Klausner says. "I'm prone to random feminine outbursts of rage, so every once in a while I will tweet something about a rape case or Olivia Munn. I'd also recently rewatched *Tootsie* and thought, 'If we were to remake it today Dustin Hoffman would be with Terri Garr's character. He wouldn't be with Jessica Lange's character. Terri Garr's character would be the female lead. She's a girl. She's not a woman.' I lamented the loss of the female adults in pop culture that are not either over the hill in a *Real Housewives/*Christine Baranski kind of way. They're either kitsch or they're fawns. I'm not saying all women that dress younger or act younger are smarter than they let on. I'm sure a great many of them are not—but I do know that there is a very strong history of women trying to make themselves less intimidating for their male counterparts, and that can involve a sort of lack of maturity, wherewithal, sophistication, and intelligence."

There were no less than three shows with *Girl* in the title debuting that fall, as the debate ran on over what a grown woman should look and behave like. As it turns out, all three, *New Girl*, *Two Broke Girls*, and *Girls*, were high-quality runaway hits. *New Girl* was more of an ensemble than most expected, with Deschanel—as Jess, a teacher recently dumped by her boyfriend—sharing the best moments with her male costars, who play the renters of an L.A. loft. Jess answers a Craigslist ad on short notice and finds herself with three male roommates. It would be Max Greenfield's Schmidt and his "douche jar" that would emerge as the show's breakout success, and a romance with Nick (Jake Johnson) that would captivate audiences in that old Sam-and-Diane, Maggie-and-David, will-they-or-won't-they fashion. In other words, Deschanel's Twee bender was well tempered, and the show succeeded as a result.

"There is a very strong female energy there," says Curtis Armstrong, who now has a recurring role. "Zooey knows comedy, has a strong sense of herself, and is wonderful at improv. People would hate me for saying this, but this show feels to me like a contemporary *Mary Tyler Moore Show*. *MTM* is considered prehistoric by *New Girl* fans, I'm sure, and obviously the humor is very different. But that single woman, accessible and attractive, surrounded by eccentrics, is an old standby in TV comedy."

It may be decades before *New Girl*, one of the most consistent and original sitcoms in years, gets its due. Each week, culture sites were on alert as they recapped the misadventures of Jess, Winston, Nick, and Schmidt; *Vanity Fair*'s site, where I was a contributor, would even grade them: "adorkable" or "tweepulsive."

After a point, in an effort to defuse the bomb, Meriwether even addressed the issue in a typically smart way. In a late-season story line involving Julia, a girlfriend of Nick's played by Lizzy Caplan, Jess gets an expensive traffic ticket and entreats Julia to argue her case. Julia is perfectly cast to take on a real-life issue in the meta-sitcom universe. Caplan is a veteran of the canceled but cult-beloved Starz comedy *Party Down,* and that show's genius—and failure—gave her credibility. When Julia reviews Jess's case, she shrugs, "You never know, the judge might go for that thing."

"What thing?" Jess asks.

"Your whole thing with the cupcakes and braking for birds. It's a great thing. The big beautiful eyes like a scared baby. I bet that gets you out of all kinds of stuff."

It sets up Deschanel's big answer-song moment. "I brake for birds," Jess admits, addressing all of the haters indirectly, but unmistakably too. "I rock a lot of polka dots. I have touched glitter in the last twenty-four hours. I spend my entire day talking to children, and I find it fundamentally strange that you're not a dessert person. That's just weird and it freaks me out. And I'm sorry I don't talk like Murphy Brown, and I hate your pantsuit and I wish it had ribbons on it to make it slightly cute. And that doesn't mean I'm not smart and tough and strong."

There were those who argued that this *was* the new feminism, and that Deschanel was indeed leading a movement toward equality. If Judd Apatow's doughy boy-men of hits like *Superbad* and *Funny People* could become major movie stars, why couldn't a ukulele-playing girl-woman do the same?

"I'm just being myself. There is not an ounce of me that believes any of that crap that they say. We can't be feminine and be feminists and be successful? I want to be a fucking feminist and wear a fucking Peter Pan collar. So fucking what?" Deschanel would later tell *Glamour*.

Blogger Tami Winfrey Harris raised another, more provocative issue in regard to Twee at this time. Her essay, called "Who Is the Black Zooey Deschanel?," brought race into the conversation. Harris noted that when a white person puts a strand of color in their hair, it's quirky, but when a woman of color does the same, there's a double standard. "What I'm really interested in is how Kool-Aid-colored dos are evaluated differently," she wrote, "based on the race of the wearer. Black Girl with Long Hair gets at this issue: 'Any black girl sporting a weave like this after 1999 would be considered GHETTO/ YARDIE/HOOD!' Making it hardly a new trend . . . Rainbow hair on a black woman provokes a whole lot of judgments about class and education, even among other black people. Meanwhile, a bright blue streak in a white woman's hair is accepted differently, I think."

Winfrey Harris found *New Girl* and Deschanel appealing, but wondered if it would be as much if there was a woman of color in the lead. There've been similar figures, the Web series *Awkward Black Girl* among them, but they remained obscure. Laina Dawes's book *What Are You Doing Here?* similarly chronicled her experience being one of the only African-American women at Punk and metal shows.

"A lot of the qualities of the 'Manic Pixie Dream Girl' are not ones that society necessarily associates with women of color," Winfrey Harris says today. "I can't think of a black actress that could ever be slotted into a kind of Zooey Deschanel role where she could play a main character where she is kind of quirky, cute, little-girlish, and needs to be taken care of by her roommates. It almost harkens back to the 'cult of true womanhood,' that nineteenth-century idea of what a proper woman should be—very chaste and very innocent and very feminine and very girlish."

There was nothing giggly or goofy about Lena Dunham, whose *Girls* launched the following year, in April 2012. An Oberlin grad, Dunham certainly had her feminist bona fides, and never had to declare them repeatedly to major magazines as Deschanel had. She was also a natural provocateur. Take this scene from "Hooker on Campus," her pre–*Tiny Furniture* short: kids are rushing to class, and she stands on the common road, dressed in trashy streetwalker garb, shrugging, "Are you interested in pussy?" In another film, made famous via YouTube, she lingers in a fountain like Anita Ekberg in *La Dolce Vita*.

"You wanna be naked in front of people that don't necessarily want to see you naked," a boyfriend once told her. Her sexuality was aggressive, bold, and positive; her writing had a winning, very Jewish wit to it. She was well versed in just about every major Twee icon, from Sendak to Stillman to Baumbach to even Miranda July.

Dunham was also hugely influenced by Bujalski and Swanberg and was a fan of mumblecore. That her character in *Girls* is named Hannah is no accident. Ultimately it's fame, not politics, that forces the audit. When Dunham debuted with *Tiny Furniture*, nobody questioned the world she was depicting. It was clearly one she knew well, of bohemian privilege and urban social jockeying.

But once Dunham's worldview was an HBO show, suddenly she had a great responsibility. They couldn't question her about sex; she had made herself clear on that topic. So the haters turned to race and privilege, the class issues raised by Simon Reynolds.

Dunham, the smartest of her peers, handled the controversy in a way that politicians might learn from: facing it head-on and using it, via guest star Donald Glover, as a major plot point in the very first episode of season two of the now hit show—and quoting Missy Elliott.

"So why don't you lay this thing down, flip it, and reverse it," she tells Glover as he tries to typify her as a curious white girl sexually slumming with a black man. It was both a bold move by Dunham and also an obvious choice. Glover, a former writer for *30 Rock* and star of *Community* who raps under the moniker Childish Gambino (pulled from an online Wu Tang Clan name generator) has all the Twee Tribe qualities himself: he does not fear sensitivity or vulnerability, having recently posted a series of confessional sketch messages on his Instagram page. "Donald is just so awkward, so uncomfortable in his own skin," writer Kyla Marshell observed some months later on *Gawker*. "In addition to his posture problems and unwillingness to blink is the fact that he's so caught up on his childhood. Childish Gambino could be fudged into simpler terms to mean Babyish Baby, and that's apt. Donald's childhood, I glean, was very similar to mine: an ethnically black child who grew up culturally white because of the surrounding school system and neighborhood. The difference between him and me, however, is that I found something else to say besides *Ow*."

"I can't think of another black male character that's very much like him," says Winfrey Harris. "He's unique—being a black male and being able to occupy that kind of quirky geek space." The inner-child imagery of Jean-Michel Basquiat's paintings, or the idealism and petulance of early-'80s Prince once he conked his late-'70s afro and began playing funky New Wave with his mixed-race, mixed-gender band, both come to mind, but that was thirty years ago now, as was the bohemianism of Cosby-era Lisa Bonet's crush object Denise Huxtable, who appealed, with her thrift-store overcoats and funky shoes, to both black and white kids (*Cosby* was all about this cultural mind melding).

The door seemed to be open for white kids to mingle in Hip-Hop culture and even profit from it—Macklemore being the most recent in a line that began thirty years ago with the Beastie Boys. *Pitchfork* readers worship African-American music and culture like the Canadian, Emo-aware Drake or the savvy Glover/Gambino (or of course, Kanye West, whose 2011 album *My Beautiful Dark Twisted Fantasy* received one of the site's rare perfect 10 reviews . . . no decimal points). It does not seem to be an even exchange when it comes to interest. Few from the Hip-Hop world seem interested or able to kick with the Twee, beyond Outkast's now decade-old stated love for the work of Kate Bush.

Romano is a bit blunt about what still seems like a schism. "Hip-Hop is automatically cooler. No black guy is going to look at Indie rock and want to aspire to be a part of that. It's sort of dorky. It's not smooth. It's not macho, it's Twee. They're boys. What black urban guy is going to look at that and want to be a part of it?" I suggest Kanye

West's collaborations with bearded singer-songwriter Bon Iver and *Pitchfork*'s TMZ-like coverage of West's every move. "The *Pitchfork* guys worship Kanye because Kanye will always be cooler than them. Kanye can fart and he will be cooler than them."

The debate had begun, but the question remains unanswered: What do you do with bullies? When the appealing actress Jenny Slate became one of the few people to utter the word *fuck* on *Saturday Night Live* during a skit in her debut season, she was piled on by haters. Slate did not give in to the negativity but rather synthesized it into a shell—"a partial shell, as you can see I have shoes," says her creation "Marcel . . . the Shell with Shoes On." The short stop-motion film she cocreated and posted on YouTube became perhaps the most talked about since *SNL*'s own Digital Short "Lazy Sunday." Slate became, in essence, as big as her former employer, if not bigger, via a sort of arch sweetness almost fueled by attack. "Marcel the Shell with Shoes On" was a phenomenon with almost twenty-five million hits and spawned sequels and an accompanying book. It's essentially the story of a google-eyed Cyclops seashell with one foot and the things it uses because it's small. "Guess what I wear as a hat? A lentil. Guess what I use to tie my skis to a car? A hair. Guess what my skis are? Toenails from a man."

Marcel is the equivalent of Pee-wee Herman doing the big shoe dance to disarm the mob that would hang him, kill him, then tattoo him in Tim Burton's *Pee-wee's Big Adventure*. The shell helped wound snark, but it would take a series from another *SNL* veteran to eradicate it forever.

Chapter 16

Culture Teasing

2011–Present

In which the Twee aesthetic's popularity is confirmed and the inevitable backlash is tempered by an affectionate and knowing sketch comedy show that even the hardest of hard-core haters cannot deny. A bird is placed on the entire youth movement by a trio who cannot forget the Indie dream of the '90s.

I'm not wearing a nerd costume for Halloween, this is how I actually dress," says Brian P., an "actual nerd," in a hilarious and heartbreaking sketch from season three of the hit IFC satire *Portlandia*. Like many who appear on the show, Brian is not a professional actor but a local, scouted by the casting director. "We thought that someone who acts like a nerd wouldn't read right," says cocreator and star Fred Armisen. "It just looks fake. We needed a real guy. Our casting director knew a guy who worked at a hardware store. He didn't want to do it at first. Which was perfect! He came to the set and we had a long speech written out for him. He couldn't memorize it. He's not an actor. So I had to write it all out on cue cards. I thought, 'That'll fix it.' I thought it was a brilliant idea, but when the editors noticed the tapes without the cue cards, where he was nervous and stumbling, were the ones that worked, that spelled out that this is a person who is a true nerd." The "Actual Nerd PSA" opens with a gorgeous model type in black horn-rims, straining to convince a dude in a hip bar, "I'm such a total nerd . . . I've been into video games and comic books and stuff." It's a typically affectionate *Portlandia* jab at those who were *never* pushed around but wear the uniform of the bullied.

When Drew Barrymore indulged her inner wannabe Twee in the late 1990s, insisting to magazine feature writers that despite being a movie star literally for her entire life, she was, deep down, a "total nerd," it was refreshing. She mined her pain (drug addiction, divorce, an initial career skid, seeing Tom Green naked) and applied it to the pain of a genuine high school Twee, and, culturally savvy as she is, did so before the onslaught. Her portrayal of the virginal Josie "Josie Grossie" Geller, who crochets pillows and talks to turtles in the otherwise by-rote romantic comedy *Never Been Kissed,* might seem brave in retrospect, whereas a few years later it would be some kind of nerd-o minstrel showcase. Drew stood, more or less alone, among movie stars of her day in nerd aspiration. I met her once or twice and she clearly has the record collection to back it up.

"A real nerd is ashamed to be called a nerd. So please, get real. If you're not a nerd, don't call yourself one," the obese, fidgety, shy Brian P. pleads on *Portlandia.*

Ultimately it would be love and unity, not hate and division, that would make the best watchdog on Twee culture. *Portlandia* debuted in January 2011 to send up the affectations, idealism, and pretension of Indie righteousness and the new green-market consumerism better than anything else, in part because its creators—Fred Armisen, Carrie Brownstein, and Jonathan Krisel—hail from the very same world. "The three of us kind of grew up around all of that," Armisen says of his Indie background. "Every city I've ever lived in, that was going on." The show sometimes blurs the line between broad, almost slapstick humor and seriousness, but it never, ever crosses over into the mean. There are no cheap shots at easy targets. "We like things to be positive," Armisen says. "That's also a very Punk aesthetic. It's a positivity that comes directly from Punk rock." As a linchpin cast member on *SNL* for nearly a decade, Armisen witnessed time and again how a low-blow joke would land dead with the audience. "No one likes to be bummed out," he says. "When that happens, you can hear it in the crowd. The more we keep it positive, the more it just makes for a fun workday."

Portlandia was born, like the best things, from a spirit of "this will never go anywhere." Armisen would spend his summers off from the late-night show in Portland to be close to his best friend, Carrie Brownstein, who was adjusting to the hiatus of her Punk trio Sleater-Kinney. The two would film clips designed strictly to crack each other up. Sometimes they'd send up some of the locals they encountered every day, such as the proprietors of a local feminist-centric bookshop. The clips were the perfect size to post on YouTube and then forget about until the next idea came along . . . or didn't.

"One thing leads to the next," Armisen says of the organic progression that eventually led to the series, now approaching its fourth season. "It's like you're in a band and you have a couple of songs and all of a sudden it turns into eight songs and you've got enough for an album. Carrie and I wanted to do it for fun. And then someone said,

'What do you guys think of doing a TV show?' 'Oh, yeah, maybe we should do it as a TV show.'" That someone was executive producer Lorne Michaels, who saw the potential in the unconnected series of sketches collected under the umbrella name Thunder Ant. Jonathan Krisel, a film student whose credits include the rapid-fire, low-budget, absurdist Adult Swim hit *Tim and Eric Awesome Show, Great Job!*, was also a fan of the video series.

"I was already a huge Sleater-Kinney fan," Krisel says, "so I was curious to know that Fred and Carrie were friends. That seemed really cool to me, since I only knew her as a musician." It was the "Feminist Bookstore" sketch, in which Armisen, in drag, plays Candace and Brownstein plays Toni, operators of Women and Women First, that convinced the director the show could work. Candace and Toni's politics are sound, but only at the expense of their business sense. They never manage to sell a book; they're too offended by their would-be customers. "Andy Samberg comes in and asks for a book at the feminist bookstore and even though Fred is touching it, he says he can't reach it. It made me laugh so hard." The sketches are improvised, but in the hands of Armisen and the surprisingly skilled comedian Brownstein they feel smooth and scripted.

Portlandia is a little like *Monty Python's Flying Circus*, a little SNL, a little *Kids in the Hall*, a little *The State*, but unlike those classic sketch shows, its target has remained focused and it functions in a sort of fixed world: the city of Portland, which is treated as a flawed but noble utopia.

"It's about people yearning," says Armisen. "They're all yearning to do better. To be a better person. A better citizen. There's a constant sense of 'We can do this the right way. We can be better. We can make the world a better place.' I've been that way. Carrie feels that way. Of course it's an uphill battle." Often the good intentions are wildly misguided, as when the recurring characters Kath and Dave, another of the show's many couples, free a tied-up dog that turns out to be a beloved family pet.

The perceived affectations of the real Portland, of course, have practical origins.

"Local people made great coffee for their neighborhood, not for franchises but because they valued their four-block radius," says Krisel. Now that these practices have been adopted by the masses and everywhere is "weird" in the bumper-sticker sense, there's a theme-park feeling to the city itself. On a recent trip to Portland to do a book reading, I stayed at the Ace Hotel, which was parodied on the show (as the Deuce Hotel). I found a stack of vinyl in my room along with the towels. Walking around the city and observing the old hippies in gray ponytails, the Punk rockers getting drunk in the middle of the day, the pierced bicyclists, the vintage toy shops, it's as if they all came after the show permeated the culture and not vice versa, and this might make some of the natives a little prickly.

"Oh, no, it's the opposite," Armisen, who spends four months of the year in the city, says. "Who knows what happens behind my back, but to my face, everyone's like, 'I know this is really *Portlandia*-ish, but I have this herb garden on my organic farm . . .' They're very sweet and proud of it. All I get is the good side. I get handed a lot of business cards. 'I do this special foot massage with needles . . .'"

In its own way, *Portlandia* is an artisanal show. It uses, whenever possible, locally sourced real Portlandians, like the aforementioned Brian P., the "actual nerd." The African-American actor who played (white) Ronald D. Moore, creator of *Battlestar Galactica,* was merely accompanying his cousin to an audition when he was cast.

Other guests are harvested from the Indie-rock community. To date the show has played host to Aimee Mann, Sarah McLachlan, Eddie Vedder, James Mercer of the Shins, Colin Meloy of the Decemberists, Joanna Newsom, St. Vincent, and Tunde Adebimpe of TV on the Radio, among many other Indie weirdos made major rock stars by *Garden State* a decade ago. Even ex-Smiths guitarist Johnny Marr, a Portland resident and onetime member of Modest Mouse, has appeared.

"I have a theory that all bands have one really funny dude in them who is dying to get in front of the camera," says Krisel. "Usually their talent is raw and not perfect, but I like putting them in front of the camera to see what happens. My goal in the beginning was very simple. I wanted the show to be something that bands watched on tour. I set my sights on that."

"That's just a matter of luck," says Armisen. "Some of them are just friends of ours."

When musicians and friends pass through town, either on tour or to visit, Fred and Carrie become ambassadors of a sort. "We take them to dinner and show them around," Armisen says. This has attracted many movie stars as well. "We just want them to have a good time."

Sometimes the roles they play (a knot salesman, in the case of Jeff Goldblum) aren't worked out until the last minute. "We don't define their characters," Armisen says. "We just say, 'Okay, why don't you be this kind of person.'" It's the antithesis to the high-pressure, round-the-clock production schedule of just about every other TV show.

And yet *Portlandia* is not ramshackle. Part of its appeal is its specific detail. Its costume, hair, and makeup staff are spot on, whether it's applying body-mod earrings to Armisen's high-strung bike messenger Spyke or underarm hair to Brownstein's macho Lance. "Costumes and sets are very important," says Jonathan Krisel. "When Fred and Carrie emerge as the character on the shoot days, we say, 'Wow, I *know* that guy.' Authenticity and attention to detail is important to all of us. We have bulletin boards with pictures of friends and references to real people who inspire the characters. Fred is a master impressionist from *SNL*, but he also stores people and behavior from all walks of life in his brain."

Today, of course, everybody knows that guy. You don't even really need to know the terrain of Portland to know that guy. "We found a show in Quebec that was a shot-for-shot ripoff of *Portlandia*," Krisel says, "but in French, and with slightly older actors."

"I went to Sweden," Armisen says, "and interviewers kept asking me if I thought it would relate to people in Stockholm. And they just knew it all. I think the world is becoming so small now. Everyone just knows it all."

All of us, in a way, are now living in a *Portlandia* sketch. "The show has become synonymous with the absurdity of modern life," Krisel says, "and that's an honor."

So did we win, us bedroom weirdos? The Lambs, did they eat the Tygers? Do we indeed rule the school? The Dream of the '90s, which stayed alive in Portland for two decades, is now alive everywhere: everywhere is Portlandia, Brooklandia, Tweelandia. Every major city is now a place "where young people go to retire," as Armisen tells Brownstein in the show's very first sketch. Everywhere "people were talking about getting piercings and getting tribal tattoos, people talking about saving the world and forming bands . . ." Is this a good thing? Or is *Portlandia* nothing more than the music on the deck as the *Titanic* lurches into the icy drink?

"Our friends and our references are largely nineties. It was an idealistic time that has become the state of affairs now," Krisel says. "It was revolutionary back then to be vegan—now it's an option on a menu. The nineties was the war, today is the implementation of those revolutionary demands."

Epilogue

The Last Donut

2013–Present

There's an old *Mr. Show* sketch called "The Last Donut," in which Bob Odenkirk and David Cross sit in a donut shop straining to have a conversation. Bob is bleeding from his left ear as he offers a donut to David, who wears a scarf and turns up his nose. "I don't eat donuts, or hamburgers, or any other food that has 'approval of the masses,'" he says.

Bob asks him if he watched *Sanford and Son* the previous night.

"I don't watch television," David says. "I don't even own a television."

Does he want to go to a movie? ("The one about the coupon," to be specific.)

"I only go and see foreign films."

Listen to some CDs?

"Please, compact discs blow. People were not meant to hear music with such clarity. People need to hear snaps and pops and that shit. This, my friend, is the only modern piece of equipment I will touch," David says, putting an old-timey contraption on the tabletop. "It's a mini Victrola, and it allows me to listen to the only decent music ever committed to *vin-yule* . . . Just listen . . . it's so pure it hurts."

The desire for purity is age-old, but if you were inclined (or a hater), you could reduce the entirety of the phenomenon chronicled in this book to a few modern events:

We got the Internet.

Barack Obama got elected.

Big business crashed and small businesses flourished, and the people took power.

And you would not be wrong. But on a slower and more subtle scale, it's that the Twee-verse is a mark of a slow evolution toward a better, kinder, humbler, more politicized, and "so pure" human race, or at least one with a better record collection. The new culture of kindness is helping us improve as Americans. Think of how we rally to every tragedy, whether it's a natural disaster or a mad gunman shooting up a mall or movie theater. We are all connected as a species, and now via our phones, and this is of a piece with the ethics of Twee. Punk has not been drained of its power, especially in culturally evolving countries: look at the sensational Pussy Riot, the all-female Russian insurgents who don't play their instruments very well but are now among the most significant Punk acts in history, literally persecuted, sent to gulags, and fomenting revolution. There's a Punk-rock quality to the mosh-pit-like gatherings in the post–Arab Spring Middle East too.

But it's Twee, I believe, that's the only movement that's going to make all these young people decent to each other. Once it's fully open to everyone and seen as appealing to people who did not go to liberal arts colleges, its potential will be limitless.

The old-school Twees (O.Twees?) are already making room.

There's a sort of cultural food coma they're suffering from as they look for rock and roll kicks in the more extreme realms.

"Within people who mostly listen to Indie rock," says the culture critic Nitsuh Abebe, "it seems like a lot more of them are interested in black metal—a little bit of a reaction against listening to pleasantly sophisticated, polished Indie-rock bands. They want to jump out into something else. You did see a lot more people starting to say, 'Oh, we're bored with Wilco. Give me something more.'"

Others simply want to achieve something beyond their Twitter feed and its careful quips and pop referencing. A fatigue is settling in that will be good for the movement, and that may see an increase in Twee Tribe activism in the coming years. "I had a certain measure of pride in my ability to know arcane stuff," says Sean Nelson, "but it isn't that hard to know trivia. The fact that IMDB exists robs you of that pride—but it also demonstrates that taking pride in that kind of knowledge is ultimately a substitute for real pride and accomplishment."

Will the children of the current Twee Tribe place their values on the former or the latter design for living? Will they be even softer than we were? Even more autodidactic and disconnected from the kind of experiences once prized by Ernest Hemingway and Norman Mailer and even, for a time, J. D. Salinger? Will they make great art or just talk about great art that's already been made?

"I live in Austin," Andrew Bujalski told me. "It's a yuppie paradise. I have a two-year-old son and I feel that raising a kid here there's no way he won't grow up soft because there's nothing to push against."

Recently I tried to find birthday gifts for my niece and my godson, who are both about six and the children of Xers.

"Has he ever seen *Fantastic Mr. Fox*?" I asked after my godson.

"He loves it," his mother said immediately.

"Does she like Edward Gorey?" I asked my sister.

"Very much."

I felt like I wanted to buy the kids a hammer and maybe a handsaw. Some nails. Take them on a trek through the woods. A vision quest was in order. They could wade into the unknown and return as men and women. But then I realized this was my problem, not theirs, and that children well versed in the weird are bound to diminish bullying, judgment, gay bashing, and even, eventually, racial divides. It used to be that the one person in your school who was into the Smiths automatically became your best friend. Now, if everyone worships at the same temple, virtue might actually come down to a question of true character. Right? Or is that very sunny, hopeful idea just another Twee trope in itself?

Still at a loss for birthday gifts, I found myself browsing Etsy.

Bibliography

Books

Alexander, Paul. *Rough Magic: A Biography of Sylvia Plath.* Cambridge: Da Capo Press, 1999.

Arendt, Hannah. *Eichmann in Jerusalem: A Report on the Banality of Evil.* New York: The Viking Press, 1963.

Azerrad, Michael. *Come as You Are: The Story of Nirvana.* New York: Doubleday, 1993.

Beghtol, L. D. *69 Love Songs: The Magnetic Fields.* London: Continuum Books, 2010.

Belsen, Ken, and Brian Bremner. *Hello Kitty: The Remarkable Story of Sanrio and the Billion-Dollar Feline Phenomenon.* Singapore: Wiley, 2004.

Blume, Judy. *Are You There God? It's Me, Margaret.* Scarsdale, N.Y.: Bradbury Press, 1970.

Brown, Len. *Meetings with Morrissey.* London: Omnibus, 2009.

Capote, Truman. *Breakfast at Tiffany's.* New York: Viking, 2011.

Carlin, Peter Ames. *Catch a Wave: The Rise, Fall and Redemption of the Beach Boys' Brian Wilson.* New York: Rodale Books, 2006.

Chbosky, Stephen. *The Perks of Being a Wallflower.* New York: MTV Books, 1999.

Clarke, Gerald. *Capote: A Biography.* New York: Carroll and Graf, 1988.

Clarke, Victoria Mary, and Shane MacGowan. *A Drink with Shane MacGowan.* London: Sidgwick and Jackson, 2001.

Colegrave, Stephen, and Chris Sullivan. *Punk: The Definitive Record of a Revolution.* New York: Thunder's Mouth Press, 2001.

Cooper, Kim. *In the Aeroplane Over the Sea.* New York: Continuum, 2005.

Cross, Charles R. *Heavier Than Heaven: A Biography of Kurt Cobain.* New York: Hyperion Books, 2001.

Dahl, Roald, and Quentin Blake. *James and the Giant Peach.* New York: Alfred A. Knopf, 1961.

Dahl, Roald, and Quentin Blake. *Matilda.* New York: Puffin/Penguin, 1988.

Eggers, Dave. *The Wild Things* (adapted from *Where the Wild Things Are* by Maurice Sendak, and based on the screenplay *Where the Wild Things Are,* cowritten by Dave Eggers and Spike Jonze). San Francisco: McSweeney's Books, 2009.

Eggers, Dave. *What Is the What.* New York: Vintage Books, 2006.

Eggers, Dave, and Jordan Bass. *The Best of McSweeney's.* San Francisco: McSweeney's, 2013.

Fagen, Donald. *Eminent Hipsters.* New York: Viking, 2013.

Foer, Jonathan Safran. *Everything Is Illuminated.* New York: HarperCollins, 2002.

Foer, Jonathan Safran. *Extremely Loud and Incredibly Close.* New York: HarperCollins, 2005.

Frank, Anne. *The Diary of a Young Girl.* New York: Pocket Books, 1953.

Gabler, Neal. *Walt Disney: The Triumph of the American Imagination.* New York: Vintage, 2006.

Goddard, Simon. *The Songs That Saved Your Life: The Art of the Smiths. 1982–1987.* London: Titan Books, 2013.

Goodrich, Frances, and Albert Hackett, adapted by Wendy Kesselman. *The Diary of Anne Frank* (play). New York: Dramatists Play Service Inc., 2001.

Heer, Jeet. *In Love with Art: Francoise Mouly's Adventures in Comics with Art Spiegelman.* Toronto: Coach House Books, 2013.

Hoffman, Abbie. *Revolution for the Hell of It.* New York: Thunder's Mouth Press, 2005.

Hughes, Ted. *The Birthday Letters*. New York: Farrar, Straus and Giroux, 1998.

Johnson, Crockett. *Harold and the Purple Crayon*. New York: Harper Festival, 1955.

July, Miranda. *No One Belongs Here More Than You: Stories*. New York: Scribner, 2007.

Knee, Sam. *A Scene in Between: Fashion and Independent Music in the UK, 1983–1989*. London: Cicada Books, 2013.

Koenig, David. *Mouse Tales: A Behind-the-Ears Look at Disneyland*. Irvine, Calif.: Bonaventure Press, 1995.

Koenig, Gloria. *Eames*. Koln: Taschen, 2005.

Long, Pat. *The History of the N.M.E.* London: Portico Books, 2012.

MacDonald, Ian. *Revolution in the Head: The Beatles Records and the Sixties*. Chicago: Chicago Review Press, 2007.

McGonigal, Mike. *Loveless*. New York/London: Continuum, 2007.

Michaels, David. *Schulz and Peanuts: A Biography*. New York: Harper, 2007.

Mitchell, Tim. *There's Something About Jonathan: Jonathan Richman and the Modern Lovers*. London: Peter Owen Press, 1999.

Morrissey. *Autobiography*. London: Penguin Classics, 2013.

Nugent, Benjamin. *Elliott Smith and the Big Nothing*. New York: Da Capo Press, 2004.

Plath, Sylvia. *Ariel: Poems by Sylvia Plath*. New York: Harper Perennial, 1961.

Plath, Sylvia. *The Unabridged Journals of Sylvia Plath*. New York: Anchor Books, 2000.

Plimpton, George. *Truman Capote: In Which Various Friends, Enemies, Acquaintances and Detractors Recall His Turbulent Career*. New York: Anchor Books, 1998.

Reed, Alexander S., and Philip Sandifer. *Flood (33 1/3)*. London: Bloomsbury Academic, 2013.

Rees, David. *How to Sharpen Pencils*. New York: Melville House, 2013.

Reynolds, Simon. *Rip It Up and Start Again: Postpunk 1978–1984*. New York: Penguin Books, 2006.

Richards, David. *Played Out: The Jean Seberg Story*. New York: Random House, 1981.

Rimner, David. *Like Punk Never Happened: Culture Club and the New Pop.* London: Faber and Faber, 2011.

Salinger, J. D. *For Esme, with Love and Squalor.* New York: Penguin Books, 2010.

Salinger, J. D. *Raise High the Roof Beam, Carpenters and Seymour: An Introduction.* New York: Little Brown and Company, 1959.

Salinger, J. D. *The Catcher in the Rye.* New York: Little, Brown and Company, 1991.

Schumacher, E. F. *Small Is Beautiful: Economics as if People Mattered.* London: Brigs and Brigs, 1973.

Seitz, Matt Zoller. *The Wes Anderson Collection.* New York: Harry N. Abrams, 2013.

Sendak, Maurice. *Higglety Pigglety Pop! Or, There Must Be More to Life.* New York: HarperCollins, 1967.

Sendak, Maurice. *In the Night Kitchen,* New York: HarperCollins, 1970.

Dr. Seuss. *The Butter Battle Book.* New York: Random House, 1984.

Dr. Seuss. *The Cat in the Hat.* New York: Random House, 1957.

Dr. Seuss. *Horton Hears a Who!.* New York: Random House, 1954.

Slawenski, Kenneth. *J. D. Salinger: A Life.* New York: Random House, 2010.

Spiegelman, Art. *Maus II: And Here My Troubles Began.* New York: Pantheon, 1991.

Spiegelman, Art. *Maus: A Survivor's Tale.* New York: Pantheon, 1986.

Spiegelman, Art. *In the Shadow of No Towers.* New York: Pantheon, 2004.

Taylor, Neil. *Document and Eyewitness: An Intimate History of Rough Trade.* London: Orion, 2011.

Thompson, Kay, and Hilary Knight. *The Ultimate Eloise Edition.* New York: Simon and Schuster, 1980.

True, Everett. *Live Through This: American Rock Music in the 90s.* London: Virgin, 2001.

Truffaut, François, and Helen G. Scott. *Hitchcock.* New York: Simon and Schuster, 1983.

Whitelaw, Paul. *Belle and Sebastian: Just a Modern Rock Story.* New York: St. Martins/Griffin, 2005.

Winthrop, Jordan. *The Americans: A History.* Boston: McDougal Littell, 1996.

Woods, Paul A., ed. *Morrissey in Conversation: The Essential Interviews.* London: Plexus, 2011.

World Book Encyclopedia, "Television." Chicago: World Book, 2003.

Zehme, Bill. *Lost in the Funhouse: The Life and Mind of Andy Kaufman.* New York: Delacorte Press, 1999.

Magazines, Websites, and Podcasts

Abebe, Nitshuh. "This Is Punk?" *New York Magazine,* April 29, 2013.

Abebe, Nitsuh. "The Decade in Indie." *Pitchfork,* February 25, 2010.

Abebe, Nitsuh. "Twee as Fuck: The Story of Indie Pop." *Pitchfork,* October 24, 2005.

Aiken, Kit. "Belle and Sebastian *Tigermilk* (reissue review)." *Uncut,* August 1999.

Aiken, Kit. "Roddy Frame." *Uncut,* September 1999.

Alani, Anaheed. "Smells Like Teen Spirit." *Bust,* Fall 2012.

Albini, Steve. "Three Pandering Sluts and Their Music Press Stooge: Letter to the Editor." *Chicago Reader,* January 28, 2004.

Anderson, Kurt. "American Icons: The Disney Parks." *Studio 360* podcast, October 16, 2013.

Aston, Martin. "Here Comes the Reign." *Mojo:* The Queen Is Dead *Anniversary Issue,* April 2011.

Aston, Martin. "Orange Juice: Where Are They Now?" *Q,* July 1992.

Azerrad, Michael. "Nirvana: Inside the Heart and Mind of Kurt Cobain." *Rolling Stone,* April 16, 1992.

Bangs, Lester. "Jonathan Richman: Town Hall, New York City." *N.M.E.,* November 13, 1976.

Beck, Richard. "5.4 Pitchfork, 1995–Present." *n+1,* January 19, 2012.

Birch, Ian. "In Love with the Modern World." *Melody Maker,* September 17, 1977.

Birch, Ian. "Jonathan Richman and the Modern Lovers: Hammersmith Odeon, London (review)." *Melody Maker*, September 24, 1977.

Birch, Ian. "The Morrissey Collection." *Smash Hits*, July 4, 1984.

Black, Bill. "Jonathan Richman and the Modern Lovers: *Jonathan Sings* (review)." *Sounds*, 1984.

Bohn, Chris. "Orange Juice: From a Postcard to a Postage Stamp." *N.M.E.*, October 2, 1982.

Bolonik, Kera. "Greta Gerwig Isn't Your Average It Girl." *The Village Voice*, May 8, 2013.

Bower, Paul. "Andrew Bujalski Interview." *Tiny Mix Tapes*, June 2012.

Brody, Richard. "The Grand Budapest Hotel: Wes Anderson's Artistic Manifesto." *New Yorker*, March 8, 2014.

Cameron, Keith. "Nirvana." *Sounds*, October 1990.

Cameron, Keith. "Nirvana: Love Will Tear Us Apart." *N.M.E.*, August 29, 1992.

Cameron, Keith. "Rip It Up." *Mojo: The Smiths, The Stone Roses and . . .*, 2011.

Cardace, Sara. "Mumblecore Muse Greta Gerwig on Nights and Weekends' and the Ugly Side of Movie Sex." *Vulture*, October 10, 2008.

Carmon, Irin. "Olivia Munn's Geek Goddess Schtick." *Jezebel*, June 8, 2010.

Carmon, Irin. "The *Daily Show*'s Woman Problem." *Jezebel*, June 23, 2010.

Cohen, Mitchell. "Altered Images: *Pinky Blue* (review)." *Creem*, January 1983.

Cohen, Scott. "Jonathan Richman Interview." *Interview*, August 1973.

Cook, Mariana. "Postscript: Wild Things." *The New Yorker*, May 2012.

Coon, Caroline. "Whatever Happened to the Buzzcocks?" *Sounds*, September 17, 1977.

Cooper, Mark. "*Orange Juice: The Best Of* (review)." *Q*, September 1992.

Cott, Jonathan. "Maurice Sendak: King of All Wild Things." *Rolling Stone*, December 30, 1976.

Dargis, Manohla. "A Youngster with a Key, a Word and a Quest (*Extremely Loud and Incredibly Close* film review)." *New York Times*, December 22, 2011.

Day, Elizabeth. "Dave Eggers: We Tend to Look Everywhere but the Mirror." *The Guardian,* January 26, 2013.

Day, Elizabeth. "Zooey Deschanel Interview." *The Guardian,* April 24, 2010.

DeCurtis, Anthony. "An Open Party: R.E.M.'s Hip American Dream." *Rolling Stone,* June 1984.

DiMartino, Dave. "Aztec Camera: *High Land, Hard Rain* (review)." *Creem,* December 1983.

Edwards, Gavin. "The Duplass Brothers Have Kidnapped Hollywood." *New York Times Magazine,* May 20, 2012.

Eggers, Dave. "A Marriage of Convenience . . . (June Brides feature)." *The Guardian,* January 26, 2006.

Evans, Paul David. "Label of Love: Postcard Records." *The Guardian,* November 10, 2008.

Fletcher, Tony. "The Boy Looked at Johnny." *Mojo,* October 2012.

Fox, Margalit. "Bill Melendez, Peanuts Animator, Dies at 91." *New York Times,* September 4, 2008.

Gerosa, Melina. "The Goddaughter." *Entertainment Weekly,* January 25, 1991.

Gertler, T. "The Pee-wee Perplex." *Rolling Stone,* February 12, 1987.

Gevinson, Tavi. "Follow What's Alive: An Interview with Greta Gerwig." *Rookie,* August 8, 2013.

Gilbert, Pat. "The Boy with the Thorn in His Side." *Mojo,* February 2013.

Gillis, Michael. "The Curators of Cool: A History of Pitchfork Media," *New City,* July 14, 2013.

Grose, Jessica. "Naked Honesty: Why Mumblecore Nudity Will Never Go Mainstream." *Slate,* April 1, 2010.

Gross, Terry. "Lena Dunham." *Fresh Air,* May 7, 2012.

Gross, Terry. "Stuart Murdoch." *Fresh Air,* March 6, 2006.

Gumprecht, Blake. "Aztec Camera (interview)." *Matter,* September 1983.

Gurley, George. "Zooey Deschanel on Love, Bullies and Revenge." *Marie Claire,* September 2013.

Hamilton, Denise. "An Interview with *Weetzie Bat* author Francesca Lia Block." *Los Angeles Times,* November 15, 2008.

Harrison, Ian. "Handsome Devils." *Mojo: The Smiths, The Stone Roses and . . . ,* 2011.

Hibbert, Tom. "Jonathan Richman: The Man Who Hates Sitting Down." *Q,* May 1993.

Hill, Logan. "Zooey Deschanel Interview." *Glamour,* January 2013.

Hoberman, J. "Proof That Critic Armond White *Did* Call for Noah Baumbach's Abortion." *The Village Voice,* March 10, 2010.

Holdship, Bill. "The Violent Femmes: *The Violent Femmes* (review)." *Creem,* October 1983.

Hull, Robot A. "Altered Images: *Happy Birthday* (review)." *Creem,* May 1982.

Hynes, Eric. "Mumblecore Masters, Enunciating Clearly." *New York Times,* July 11, 2013.

Irwin, Colin. "The Outsider." *Mojo '60s,* 2011.

July, Miranda. "Girls on Fire (Lena Dunham interview)." *Interview,* February 2013.

Kael, Pauline. "*Fast Times at Ridgemont High* (film review)." *The New Yorker,* 1982.

Keh, Dave. "*Pee-wee's Big Adventure* film review." *Chicago Reader,* 1985.

Keller, Joel. "Fred Armisen and Carrie Brownstein Interview." *The A.V. Club,* January 5, 2012.

Ken, Nick. "XTC: Making Plans for Andy, Colin, Terry and Dave." *N.M.E.,* October 20, 1979.

Kent, Nick. "Jonathan Richman Melts an Old Cynic's Heart." *N.M.E.,* October 1, 1977.

Kent, Nick. "Talking Heads: Are These Guys Trying to Give Rock a Bad Name?" *N.M.E.,* June 25, 1977.

Klausner, Julie. "Don't Fear the Dowager: A Valentine to Maturity." *Jezebel,* June 10, 2011.

Knopper, Steve. "It Takes 2 to Be They Might Be Giants." *Chicago Tribune,* March 14, 2013.

Kompanek, Chris. "Jonathan Ames Interview." *The A.V. Club,* September 21, 2010.

Kopf, Biba. "A Suitable Case for Treatment: The Smiths." *N.M.E.,* December 22, 1984.

La Ferla, Ruth. "The Once and Future Pee-wee." *New York Times,* May 20, 2007.

Lahr, John. "Varieties of Disturbance." *New Yorker,* September 9, 2013.

Lester, Paul. "Clare Grogan (interview)." *Uncut,* February 1998.

Leyshon, Cressida. "Talking with Dave Eggers About 'A Hologram for the King.'" *The New Yorker,* June 19, 2012.

Lim, Dennis. "A Generation Finds Its Mumble." *New York Times,* August 19, 2007.

Lloyd, Robert. "2 Good 2 Be 4Gotten: The Oral History of Freaks and Geeks." *Vanity Fair,* January 2013.

Lovell, Joel. "Love's Labours, Published: David Rakoff's Last Deadline." *New York Times,* July 3, 2013.

Lumenick, Lou. "*Extremely Loud and Incredibly Close* (review)." *New York Post,* December 22, 2011.

Marche, Stephen. "All the Rebels Are Fey in Quirky America." *Esquire,* May 2012.

Marshall, Kyla. "Two Years Ago, I Saw a Sad Black Boy Named Donald Glover." *Huffington Post,* December 17, 2013.

Maslin, Janet. "Mr. Jealousy: Therapy as a Front for Snooping." *New York Times,* June 5, 1998.

McGonigal, Mike. "Neutral Milk Hotel Interview." *Pitchfork,* February 11, 2008.

Meir, Christopher. "Bill Forsyth Profile." *Sense of Cinema,* October 28, 2004.

Monte Smith, Christopher. "Art Spiegelman Interview." *Indiebound.com,* 2008.

Morley, Paul. "Altered Images: The Altered State of Pop Art." *N.M.E.,* February 13, 1982.

Morley, Paul. "Buzzcocks: Teen Rebel Scores 250 (Pounds) from Dad." *N.M.E.,* February 5, 1977.

Morley, Paul. "Orange Juice: The Sneer That Says 'Wish You Were Here.'" *N.M.E.*, October 4, 1980.

Morley, Paul. "The Last Temptation of Morrissey." *Uncut*, May 2006.

Morley, Paul. "Wilde Child." *Blitz*, April 1988.

Morley, Paul. "XTC: Last Exit to Catalonia." *N.M.E.*, September 20, 1980.

"Morrissey and the Story of Manchester." *Mojo Classic*, 2006.

"Morrissey Answers 20 Questions." *Star Hits*, 1985.

Moskin, Julia. "Good Trucks Add American Flavor to Paris." *New York Times*, June 3, 2012.

Needs, Kris. "Jonathan Richman Interview." *Zig Zag*, November 1977.

Needs, Kris. "The Buzzcocks." *Zig Zag*, September 1978 .

Nussbaum, Emily. "*Girls* Is the Ballsiest Show on TV." *New York Magazine*, April 2, 2012.

Nusser, Richard. "The Velvets at Max's (review)." *The Village Voice*, July 2, 1970.

O'Neill, Luke. "Proof Charlie Brown and Morrissey Are Really the Same Person: Interview with Lauren Loprete." *Esquire*, August 15, 2013.

Onstad, Katrina. "Miranda July Is Totally Not Kidding." *New York Times Magazine*, July 14, 2011.

Page, Betty. "Altered Images: *Pinky Blue* (review)." *Sounds*, May 8, 1982.

Parker, Ian. "Happiness: Noah Baumbach's New Wave." *The New Yorker*, April 29, 2013.

Paskin, Willa. "Liz Meriwether Interview." *Salon*, May 15, 2013.

Paytress, Mark. "Do It Yourself." *Mojo: The Smiths, The Stone Roses and . . .*, 2011.

Persky, Lisa. "Jonathan Richman at Town Hall, New York, NY." *New York Rocker*, December 1976.

Preston, John. "Dave Eggers: The Heartbreak Kid." *The Telegraph*, December 29, 2009.

Push. "Nirvana Heaven Can't Wait." *Melody Maker*, December 15, 1990.

Puterbaugh, Parke. "R.E.M.'s Southern Rock Revival." *Rolling Stone,* July 9, 2013.

Raab, Scott. "Fred Armisen: The ESQ and A." *Esquire,* January 2012.

Rambali, Paul. "Jonathan Richman and the Modern Lovers: *Rock 'n' Roll with the Modern Lovers.*" N.M.E., August 3, 1977.

Reynolds, Simon. "Nirvana: *Nevermind* (review)." *New York Times,* November 24, 1991.

Reynolds, Simon. "Younger Than Yesterday: Indie Pop's Cult of Innocence." *Melody Maker,* June 28, 1986.

Richman, Jonathan. "New York Art and the Velvet Underground." *Vibrations,* September 1967.

Robbins, Ira. "Jonathan Richman: *Back in Your Life* (review)." *Trouser Press,* June 1979.

Rogan, Johnny. "Once Upon a Time in the West." *Mojo 60's,* 2011.

Rosen, Jody. "Why Taylor Swift Is the Biggest Pop Star in the World." *New York Magazine,* November 25, 2013.

Savage, John. "Sounds Dirty: The Truth about Nirvana." *The Observer (UK),* August 15, 1993.

Savage, Jon. "Jonathan Richman: Hammersmith Odeon, London." *Sounds,* September 24, 1977.

Savage, Jon. "The Enemy Within." *Mojo: The Queen Is Dead Anniversary Issue,* April 2011.

Scocca, Tom. "On Smarm." *Gawker,* December 5, 2013.

Scott, A. O. "Bittersweet Chocolate on the Pillow." *New York Times,* March 6, 2014.

Sheffield, Rob. "Hawke's Labor of Love." *Rolling Stone,* June 6, 2013.

Sisario, Ben. "Records Are Dying? Not Here. Rough Trade, NYC." *New York Times,* November 21, 2013.

Smith, Damon. "The Low-Key Jester: An Interview with Andrew Bujalski." *Senses of Cinema,* May 2007.

Snow, Mat. "Orange Juice/The Go Betweens: Lyceum, London." *N.M.E.,* April 9, 1983.

Spitznagel, Eric. "Sarah Vowell interview." *Vanity Fair,* March 13, 2011.

St. Clair, Stacy. "Glen Ellyn Board Listens to Blume, Reinstates YA Novel." *Chicago Tribune,* June 12, 2013.

Stein, Joel. "Lonely Boy." *Time,* January 20, 2014.

Swanson, Carl. "Jane Pratt's Perpetual Adolescence: Why She's Still Talking Teen Three Decades after *Sassy.*" *New York Magazine,* August 14, 2012.

Talbot, Margaret. "Stumptown Girl." *The New Yorker,* January 2, 2012.

"The 500 Greatest Songs of All Time." *Rolling Stone,* December 9, 2004.

"*The Queen Is Dead,* 20 Years On." *N.M.E. Special Smiths Anniversary Issue,* June 10, 2006.

"*The Queen Is Dead,* 25 Years On." *N.M.E. Smiths Anniversary Special,* June 18, 2011.

The Smiths, Special Collector's Magazine, from the Makers of NME and Uncut, Winter 2011.

Tobias, Scott. "Andrew Bujalski Interview." *The A.V. Club,* August 5, 2009.

True, Everett. "Nirvana: In My Head, I'm So Ugly." *Melody Maker,* July 18, 1992.

True, Everett. "Nirvana: Station to Devastation." *Melody Maker,* November 2, 1991.

Tsoulis-Reay, Alexa. "The Judy Blume File." *New York Magazine,* May 27, 2013.

Vilkomerson, Sara. "Are You There Hollywood? It's Me, Judy Blume." *Entertainment Weekly,* May 17, 2013.

Vineyard, Jennifer. "Paul Feig Explains His Cultural Influences." *Vulture,* June 16, 2013.

Vishnevetsky, Ignatiy. "Matters of Opinion: An Interview with Andrew Bujalski." *Notebook,* February 4, 2010.

Wallace, Benjamin. "The Twee Party: Is Artisanal Brooklyn a Step Forward for Food or a Sign of the Apocalypse . . . ?" *New York Magazine,* April 2, 2012.

Williams, Mary Elizabeth. "Zooey Deschanel Declares Her Feminism." *Salon,* January 14, 2013.

Winfrey Harris, Tami. "Who Is the Black Zooey Deschanel?" *What Tami Said*, June 13, 2011.

Wolcott, James. "Punk Is in the Air." *Vanity Fair*, May 2013.

Wolf Shenk, Joshua. "Jonathan Safran Foer (interview)." *Mother Jones*, May 2005.

Wyman, Bill. "Not from the Underground: 1993 in Review." *Chicago Reader*, January 7, 1994.

Yuan, Jada. "The Pin-up of Williamsburg." *New York Magazine*, September 11, 2011.

Interviews

Zach Condon, September 19, 2006. Originally for *Uncut*.

Sufjan Stevens, September 11, 2007. Originally for *Uncut*.

Jack White, June 18, 2009. Originally for *Uncut*.

Tavi Gevinson, June 10, 2011. Originally for *Spin*.

Krist Novoselic, August 12, 2011. Originally for *New York Times*.

Chris Eigeman, October 4, 2012.

Nick Kent, October 21, 2012.

Clare Grogan, November 13, 2012.

Steven Daly, November 20, 2012.

Simon Reynolds, November 27, 2012.

John Gordon Sinclair, December 6, 2012.

Josh Hamilton, December 18, 2012.

Asa Brebner, December 19, 2012.

Whit Stillman, February 19, 2013.

Andrew Bujalski, February 25, 2013.

Justin Rice, March 30, 2013.

Matt Haynes, March 31, 2013.

Joe Swanberg, April 2, 2013.

Alex Karpovsky, April 8, 2013.

Matthew King Kaufman, April 8, 2013.

Julie Klausner, April 17, 2013.

John Hodgman, April 19, 2013.

Zoe Lister Jones, April 24, 2013.

Lloyd Cole, April 26, 2013.

Clare Wadd, April 28, 2013.

Glen Matlock, April 29, 2013.

Sarah Vowell, May 6, 2013.

Nils Bernstein, May 9, 2013.

Dean Wareham, May 9, 2013.

Jonathan Ames, May 13, 2013.

Phil Wilson, May 13, 2013.

Stephen Chbosky, May 20, 2013.

Shirley Manson, May 29, 2013.

Slim Moon, May 30, 2013.

Calvin Johnson, June 3, 2013.

Joel Kastelberg, June 5, 2013.

Fred Armisen, June 6, 2013.

Jonathan Krisel, June 7, 2013.

Alan Pafenbach, June 7, 2013.

Eric Stoltz, June 18, 2013.

Stephen Pastel, June 24, 2013.

Amy Heckerling, June 26, 2013.

Curtis Armstrong, July 2, 2013.

Stefano D'Andrea, July 2, 2013.

Ryan Schreiber, July 24, 2013.

Daniel Waters, August 8, 2013.

Paul Morley, August 11, 2013.

Gina Birch, August 12, 2013.

Mark Duplass, August 29, 2013.

Lynn Shelton, August 30, 2013.

Richard Boon, September 9, 2013.

Joe Boyd, September 18, 2013.

Tricia Romano, October 18, 2013.

Nitsuh Abebe, October 22, 2013.

Sean Nelson, October 22, 2013.

Brian Ritchie, October 22, 2013.

Todd Solondz, October 23, 2013.

Tamara Winfrey Harris, October 23, 2013.

Barry Katz, November 1, 2013.

John Flansburgh, November 8, 2013.

Geoff Travis, January 5, 2014.

Devon Gummersall, January 16, 2014.

Ian Whitcomb, January 31, 2014.

Appendices

A Thoughtful but Danceable Playlist

"This Is Just a Modern Rock Song"
 —Belle and Sebastian

"Thirteen"—Big Star

"Birdhouse in Your Soul"
 —They Might Be Giants

"In the Aeroplane Over the Sea"
 —Neutral Milk Hotel

"Pretty Ballerina"—The Left Banke

"Here's Where the Story Ends"
 —The Sundays

"We Are Going to Be Friends"
 —The White Stripes

"Waterloo Sunset"—The Kinks

"Handlebars"—The Desperate Bicycles

"I Know Where Syd Barrett Lives"
 —Television Personalities

"Still Ill"—The Smiths

"After Hours"
 —The Velvet Underground

"Hospital"—The Modern Lovers

"When You Wish Upon a Star"
 —Cliff Edwards

"I Could Be Happy"—Altered Images

"Emma's House"—The Field Mice

"Indian Summer"—Beat Happening

"Been Teen"—Dolly Mixture

"Moon River"—Andy Williams

"Lee Remick"—The Go-Betweens

"Stretch Out and Wait"—The Smiths

"Somewhere in China"
 —The Shop Assistants

"In My Room"—The Beach Boys

"Love You More"—The Buzzcocks

"Nature Thing"—Close Lobsters

"Oxford Comma"—Vampire Weekend

"Happy All the Time"—The Flatmates

"Bummer in the Summer"—Love

"My Back Pages"—The Byrds

"New Slang"—The Shins

"It's Only Obvious"—The Orchids

"Sunlight Bathed in the Golden Glow"
—Felt

"Tripping Wires"—Velocity Girl

"Fill Your Heart"—David Bowie

"When the World Was Young"
—Blossom Dearie

"Free to Be You and Me"
—The New Seekers

"Nature Boy"—Big Star

"Christmas Time Is Here"
—The Vince Guaraldi Trio

"Tonight, You Belong to Me"
—Steve Martin and Bernadette
Peters

"Simply Thrilled Honey"
—Orange Juice

"The Boy with the Perpetual
Nervousness"—The Feelies

"Anyone Else but You"
—The Moldy Peaches

"God Only Knows"—Beach Boys

"Sixteen Dreams"—Loop

"The Headmaster Ritual"—The Smiths

"Don't Worry About the Government"
—Talking Heads

"Butterfly"—Weezer

"Actor Out of Work"—St. Vincent

"Listen the Snow Is Falling"
—Galaxie 500

"Rory Rides Me Raw"—The Vaselines

"Me and My Arrow"—Harry Nilsson

"A Place in the Sun"—Marine Girls

"Contender"
—The Pains of Being Pure of Heart

"Just Like Honey"
—The Jesus and Mary Chain

"Flagpole Sitta"—Harvey Danger

"Everybody's Gotta Learn Sometime"
—Beck

"Imperial Teen"—Imperial Teen

"River Man"—Nick Drake

"Hypnotized"—Spacemen 3

"Unfair Kind of Fame"—The Pastels

"Space Oddity"
—Langley Schools Music Project

"Since Yesterday"
—Strawberry Switchblade

"It's Oh So Quiet"—Bjork

"O Valencia!"—The Decemberists

"Are You Ready to Be Heartbroken?"
 —Lloyd Cole and the Commotions

"Life Begins at the Hop"—XTC

"Sugar Water"—Cibo Matto

"I Put a Spell on You"—She & Him

"Lazy Sunday"—The Small Faces

"Strawberries Are Growing in My
 Garden (And It's Wintertime)"
 —The Dentists

"Old Friends"—Simon and Garfunkel

"The Book of Love"
 —The Magnetic Fields

"Up the Junction"—Squeeze

"Pure Imagination"—Gene Wilder

"Through Being Cool"—Devo

"If You Wanna Sing Out"
 —Cat Stevens

"Elephant Stone"—The Stone Roses

"Eating Noddemix"
 —Young Marble Giants

"Lola"—The Raincoats

"Crash"—The Primitives

"The Lovecats"—The Cure

"Sunday to Saturday"
 —The June Brides

"Happy Hour"—The Housemartins

"Crashed the Wedding"
 —The Wedding Present

"We Will Become Silhouettes"
 —The Postal Service

"Lorelei"—Cocteau Twins

"Sorry for Laughing"—Josef K

"Sunny Goodge Street"—Donovan

"Timeless Melody"—The La's

"Randy Scouse Git"—The Monkees

"The Concept"—Teenage Fanclub

"Rain"—The Beatles

"Really Rosie"—Carole King

"Coconut Grove"
 —The Lovin' Spoonful

"Velocity Girl"—Primal Scream

"Lua"—Bright Eyes

"Peach, Plum, Pear"—Joanna Newsom

"Ice Cream Man"
 —Jonathan Richman and
 the Modern Lovers

"Pilgrimage"—R.E.M.

"Get Up and Use Me"—Fire Engines

"Twist Barbie"—Shonen Knife

"Life on Mars"—Seu Jorge

"Walking the Cow"—Daniel Johnston

"L.E.S."—Childish Gambino

"Please Do Not Go"—Violent Femmes

"My Name Is Tallulah"—Jodie Foster

"The Beatles and the Stones"
—The House of Love

"When You Were Mine"—Prince

"Tally Ho"—The Clean

"Eighties Fan"—Camera Obscura

"In the Rain"—The June Brides

"Say Yes"—Elliott Smith

"Losing My Edge"
—LCD Soundsystem

"Chicago"—Sufjan Stevens

"Postcards from Italy"—Beirut

"Rebellion (Lies)"—The Arcade Fire

"You Turn Me On"—Ian Whitcomb

"Pretty Flamingo"—Manfred Mann

"Daydream"—The Lovin' Spoonful

"You Should All Be Murdered"
—Another Sunny Day

"Please Rain Fall"—The Sea Urchins

"Lady Jane"—The Rolling Stones

"Lust in the Movies"—The Long
Blondes

"This Must Be the Place (Naïve
Melody)"—Talking Heads

"Roller Girl"—Anna Karina

"Le Hotel Particulier"
—Serge Gainsbourg

"Suzanne"—Françoise Hardy

"Sliver"—Nirvana

"So Sad About Us"—The Who

"Bus Stop"—The Hollies

"This Will Be Our Year"—The Zombies

"He's Frank"—The Monochrome Set

"My Favorite Things"—Julie Andrews

A Reader, Books Both Joyful and Sad

The Catcher in the Rye—J. D. Salinger

Where the Wild Things Are
—Maurice Sendak

Anne Frank: the Diary of a Young Girl
—Anne Frank

Ferdinand the Bull
—Munro Leaf and Robert Lawson

The Bell Jar—Sylvia Plath

The Gashlycrumb Tinies—Edward Gorey

Are You There God? It's Me, Margaret
  —Judy Blume

The Nutshell Library—Maurice Sendak

Charlotte's Web
  —E. B. White and Garth Williams

Franny and Zooey—J. D. Salinger

*A Heartbreaking Work of Staggering
  Genius*—Dave Eggers

*The Last Days of Disco with Cocktails at
  Petrossian Afterwards*
  —Whit Stillman

Extremely Loud and Incredibly Close
  —Jonathan Safran Foer

Assassination Vacation—Sarah Vowell

Eloise: The Ultimate Edition
  —Kaye Thompson and Hilary Knight

The Doubtful Guest—Edward Gorey

Ariel—Sylvia Plath

Maus and *Maus 2*—Art Spiegelman

The Phantom Tollbooth
  —Norton Juster and Jules Feiffer

Weetzie Bat—Francesca Lia Block

The Night Kitchen—Maurice Sendak

A Scene In Between—Sam Knee

Forever . . .—Judy Blume

The Awful Rowing Toward God
  —Anne Sexton

Where the Sidewalk Ends
  —Shel Silverstein

Breakfast at Tiffany's—Truman Capote

Peanuts: The Complete Collection
  —Charles M. Schulz

*Raise High the Roof Beam, Carpenters
  and Seymour: An Introduction*
  —J. D. Salinger

Candy Girl—Diablo Cody

Higglety Pigglety Pop!
  —Maurice Sendak

Charlie and the Chocolate Factory
  —Roald Dahl

Eightball—Daniel Clowes

The Red Balloon—Albert Lamorisse

The Little Prince
  —Antoine de Saint-Exupéry

Frog and Toad Are Friends
  —Arnold Lobel

The Cat in the Hat—Dr. Seuss

Goodnight Moon
  —Margaret Wise Brown and
  Clement Hurd

The Wind in the Willows
  —Kenneth Grahame

How to Sharpen Pencils—David Rees

The Lion, the Witch and the Wardrobe
  —C. S. Lewis

Live Forever—Elizabeth Peyton

The Wes Anderson Collection
   —Matthew Zoller Seitz

Rookie Yearbook One
   —*Rookie* staff, Tavi Gevinson, editor

The Double Life Is Twice as Good
   —Jonathan Ames

Autobiography—Morrissey

My Areas of Expertise—John Hodgman

How the Grinch Stole Christmas
   —Dr. Seuss

Rip It Up and Start Again
   —Simon Reynolds

Matilda—Roald Dahl

Nine Stories—J. D. Salinger

A Cricket in Times Square
   —George Selden and
   Garth Williams

Revolution in the Head
   —Ian MacDonald

England's Dreaming—Jon Savage

The Pitchfork 500—Pitchfork staff

Our Band Could Be Your Life
   —Michael Azerrad

The Songs That Saved Your Life
   —Simon Goddard

A Queue for Many Warm and Quiet Evenings In

Moonrise Kingdom—Wes Anderson

The Graduate—Mike Nichols

A Charlie Brown Christmas
   —Bill Melendez

Breathless—Jean-Luc Godard

Rudolph the Red-Nosed Reindeer
   —Rankin and Bass

The Royal Tenenbaums—Wes Anderson

Kicking and Screaming
   —Noah Baumbach

Gregory's Girl—William Forsyth

Rushmore—Wes Anderson

The 400 Blows—François Truffaut

The Ice Storm—Ang Lee

Garden State—Zach Braff

Harold and Maude—Hal Ashby

Superbad—Greg Mottola

The Diary of Anne Frank
   —George Stevens

Grey Gardens
   —Albert and David Maysles

Funny Ha Ha—Andrew Bujalski

Juno—Jason Reitman

The Virgin Suicides—Sofia Coppola

Willy Wonka and the Chocolate Factory
   —Mel Stuart

Pinocchio
   —Ben Sharpstein and
   Hamilton Luske

Donnie Darko—Richard Kelly

Bugsy Malone—Alan Parker

(500) Days of Summer—Marc Webb

The Puffy Chair—Mark and Jay Duplass

Metropolitan, Barcelona, and *The Last
   Days of Disco*—Whit Stillman

The Squid and the Whale
   —Noah Baumbach

Me and You and Everyone We Know
   —Miranda July

The Future—Miranda July

Humpday—Lynn Shelton

Fast Times at Ridgemont High
   —Amy Heckerling

Tiny Furniture—Lena Dunham

Powers of Ten—Charles and Ray Eames

Napoleon Dynamite—Jared Hess

Young Adult—Jason Reitman

Daria: The Complete Animated Series

Fans Only—Belle and Sebastian

Splendor in the Grass—Elia Kazan

Yellow Submarine—George Dunning

The Magnificent Ambersons
   —Orson Welles

The 5,000 Fingers of Dr. T
   —Dr. Seuss

Pee-wee's Big Adventure—Tim Burton

Heathers—Michael Lehman

Eternal Sunshine of the Spotless Mind
   —Michel Gondry

Clueless—Amy Heckerling

The Fantastic Mr. Fox—Wes Anderson

A Taste of Honey—Tony Richardson

Greenberg—Noah Baumbach

Amelie—Jean-Pierre Jeunet

Welcome to the Dollhouse—Todd Solondz

Lost in Translation—Sofia Coppola

Be Kind Rewind—Michel Gondry

Bambi—David Hand

The L-Shaped Room—Bryan Forbes

Hotel Chevalier/The Darjeeling Limited
   —Wes Anderson

Hannah Takes the Stairs—Joe Swanberg

Beginners—Mike Mills

Rebel Without a Cause—Nicholas Ray

Henry Fool—Hal Hartley

Storytelling—Todd Solondz

The Do-Deca-Pentathlon
  —Jay and Mark Duplass

High Fidelity—Stephen Frears

Your Sister's Sister—Lynn Shelton

Lady and the Tramp
  —Clyde Geronimi

Girls (seasons 1–3)
  —Lena Dunham

Cyrus—Jay and Mark Duplass

*The Loneliness of the Long Distance
  Runner*—Tony Richardson

Dark Horse—Todd Solondz

The Science of Sleep—Michel Gondry

Frances Ha—Noah Baumbach

Touchy Feely—Lynn Shelton

Drinking Buddies—Joe Swanberg

Computer Chess—Andrew Bujalski

The Grand Budapest Hotel
  —Wes Anderson

Acknowledgments

Special thank you to James Fitzgerald and Carrie Thornton for being my partners on this book and the calm voices through my strange and loud career. The following people look like kittens: Calvert Morgan, Lynn Grady, Kevin Callahan, Michael Barrs, Brittany Hamblin, Amanda Kain, Joseph Papa, Trina Hunn, Tracey Pepper, Lizzy Goodman, Joni Mitchell and Jerry Orbach (Basset kittens), my parents, Sid Spitz, Al Josephberg and Ricki Josephberg, Chris Eigeman, Maureen Callahan, Robert Cox, Adam Kersh, Megan Davey, Joshua Seftel, Nils Bernstein, Justin Rice, Brian Bumbery, Joan Uhelszkin, Matthew King Kaufman, Bonnie Thornton, Marc Maron, George Gurley, Dr. Dori Fromer, Dr. Robert Levine, Lauretta Charlton, Michael Bonner, Michael Hogan, Roger Greenberg, Fisher & Sons, Steven Daly, Simon Reynolds, Rob Gelardi and all at XOU, Richard Allen and everyone at Black and White, Nick Bodor and everyone at the Library, Soho, Hal Horowitz, Felder and Schustack Mgmt, Kirsten Ames, Jill Landaker, and Steven Barclay.

Please visit www.marcspitz.com for information on all of
Marc Adam Spitz's books, plays, journalism, and other writing,
as well as weekly essays and special features.

Follow Marc at @marcspitz on Twitter and on Facebook at
https://www.facebook.com/pages/Marc-Spitz/179985432068973

MARC SPITZ is an author, playwright, and journalist. His books include *Bowie: A Biography* and *Jagger: Rebel, Rock Star, Rambler, Rogue*, as well as two novels: the cult classic *How Soon Is Never?* and *Too Much, Too Late*. He has also published a memoir, *Poseur: A Memoir of Downtown New York City in the '90s*. He was formerly a senior writer at *Spin* magazine, and his work has appeared in *Rolling Stone, Maxim, Vanity Fair, New York, Uncut,* and the *New York Times*. He lives in New York City.